# RUSSIAN
# CIVIL-MILITARY
# RELATIONS

# RUSSIAN
# CIVIL-MILITARY
# RELATIONS

DALE R. HERSPRING

INDIANA UNIVERSITY PRESS
*Bloomington and Indianapolis*

**Library of Congress Cataloging-in-Publication Data**

Herspring, Dale R. (Dale Roy)
    Russian civil-military relations / Dale R. Herspring
        p.    cm.
    Includes bibliographical references and index.
    ISBN 0-253-33225-7 (cl : alk. paper)
    1. Civil-military relations—Soviet Union—History. 2. Civil-military relations—Russia (Federation)—History. 3. Soviet Union—Politics and government—1917–1936. 4. Soviet Union—Politics and government—1985-1991. 5. Russia (Federation)—Politics and government—1991-
I. Title.
UA770.H4797     1996
322'.5'0947—dc20                                                    96-11635


1  2  3  4  5      01  00  99  98  97  96

*To the Memory of My Father*
*Frank E. Herspring*

One measure of a theory is the degree to which it encompasses and explains all the relevant facts.

Samuel Huntington

# CONTENTS

# PREFACE

Yeltsin's resounding victory in the July 1996 elections, his precarious health, the unstable political situation in the country, and the emergence of General Lebed—together with the resulting shake-up in the senior ranks of the Russian military—make civil-military relations one of the most important and critical components of Russian politics today. The military is deeply split, demoralized, falling increasingly behind the West in the area of military technology and training, and highly politicized. With the appointment of General Lebed as national security advisor and the resultant increased attention being given to military reform, training, and modernization, however, there is a real possibility that the downward spiral the military has found itself in since the collapse of the Soviet Union may begin to be reversed. Organizational cohesion and combat readiness, which were at all-time lows in mid-1996, may slowly begin to improve. It will take time, but in five or ten years we may begin to see the emergence of a new Russian military that more closely resembles its Soviet predecessor in terms of its importance both as a combat-capable armed force and as a political interest group.

Given the political, economic, social, and moral instability in Russia today, together with the possibility that various parts of the civilian leadership will almost certainly continue their efforts to use the military for their own political ends, how this process develops is a matter of major concern. Indeed, I would argue that the way in which civil-military relations develop over the next five years is the most important issue in Russian politics today. Given the present deep divisions within the military, the chances of a military coup are almost zero. However, the emergence of a highly charismatic military figure such as Aleksandr Lebed could change things significantly. He—or someone like him—could provide the political influence and the spiritual cohesion needed to make the Russian military into a very important actor on both the internal and external political scenes.

In the past, Yeltsin tended to play off one military officer against another. For example, during the first half of 1996 he seemed to be courting simultaneously two senior military officers—Pavel Grachev, the defense minister, and Boris Gromov, the hero of Afghanistan and Grachev's bitter enemy. And then just prior to the second-round presidential run-off election, Yeltsin surprised everyone by appointing Lebed to a key position in the national security hierarchy. While at this writing (July 1996) it is too soon to say how long Lebed will remain a key actor in the Russian government, the fact that he has been given such a major portfolio suggests that even if he should be removed, his highlighting of the critical need to rebuild the military could make the process irreversible. In short, Yeltsin—or his successor—may discover that with a rebuilt army it is difficult to divide and conquer when dealing with senior officers. The organization may become too cohesive for such vulnerability to persist.

Before the military can become a unitary force, able to speak with something resembling one voice, much work remains to be done. As this book went to press, tensions were high throughout the armed forces. Russian generals openly clashed with each other over Moscow's policies on a variety of issues—a situation that would have been unthinkable ten years ago. Even more alarming was the refusal of Russian generals to carry out some of Yeltsin's orders. In the battle for Chechnya, for example, Russian generals repeatedly ignored cease-fires declared by Yeltsin—another development that would have been unthinkable ten years ago. One got the impression that the generals saw civil-military relations as a replay of the old Soviet joke, "They pretend to pay us, and we pretend to work." Yeltsin pretended to issue orders and the generals pretended to obey them. In some cases, Russian officers even refused to carry out orders issued by their own military chain of command.

Conditions among the military rank and file were, if anything, even more demoralizing. Stories abounded of officers and soldiers going for three months and more without pay, and of wretched living conditions for personnel and their families. Tales circulated of pilots who could not fly for lack of fuel, tankers whose tanks could not operate because of a lack of spare parts, and sailors who starved to death at remote posts in the Pacific because they were not supplied with food. Meanwhile, junior officers, upon whom every army relies, were resigning in droves.

The war in Chechnya caused far more casualties than the Russian military was prepared to admit. Indeed, the military's position in Chechnya was so desperate that the General Staff was forced to send to Chechnya units such as Russian marines who were trained for an entirely different task. Quite simply, there was no one else to send. The resulting deep dissatisfaction and frustration on the part of military personnel were one of the main reasons for widespread support within the military for nondemocratic presidential candidates.

One of the key problems facing Russian military and political leaders as they moved into the post-Soviet period was the lack of a "model" of civil-military relations to guide them. In economics and politics, Western observers urged the Russians to emulate "Western democratic models." However, it quickly became apparent that "outside" models that did not fit with Russian political culture would not succeed. When it came to building a new basis for civil-military relations, factors such as historical precedent had to be taken into account. The Russian military was not born in a vacuum. It was part and parcel of Russian and Soviet culture and has been heavily shaped by its external environment.

With this in mind, this book asks the question: how useful is any model at the present time in trying to understand where Russian civil-military relations are headed? On the premise that political culture plays a key role in this area, this book looks at the Soviet period as well as the post-communist period. After all, it was clear from the statements of Russian military officers that the Ministry of Defense did not disown its Soviet past. Uniforms have changed only slightly. Although communist propaganda and the party-political apparatus were gone and there was a renewed search of the pre-communist military past for historical inspiration, the Russian military continued to resemble its Soviet predecessor when it came to such matters as military strategy, operational art and tactics, and attitudes toward subordinates and civilians, to mention only a few.

Taking the importance of Russian political-military culture as its point of departure, this book examines some of the models developed by Western social scientists to explain civil-military relations at key times during the Soviet period, notably the 1920s, when Soviet power was being established, and the 1980s, when Gorbachev tried to regain civilian control over military-security issues. In analyzing events in these critical periods of change, it asks the question, just how useful were these models in helping us understand the nature of civil-military relations during the Soviet period? What aspects of these models, if any, might aid us in analyzing the evolution of civil-military relations in the post-Soviet era and in foreseeing future directions? By identifying key variables influencing the development of civil-military relations in the past, the book aims to provide historical and analytical perspectives for confronting the chaotic situation currently prevailing in Russian civil-military affairs.

# ACKNOWLEDGMENTS

This book would not have been written were it not for the help of a number of individuals. First and foremost, I am indebted to Kurt Campbell, who suggested the idea for this book during a visit we made together to the former Soviet Union. In addition, I was fortunate enough to convince a number of my colleagues to read the manuscript in whole or in part. Their patience, helpful criticisms, and suggestions were invaluable. Whatever merit this manuscript has is largely due to their comments. (Likewise, any errors of omission or commission are mine alone.) Among those who helped in the process I wish to especially thank John Daly, Robin Remington, Mark von Hagen, Jack Snyder, Bruce Parrott, Jake Kipp, Howard Wiarda and Richard Melanson. I would also like to express my appreciation to Janet Rabinowitch of Indiana University Press for her help in editing this book.

I should also like to take this opportunity to express my appreciation to the Woodrow Wilson Center, and especially the director of its Kennan Institute, Blair Ruble. The year I spent at the Wilson Center played a key role in helping me conceptualize and research this issue. The many conversations I had with my colleagues at the center also played a critical role in helping me clarify my ideas. In addition, I want to thank the United States Institute of Peace and its Director of Grants, Hrach Gregorian, for financial support during the year I spent at the Woodrow Wilson Center. The confidence both of these institutions placed in me and my idea is deeply appreciated.

The research and writing of this book took three years. During that time, my wife of thirty years and my three children put up with all of the discomforts and difficulties that came in living with someone whose mind was often on more—to them—esoteric matters. Without their support and help this book could not have been written.

In conclusion, I want to acknowledge the encouragement and help that I received over a lifetime in my academic pursuits from my father, who passed away while this book was in preparation. Although he was not a scholar himself, his faith in me and my work over the years meant more than he ever knew. Most of all, however, I want to thank him for teaching me some of the most important lessons of life: those that do not come from reading books. In appreciation for his help and understanding, this book is dedicated to my father, Frank E. Herspring.

# ABBREVIATIONS

| | |
|---|---|
| *VIZ* | *Voenno-istoricheskiy zhurnal* |
| *VM* | *Voennaya mysl'* |
| *VV* | *Voennyy vestnik* |
| *JSMS* | *Journal of Soviet Military Studies* |
| *KZ* | *Krasnaya zvezda* |
| *MR* | *Military Review* |
| *VD* | *Voennoe delo* |
| *JPRS SU* | *JPRS, The Soviet Union* |
| *FBIS SU* | *FBIS, The Soviet Union* |
| *FBIS CE* | *FBIS, Central Eurasia* |
| *MN* | *Moskovskie novosti* |

# INTRODUCTION

> Not all countries have an understanding of
> military doctrine. For example, in the West
> any military-theoretical views are called
> doctrine, while military doctrine proper does
> not include all existing military-theoretical
> views . . . but only basic, guiding, officially
> accepted provisions of military theory and
> practice . . .
>
> Gen. Makhmut Gareyev

The Gorbachev period and the collapse of the former Soviet Union raised
serious questions about many, if not most, of the traditional assumptions
of Western scholars about the nature of politics in Russia. In hindsight, it is
now clear that our understanding of politics under the Communists was
far from accurate, and equally important, that we were totally unprepared
to deal with the collapse of communism as well as with Russian politics in
the post-Communist era. This is particularly true in the area of civil-military relations.

The nature of civil-military relations constantly changed under the Communists. During the 1920s, for example, the military increasingly lost its
autonomy, and relations with civil authorities often were characterized by
conflict, while under Brezhnev military autonomy reached an all-time high
and cooperation between civil and military authorities was the norm. By
and large, however, Western analysts failed to note that the mixture of conflict and cooperation shifted over time.

One of the main reasons why Western analysts misread the situation in
the former Soviet Union was that the various models developed by political scientists were based on assumptions that tended to oversimplify the
nature of civil-military relations in the former Soviet Union. For example,
some writers assumed that the relationship between the military and civilian worlds was inherently conflictual, while others focused on the cooperative nature of the relationship. In addition, some assumed that these
two institutions were easily identifiable structures. These latter individuals further assumed that one could tell who was a military professional
and who was a civilian, and that based on that knowledge, one could pre-

dict with a fair degree of accuracy how each would react on certain issues. In reality, however, the situation was more complex. The relationship between the two structures was sometimes conflictual. In other instances it was more cooperative. Furthermore, often it was difficult to determine the boundary between the civilian and military worlds.

## Conceptualizing Civil-Military Relations

While a number of individuals wrote about the nature of civil-military relations during the Communist period, three stand out because of their intellectual and policy importance: Roman Kolkowicz, William E. Odom, and Timothy J. Colton.[1] The key question that will be asked here is to what degree these models were useful in explaining civil-military relations in the former Soviet Union. If a model was not useful, why not? What does the usefulness or non-usefulness of these models say about the overall utility of models in general? Is there anything that can be learned from these models to help us understand civil-military relations in the post-Communist period? Do we need to develop completely new models? If so, what kind? Or, based on the Soviet experience, is there reason for us to shy away from the use of models altogether?

*Kolkowicz.* The most complete expression of Kolkowicz's ideas is found in his influential book, *The Soviet Military and the Communist Party.*[2] Kolkowicz's approach focused on the military as a "closed" institution and relied heavily on the methodology developed by Samuel Huntington in his classic study of U.S. civil-military relations, *The Soldier and the State.*[3] In Huntington's view, the military is characterized by a high degree of expertise, responsibility, and corporateness. He sees a clear and distinct boundary between the military and civilian worlds.

Kolkowicz applied Huntington's paradigm to the Soviet Union and argued that Soviet military expertise led to greater demands for professional autonomy; that its sense of professional responsibility resulted in a strict code of honor and discipline, and that the bureaucratic nature of the military's organizational structure appeared in its "easily discernable and stable" levels of authority.

These attributes clashed with the Communist party's ideal image of "an open institution, one easy to penetrate and manipulate."[4] The Communist party adamantly opposed military autonomy. For the Bolsheviks, autonomy raised the specter of a military acting independently of the Soviet party/state: a situation which they could not accept. Thus from the party's standpoint, civil-military relations should be characterized by the complete penetration of the military by the party. The party believed it had both the right and obligation to interfere in military affairs at will.

According to Kolkowicz, this deep-seated difference in bureaucratic orientation led to a constant battle between military and civilian authorities. The former tried to fend off efforts to limit their autonomy, while the latter constantly interfered in military matters: "The incompatibility between the party's ideal model of a thoroughly politicized instrument of the socialist state (which also must be militarily effective and disciplined) on the one hand, and the military's 'natural' tendencies toward orthodoxy on the other, created friction and tension between the two institutions."[5] In essence, Kolkowicz saw civil-military relations as a zero-sum game.

*Odom.* Odom fundamentally disagreed with Kolkowicz.[6] To begin with, he did not see Soviet politics as a zero-sum game. Odom agreed that there was a sense of corporateness with "most military establishments," but he maintained with Morris Janowitz that military and civilian occupations were becoming increasingly interchangeable. Military officers were becoming what Janowitz called "military managers."[7]

The key to Odom's approach was totalitarian theory. He argued that because of their commitment to Marxism-Leninism, both military and civilian officials shared allegiance to the same ideological system. Likewise, they both had a stake in its perpetuation. In essence, they believed that the Soviet military-civilian complex was one large bureaucratic organization. Political conflicts took place, but within the context of one bureaucratic structure. All were subordinated to the political leadership: "In short, . . . behavior in the Soviet military is viewed as fundamentally a bureaucratic political matter; and politics within bureaucracies is essentially a struggle by the top leadership to impose its value preferences on the lower bureaucratic levels." He admitted that there was a bureaucratic boundary between the civilian and military worlds, but he argued that Western scholars exaggerated its importance. As a consequence, as party members and military officers, the marshals were "executants." They carried out policy, they did not frame it.[8]

*Colton.* Another approach, suggested by Timothy Colton, argued that Kolkowicz overstated the magnitude of the control/conflict problem. He also raised questions about Odom's paradigm, arguing that his own work suggested that even during the worst periods, "clusters of military and party officials are bound together on particular issues and pursue their interests on such issues cooperatively." Colton maintained that Odom was wrong in suggesting that there was no bureaucratic difference between the military and civilian worlds.[9]

As an alternative approach, Colton suggested that the analyst focus on military participation in the political process. He agreed with Kolkowicz to the degree that the two institutions, the party and the military, were distinct bureaucratic entities. At the same time, he maintained that conflict did not necessarily pervade the relationship, as Kolkowicz suggested. Looking especially at the Brezhnev period, Colton argued that the primary reason why the Kremlin had avoided conflict was that up to that point (i.e.,

1978) the military's core interests (e.g., pay and status) had been satisfied. The probability of conflict would rise if the party tried to undermine these core interests.

Conversely, according to Colton, the boundary between civilian and military arenas tended to become more permeable the further one moved from these basic interests (e.g., toward national industrial policy and foreign policy). Furthermore, he maintained, the nature of the relationship between civilian and military authorities depended on the situation. In one instance an issue might lead to conflict, while in another cooperation could be the norm.

Future analysts, Colton advised, should concentrate on areas where the military was involved in dealing with political issues. Toward this end, he developed a matrix which showed patterns of military participation arranged according to the scope of the issues and the means employed.

Looking at these models, the Kolkowicz approach was characterized by the greatest degree of conflict. The party worked constantly to limit autonomy in the military through an elaborate system of direct control mechanisms—while the military worked just as hard to limit party interference in the military's internal affairs.

Odom's model differed from Kolkowicz's paradigm primarily because of Odom's insistence that the relationship between military and civilian authorities was more cooperative. Unlike Kolkowicz, he saw a permeable boundary between the military and civilian worlds. The party did not have to work to penetrate the military; this had already been accomplished by the common ideology and the joint commitment to the maintenance of the system shared by military and political officials. The important point, for purposes of this study, was that Odom saw the military to be a fully penetrated organization.

In the Colton model the relationship was characterized by both conflict and cooperation. When it came to non-core issues, Colton agreed that the military was penetrated; i.e., that its participation in issues such as foreign policy could be limited. On the other hand, the military maintained considerable autonomy when it came to core issues such as discipline, promotions, tactics, etc. The difficult part of applying the Colton model was to determine exactly what were core and non-core issues. The boundary between the two shifted over time. Stalin, for example, limited the military's core values. Indeed, they were almost nonexistent. Later, under Khrushchev and Brezhnev, they expanded considerably.

This book will argue that over time, the nature of civil-military relations in the Soviet Union changed dramatically. During the early 1920s, for example, conflict characterized the relationship. The party had to control a largely hostile officer corps, while at the same time it worked to build a more loyal armed forces. To this end, the party penetrated all aspects of life in the armed forces. This was not done blindly, however, in accordance with some preexisting ideological imperative. The Bolshevik leaders were realistic, and when threatened by an outside force, they never permitted ideological purity to get in the way of military efficiency.

By the end of the 1920s, however, it was becoming obvious that Moscow had largely succeeded in building a loyal military. There was greater congruence in political and social values between the Bolsheviks and the country's military officers than had been the case in 1917. Thus, while the Kolkowicz model most aptly applied to the early 1920s, it was less useful as a tool for explaining the situation at the end of that decade.

During the Stalinist period military autonomy was almost totally destroyed as most of the senior leadership was either imprisoned or killed, and all aspects of military life were subjected to outside interference. However, the situation changed under Khrushchev and Brezhnev. Slowly, the party permitted the military to regain its autonomy in core areas. Indeed, when it came to issues such as doctrine or force structure, the military gradually gained tremendous authority—to the point where most civilians were excluded from involvement or even knowledge of what was going on in these areas. Military participation, to use Colton's phrase, was at an all-time high, especially in terms of the scope of the issues it was involved in. The relationship became more cooperative than conflictual, but contrary to the situation suggested by Odom, the boundary line between the military and civilian worlds was clearly drawn.

By the time Gorbachev came to power in 1985, the definition of core military interests had expanded to cover almost all areas of military affairs. Indeed, as he looked at the Soviet Army's leadership, Gorbachev was faced with a highly autonomous institution, one which, although officially subordinate to the Kremlin, acted with a high degree of autonomy in areas such as military doctrine. Indeed, the degree of autonomy enjoyed by the Soviet military in such areas exceeded that of many Western militaries.

Gorbachev thus had to reimpose civil control over the military. His assertion of command was not as extensive, nor as brutal as that practiced in the 1920s. Nevertheless, in order to implement his policy of "new political thinking," he had no alternative but to undercut the generals' ability to determine policy in areas such as doctrine, force structure, and nationality relationships. The period from May 1985 to August 1991 was marked by Gorbachev's successful efforts to limit military autonomy. Insofar as the three models were concerned, a close look at events suggests that none of them was able to provide a complete explanation of civil-military relations during that period. Each was partially useful, but the situation was far too complex and fluid to fit within the parameters of any model.

With the collapse of the Soviet Union, the utility of these models ended. Boris Yeltsin had to devise a new system of civil-military relations. At the same time, it is important to keep in mind that Yeltsin inherited a military organization and traditions that were based on the Soviet experience. Some important aspects changed (i.e., the party's monopoly was ended for good), while other aspects (e.g., the military's suspicion of civilians) remained.

One of Yeltsin's first actions was to purge officers clearly opposed to the new system. Those tied too closely to the values of the old system had to go. In addition, he granted the military considerable autonomy—in some cases, more than was the case with Gorbachev. Later, however, he moved to tighten his control over the military—primarily through the budget. He relied little on direct political controls such as the network of political officers that characterized the Soviet period. His primary tools were public structures such as the executive, the press, and the legislature. As in other democratic polities since the emergence of democracy in Russia, the relationship has alternated between cooperation and confrontation.

## Issues

In analyzing the evolution of Soviet and Russian civil-military relations, I will focus on four interrelated variables: the debate over a defensive versus an offensive doctrine, the nature of the force structure, the issue of national armies, and the question of how to produce a politically loyal and militarily competent officer corps.

1. *Military Doctrine.* Of the four issues analyzed in this book, this is the most important one, because it lays the groundwork for topics such as force structure, weapons acquisition, and personnel policies. Decisions in this area influence heavily actions in other areas. An offensive doctrine requires one type of force structure, a defensive one another.

There are several key questions. First, how autonomous is the High Command in determining the country's military doctrine? Have political authorities dominated military decision making in this area? If so, to what degree?

In this study, the offense (or *strategiya sokrusheniya*—a strategy of destruction) refers to a battle plan that foresees one side initiating operations to be carried out on the opponent's territory. The goal is to defeat the enemy by seizing his territory and vital assets, whether they be economic, military, or political. Factors such as surprise, mobility, and maneuverability play key roles.

Defensive strategy, on the other hand, (*strategiya izmora*, or a strategy of attrition) is a poor man's strategy. It aims at forcing the other side to attack first. The goal is to wear down the opponent by forcing him to expend resources (in both equipment and men) as he attempts to invade the USSR/Russia. A series of fixed defenses running from the border deep into the USSR figure prominently in such a strategy. Eventually, the invader will have suffered so many casualties that he will be forced to withdraw. Given the lower economic costs involved, the defensive strategy is attractive during a period of economic scarcity.[10]

2. *Force Structure.* As will be the case with the other issues, the first question to ask is who is making the primary decisions in this area? Under Kolkowicz or even Colton's model, one would expect the generals to fight very hard to control decisions in this area—especially since force structure is generally recognized to be a "core" interest. From Odom's standpoint, these kinds of decisions would be reached on a consensual basis with both civilian and military officials fully involved.

The main policy issue—one which is strongly influenced by the outcome of the debate on doctrine—is what kind of a force structure? Should the country rely primarily on a small, but proficient professional military? Or should it place its bets on a large, but loosely organized and not as well trained militia? Or perhaps it should opt for a mixed system made up of a professional military backed by a militia? While there are exceptions, by and large a large well-equipped, standing army is better suited for offensive actions; a smaller one backed up by less well-trained reserves is more appropriate for a defensive strategy.

3. *National Armies.* National armies are especially useful as a device to back up a small professional military. These formations (i.e., military units composed of individuals who speak a language other than Russian—the USSR recognized more than 100 official languages—in which the native language is the command language) are a way of ensuring a larger mobilization potential in the event of a conflict.

From the standpoint of the High Command, however, such units present at least two problems. The first is that, like militias, they will not possess the same level of training and readiness as a professional military. In fact, since many in the national units will not speak and read Russian, their ability to work closely with Russian units will be limited. The second is that there is always a danger that they will develop into nationalistic forces, pushing for independence from the Russian center. As a consequence, the generals are likely to oppose such forces, preferring instead to put resources into a regular standing army.

4. *Personnel Issues.* Of all the core issues faced by the military leadership, none were more sensitive and aggressively protected than personnel questions. Who gets to the top is a question in which all military officers have a keen interest. What are the criteria for promotion? To what degree is there outside interference?

Similarly, the role played by political structures is a major concern. Do they serve as a control mechanism, or is their primary purpose to support the armed forces? How do regular officers view these structures? Do they believe they are helpful? Or do they see them as unwanted interference in internal military matters?

## Time Frame

The time periods covered by this study, 1917-1930, 1985-1990, and 1990-1994, were selected because they provided an opportunity to evaluate the utility of the various models during the Soviet period as well as to take a look at the emerging post-Communist period. Change is central to all three of these time periods.

The first period is characterized by a move from an autocratic regime to a Marxist-Leninist system. The task for the Bolsheviks was to introduce a new system of civil-military relations while at the same time ensuring the loyalty and efficiency of the armed forces.[11]

The second or Gorbachev period was also marked by change. Here the problem was not so much the creation of a new polity as it was introducing major reforms in the preexisting one. Gorbachev wanted to keep the Marxist-Leninist system, but to do so he believed that radical changes had to be made, especially in civil-military relations. In short, he had to change the relationship; he could not accomplish his goals if the generals continued to enjoy such a high degree of autonomy in military affairs.

Finally, the post-Communist period presented another problem: how to construct a new form of civil-military relations without destroying the preexisting military, as happened in the aftermath of the 1917 October Revolution? One could not simply smash the preexisting military system—especially since Yeltsin depended on senior military officers for political support.

These three periods also fit together nicely from a historical standpoint. First, the 1920s were constantly referred to by military as well as civilian writers during the Gorbachev period. Indeed, they figured prominently in the debates over the future of the Soviet armed forces. Second, even in the post-Gorbachev era Russian military writers constantly returned to the 1920s and even earlier periods in discussing the need to construct a new Russian military. In short, the Russian military is being built on the traditions not only of the pre-Communist Tsarist Army, but of the Red Army as well.

## Organization of the Study

This book is divided into three parts. Part I deals with the 1920s and sets the stage for the remainder of the study. Its purpose is, first, to provide the reader with an understanding of the debates and issues that figure so prominently during the Gorbachev and post-Gorbachev periods. Second, this section offers an opportunity to apply the three models and discover how useful they were in explaining how civil-military relations evolved during the 1920s.

Part II looks at the Gorbachev period, focusing on Gorbachev's effort to reassert control over the armed forces. Part III looks at the post-Gorbachev period, asking the question: How useful are models in understanding civil-military relations in a country like the former Soviet Union? Finally, the conclusion ties this discussion together by analyzing the overall utility of models for understanding Soviet and post-Soviet civil-military relations.

## The Sources

Three kinds of sources were utilized in this study. First, I carefully reviewed the relevant Western literature. I included not only recent articles and books, but works published during the 1930s, 1940s, and 1950s as well. Unfortunately, with a few exceptions (e.g., the now-classic work by Dmitri Fedotoff-White, *The Growth of the Red Army*), very little of value was written until the pioneering works by Rand analysts such as Garthoff, Dinnerstein, and Wolfe in the 1950s.[12]

*The 1920s.* One of the most important Western historical works dealing with the 1920s is John Erickson's 1962 study, *The Soviet High Command.* Since that time a number of works of varying quality and importance on the evolution of the Soviet armed forces have been written. Among the most important is Mark von Hagen's *Soldiers in the Proletarian Dictatorship: The Red Army and the Soviet Socialist State, 1917-1930.*[13]

Russian language works provided the second source of materials for this book. Reflective of the importance that Soviet writers assigned to the 1920s is the wide variety of works that have been published on this period. While a number of these sources were important in the preparation of this book, one was of special significance. This was I. B. Berkhin's *Military Reform in the USSR (1924-1925).* In spite of the title, this book covers the entire period of the 1920s, not just 1924-1925. It dealt not only with the ethnic question, but with the debate over a professional military, the role of the party and political organs, as well as military doctrine. It was indispensable for an understanding of the period. A second Russian book of importance was A. G. Kavtaradze's *Military Specialists in the Service of the Republics of the Soviets, 1917-1922.* When it came to the issue of territorial forces, V. N. Konyukhovskiy's *Territorial System of Military Development* was the most authoritative work in the field. The speeches and the collected writings of the major actors were also important. In addition, for the 1920s, journals such as *Voennaya mysl' i revolyutsiya, Voennaya nauka i revolyutsiya, Voyna i revolyutsiya, Voennoe delo,* and *Voennyy vestnik* were invaluable sources of information.[14]

*The 1980s and 1990s.* Although a number of books and articles deal in part with the role of the military in the Gorbachev and post-Gorbachev period, few, however, attempt to conceptualize the evolution of military politics in the former USSR. In addition to this writer's *The Soviet High Command, 1967-1989; Personalities and Politics*, the list includes the volume edited by Timothy Colton and Thane Gustafson, *Soldiers and the Soviet State*, as well as the work edited by Bruce Parrott, *The Dynamics of Soviet Defense Policy*. Another, more recent work of note, is Thomas M. Nichols, *The Sacred Cause: Civil-Military Conflict over Soviet National Security*. In addition, journals such as *Voenno-istoricheskiy zhurnal, Voennaya zhurnal, Voennaya mysl', Voennyy vestnik, Morskoy sbornik*, as well as newspapers such as *Krasnaya zvezda, Izvestiya,* and *Pravda* were of considerable use.[15]

The third source of material for this book was discussions both in this country and abroad with Russian and Soviet civilian and military authorities. While asking to remain anonymous, senior Soviet and Russian military officers were particularly helpful and patient in enabling this writer to better understand how they viewed the nature of civil-military relations during both the Communist and post-Communist periods.

# I

## The 1920s

# *I*

# DEVISING A NEW MILITARY DOCTRINE
## OFFENSE VS. DEFENSE

> A strategy of attrition in no way renounces
> in principle the destruction of enemy
> personnel as a goal of an operation. But in
> this it sees only a part of the mission of the
> armed front rather than its entire mission.
>
> Col. Aleksandr Svechin

> As in the past, superiority lies with the
> offense, which includes the possibility of
> delivering in a specific direction overwhelm-
> ing concentrations of organized strikes, and
> thereby inflicting a serious defeat.
>
> Marshal Mikhail Tukhachevsky

### The Problem

When they came to power in 1917, the Bolsheviks faced a dilemma. On the
one hand, they needed a new doctrine more in accord with their revolutionary goals and beliefs. From a doctrinal standpoint, this meant an offensive strategy because an offensive strategy would permit the Bolsheviks to
portray themselves as moving forward, climbing new mountains, conquer-
ing new heights, exporting the revolution to other parts of the world. Positional warfare, characteristic of World War I, was the type of strategy followed by capitalist armies. Given its revolutionary, unique nature, the Bolsheviks needed a *new* strategy to distinguish themselves from others in the
world.

*The Nature of Doctrine.* The problem that faced the Bolsheviks at that
time was that the majority of the officers from the old army, who played a
key role in the new Red Army, believed that an offensive strategy required
a high degree of mechanization, close coordination between troops, the
presence of armored forces as well as an air force, and a large, well-trained

army equipped with the latest in modern technology. They argued that such a force structure was expensive and required a strong industrial base.

On the other hand, these officers claimed that a defensive strategy was much cheaper. History had shown that fighting a defensive war did not require the high degree of mechanization, technical training, modern equipment, and coordination of an offensive strategy. In essence, Soviet troops would occupy a series of defensive positions and wait for an opponent to wear itself out (in terms of casualties and the loss of weapons). Once the enemy was exhausted, the Red Army would then be in a position to expel the invader and perhaps even export the revolution abroad. This strategy did not require a large standing army and the demands on the technological training of those in the military were much lower—an important consideration, given the illiteracy that pervaded the Soviet Union. It would be costly in terms of the destruction that the Soviet Union would suffer, but the former Tsarist officers believed that the USSR had little choice. The country was in chaos. Not only was the economy a mess, the political and social situation was also disastrous. These officers argued that ideology would have to take a backseat to historical, economic, and social realities. In the 1920s it was a luxury the country could not afford—politicizing military doctrine would threaten the country's security.

*An Open Discussion?* A second, closely related issue was how to define military doctrine. On the one hand, those who were out to politicize military doctrine argued for a very tight, comprehensive definition, one which would guide the future of Soviet force structure, and provide the leaders of the Red Army with a vehicle for socializing the new army's recruits and officers. Officers from the old army, on the other hand, feared that if doctrine were comprehensively defined it would lead to stagnation in the intellectual thought process. Such a definition would not only include a number of key variables, it would also exclude others. History, for example, would be very selectively interpreted. The possibility of using it as the basis for an open discussion of these questions would be gone. Given the dynamic, changing nature of military affairs, and the danger that ideological orthodoxy could intrude into this area, opponents maintained that a working definition which permitted a free and open use of the past was the best approach.

## The Civil War—The Basis for a "New" Doctrine?

The Civil War differed significantly from the positional type of warfare characteristic of World War I. Instead of two giant military machines facing each other across a no-man's land, fronts in the Russian Civil War were more fluid. Troops lived off the land, made deep penetration raids into the enemy's rear, failed to coordinate attacks, and organization was weak. Once an attack or an offensive lost momentum, a counterattack would be launched, thereby forcing the formerly victorious army to retreat.

Among the newly converted Communists there were a large number who had fought in the Civil War, and who believed that the war had laid the foundation for a unique proletarian form of military science. As Fedotoff-White put it, "The young Red commanders, victorious in the field against their White enemies, thought they had discovered the foundations of a new revolutionary doctrine of the proletariat, which relegated to the scrap heap the theories of the old generals, based on the experience of World War I and the study of its history." These men believed that strategy and tactics were dependent on Marxist theory, not on historical precedent or traditional military science. In practice this meant putting primary emphasis on the offensive. Just as Red Army units avoided positional warfare during the Civil War, so should the future Soviet military. Ideological conviction, together with mobility and maneuverability, would be the cornerstones of the new military science. Defensive tactics, such as the construction of fortifications, had to be avoided at all costs.[1]

Meanwhile, in good "Kolkowiczian" fashion, the majority of professional military officers resisted this effort to politicize military doctrine, arguing that while the Civil War led to some interesting changes in tactics, it did not seriously affect strategy and doctrine. Mikhail Tukhachevsky set out these two positions in a lecture in 1919:

> One opinion maintains that the conditions under which the Civil War was conducted resulted in several special strategic concepts that must be mastered. The second position, which is juxtaposed to the first, argues that the laws of strategy are unshakable and for that reason there is nothing new in our Civil War and that if we master these laws, which were mastered earlier, then our actions will be completely correct and we will avoid mistakes.[2]

During the early 1920s, these two points of view gave rise to three identifiable schools of thought. The first maintained that the Civil War had little relevance for Soviet military thought. Furthermore, representatives of this school—Aleksandr Svechin was the most famous—argued that given the country's dire economic situation, a defensive strategy was the only viable alternative. The second, headed by Mikhail Frunze, idealized the Civil War experience by placing primary emphasis on maneuverability and the offense. The third was Leon Trotsky's changing, non-dogmatic approach which tried to combine the two. For him, both ideology and history were important. In evaluating this situation, however, it is important to note, first, that a power struggle was going on between Stalin and Trotsky. Second, by the end of the 1920s the issue had become so politicized that much of the discussion had little to do with military strategy. And third, once the ideological veneer was wiped away, none of the positions were as simplistic as their opponents claimed. Svechin, for example, favored defense, but he also recognized the importance of the offense. Similarly, while Frunze emphasized the offense, he too realized that a war could not be won without a solid defense.

### Framing the Issues

Frunze and S. I. Gusev fired the first salvo in the debate over the politicization of doctrine in the twenty-one theses, which they had planned to submit to the Tenth Party Congress (the first fifteen were written by Gusev, the last six by Frunze). While Trotsky's opposition prevented the presentation of these theses to the congress, they were important because they illustrated Frunze's early thinking.[3]

Three of the theses presented by Gusev and Frunze dealt directly with military doctrine. Thesis ten stated that the military should pay more attention to "mounted" infantry because of its maneuverability. Thesis eleven stated that the Civil War showed the increased importance of cavalry in modern warfare—primarily because of its maneuverability. Close coordination of cavalry with other units would produce "tremendous fire-power and transform it into a new branch—armored cavalry." Finally, thesis nineteen argued that work toward the development of a "unified proletarian doctrine" should not be the preserve of officers from the former Tsarist Army. Rather, it could only be built by "the joint efforts of military specialists as well as all political workers who have sufficient background in the construction of the Red Army and its struggle to utilize the revolutionary experience of the masses as its base." The latter reference both attempted to legitimate non-military specialists and to politicize doctrine.[4]

Frunze returned to the offensive in July 1921 with an article entitled "A Unified Military Doctrine and the Red Army." Turning to the question of defining doctrine, Frunze argued for an all-encompassing definition. Otherwise, he argued, the Soviet military was faced with chaos. The new state required a comprehensive definition of doctrine not only because it needed to differentiate itself from the old order, but because without it the Kremlin's attempt to inculcate new values in the military would be hurt. As he put it,

> It will above all point to the character of military clashes which we can expect. Should we accept the idea of passive defense of the country, not adopting or pursuing an active approach or should we keep the latter in mind. On the nature of the answer we give to this question will depend the entire character of the development of our armed forces, the character and system of training of individual soldiers and large military units. . . .[5]

In Frunze's eyes, doctrine would both determine the nature of the country's force structure and provide the sense of coherence needed to interrelate all of the factors involved. "It should above all explain the character of those combat encounters which await us." Frunze defined military doctrine as:

> a unified set of teachings, accepted by an army of a given state, which fix the form of constructing the armed forces of that country, and the methods of training and directing the troops (militarily) on the basis of those views which predominate in the given state and on the basis of the methods of solving them which flow from the class essence of the state and the level of development of its productive forces.

Since the economic basis of the new state was different from all other existing states, its political and military structure and doctrine also had to be qualitatively different. Indeed, it was the interaction of the technical and political sides of military affairs that gave the USSR its unique military doctrine. This was why senior officers in the Red Army had to understand both political and military factors. Only then would they be able to construct a class-based military doctrine.[6]

Turning to the issue of defense versus offense, Frunze argued that in view of the political (i.e., proletarian) nature of the new state, "Only he who finds in himself the resoluteness to attack will win; the side that always defends itself is inevitably doomed to defeat. The entire revolutionary historical process of the working class makes it necessary to go over to the offense when conditions are right." This made it important to educate the masses of soldiers in the spirit of the offensive. "The proletariat will attack and together with them as their main weapon will be the Red Army." In fact, Frunze not only saw the offense as the ideological basis of military, he also viewed it as the key to operational success.[7]

In light of the USSR's boundless spaces, the maneuver principle was perfect for the Soviet Union. "Our command staff must teach the superiority of maneuver of a strategic character, and the entire Red Army must learn quickly this art and adopt the march-maneuver in a planned manner." Indeed, Frunze went so far as to argue that in the future defense in the form of fortresses "will be completely insignificant in our operations." Instead focus would be on field armies—especially the cavalry.[8]

For his part, Svechin argued against what he considered to be party influence in military affairs, maintaining that military science exists independently of ideological considerations.[9] He admitted that political authorities must be in control during a war: "A politics that would renounce the retention of its authority over the leadership of a war and acknowledge the primacy of military specialists and silently conform to their requirements would itself acknowledge its own bankruptcy."[10] However, there was no such thing, he argued, as a "class-based" military science. There was only military science and history. To quote Svechin, "Doctrine is defined as that point of view that understands military history and incorporates its experience and lessons. Doctrine—that is the daughter of history."[11] If the new Soviet state insisted on injecting Marxism into its military science, it ran the risk of politicizing an apolitical undertaking. To quote Fedotoff-White, "Svechin's idea was thus of a national, not a class army, subordinated to the government, of course, but left free to develop what he called the specifically soldierly viewpoint, instead of being permeated with political ideas and influences."[12] Svechin also feared, correctly as it turned out, that the politicization of military science would dogmatize the study of strategy and history and penalize those who wanted to engage in independent analysis. What was needed was a willingness to adopt military doctrine to changing conditions; something that would be impossible if politics became the primary concern in devising doctrine. Svechin made this point in the preface to the first edition of his classic work, *Strategiya*, when he noted that "a particular strategic policy must be divined for every war; each war is a special case, which requires its own particular logic rather than any kind of stereotype or pattern, no matter how splendid it may be."[13] Needless to say, Svechin's opposition to outside interference in military affairs was not popular among officers whose primary raison d'etat was their ideological commitment.

In responding to the positions articulated by Frunze and Svechin, Leon Trotsky criticized—and alienated—both sides. To the professional military officers he was an amateur interfering in military affairs, while to the Communists he was defending ideas and views which most of them considered reactionary and suspect.

To begin with, Trotsky rejected Svechin's attempt to depoliticize military doctrine. Soviet military doctrine was based on Marxism-Leninism. Marxism rejected the idea that any aspect of the socio-economic superstructure could be apolitical. At the same time, it was critical not to over-politicize society in general and military doctrine in particular. Marxist theory provided a basis for dealing with military problems. As he put it in December 1921, "Marxism does not supply ready-made prescriptions, least of all in the sphere of military construction. But here, too, it provides us with the method." Thus while the significance of Marxism could not be denied in military affairs, there was no need to develop a special Marxist military science. Politicizing military doctrine made no sense.

> A military doctrine that declares "We'll crush our enemies beneath a barrage of red caps," is of no use to us. We must eradicate such bravado and revolutionary snobbery. Chaos results whenever strategy is developed from the standpoint of revolutionary youth.[14]

Trotsky admitted that defining doctrine was important, but he maintained that the current search for a Marxist military doctrine in the Soviet Union was leading to silliness.

> But under discussion is what kind of doctrine *are we lacking*? That is, what are these *new* principles, which must enter into the program of military construction, and just what is their content? And it is precisely here that the muddling begins. One individual makes the sensational discovery that the Red Army is a *class* army, the army of a proletarian dictatorship. Another one adds to this that inasmuch as the Red Army is a revolutionary, internationalist army, it must be an offensive army. A third proposes in behalf of the spirit of the offensive that we pay special attention to cavalry and aviation. And, finally, a fourth proposes that we don't forget to apply Makhno's hand-carts (tachanka). Around the world in a hand-cart—there is a doctrine for the Red Army!

In reality, Trotsky argued "it is useless to seek logical definitions" of military doctrine. The way out of this dead-end was to continue historically based analytical work while avoiding scholastic definitions. Indeed, Trotsky was beginning to sound like Svechin on this topic. For example, he argued that "the army should be an independent organism, be capable of critical thinking, and be able to evaluate the situation."[15]

Meanwhile, Trotsky argued, the Red Army must swallow its pride and recognize that it was behind the West in military affairs. Indeed, to have a competitive military it had to learn from the West: ". . . in order to invent anything except a hand-cart (tachanka), it is necessary to go to school to the bourgeoisie." Given the current situation in the country, Trotsky maintained that the Red Army would have to concentrate on more mundane things.

> I maintain that our military doctrine begins with this, that we must tell the Red Army soldier; learn to grease your boots and oil your rifle. If in addition to our will to victory and our readiness to self-sacrifice we also learn to grease boots, then we shall have the best possible military doctrine.[16]

Turning to operations, Trotsky attacked Frunze's tendency to mythicize the Civil War experience while ignoring other equally important aspects of history. After all, Trotsky argued, the Soviets did not "invent" the maneuverist principle.

> Was the Red Army alone distinguished by maneuverability? No. The Strategy of the Whites was without exception maneuverist. In most in-

stances their troops were inferior to ours in numbers and in point of morale, but they were superior in military skill. Hence the need for a maneuverist strategy was felt most urgently by the Whites. During the initial stages we learned about maneuverability from them.

Trotsky charged that men like Tukhachevsky, who argued that positional warfare was no longer relevant, were wrong. "Only a daredevil cavalry man is of the opinion that one must always attack." The need "is to go beyond this stage of maneuvering which is only the obverse side of guerilla warfare."[17]

Despite the military soundness of Trotsky's position on avoiding a comprehensive definition of an offensive doctrine, the vast majority of the new Communist officers opposed him:

> The young zealots, fresh converts to the gospel of Marx were enraged. They were told, and had come to believe, that there was a universal sesame at their disposal to solve any new problem in a revolutionary Bolshevik way. And here was Trotsky saying that the key could not open the book of war! That instead of a logical well-rounded-out theory of a Marxian science of war, the conquerors of Denikin and Wrangel had to be content with drilling sections and waiting patiently for Soviet economic life to rise to a higher level.

The approach advocated by Frunze and Gusev was much more to their liking. It fed their egos and meant that the study of strategy and tactics would not be the exclusive purview of the "military specialists," those hated officers from the imperial army.[18] Indeed, if military affairs were accepted as a science, "The self-made military men, the former noncommissioned officers commanding army divisions in the Soviet forces, could not compete with them (i.e., military professionals) in that field."[19]

### The Debate Intensifies

The debate came to a head in March 1922. Frunze, just back from an assignment in Turkey, spoke at a meeting of commanders and commissars of the Red Army. On the surface, he seemed to be attempting to resolve his dispute with Trotsky as he retreated from his more radical earlier statements.

Frunze adamantly denied that any attempt was being made to politicize or dogmatize military doctrine. The problem, however, was that the Red Army needed a unified set of political/technical concepts not only to educate cadre in the armed forces, but also to provide the logical planning system necessary to build a modern military. Without it, training would come to a halt. One had to go beyond the technical approach advocated by Svechin and Trotsky. Indeed, if one focused only on the technical side of things, Frunze admitted, the Civil War experience contributed very little. The two must be combined. And Frunze emphasized that the basis for such a doctrine clearly existed. "It includes the experiences of all those in the Red Army taken together."[20] He went further in a speech to the Eleventh Party Congress:

> I have never been and I am not a supporter of the idea that we created a special proletarian strategy and tactics. When on the pages of the late journal *Voennoe Delo*, there appeared several articles by communists which suggested that we made a complete revolution, that we have overthrown all of the old principles and created a new strategy and tactics, it seemed ludicrous to me.

From Frunze's perspective, the country would have a proletarian military doctrine, but only when it had the wherewithal to create one. To be effective, the Red Army had to be pragmatic. For that reason, Frunze maintained, "We will wage war with the same methods and means as is done in bourgeois armies." Despite his more pragmatic approach, however, Frunze did not give up in his effort to construct a politicized definition of military doctrine, one which clearly favored the offense. Indeed, in his concluding speech to the Eleventh Party Congress, he stated, "I want to once again reiterate that I consider the basic questions concerning our doctrine resolved." The task now was to fill in the blanks.[21]

Frunze's speech made it clear that whatever Trotsky or Svechin might have thought, the blanks still to be filled in were few in number. Speaking at a meeting of commanders and commissars during the early part of March, he admitted that "maneuverability is not an end in itself." It was only one of the ways in which goals could be achieved. Positional warfare was also possible. "Maneuverability by no means excludes positional military formations. Quite the opposite, correct maneuvers are unthinkable without the broad utilization of positional methods of battle." Nevertheless, this was not the preferred approach, it was not the way to victory.[22]

Conceptually, Frunze was arguing that despite the importance of military technology, it was the "spiritual force" of "proletarianism" that played the decisive role in the Civil War. The basis of this force in a proletarian political system was the offensive: "another characteristic action of our Red Army is its offensiveness. Only maneuverability will enable us to overcome the weaknesses of our technology." Finally, in his closing speech to the Eleventh Party Congress, he listed fifteen areas on which the Red Army should be based. Again the underlying theme was the primacy of the offense. In some cases the Red Army might be forced to accept positional warfare. But ideologically, the offense was preeminent.[23]

Mikhail Tukhachevsky, the young officer who had risen to the top ranks of the Red Army after having served in the Imperial Army during World War I, weighed in on Frunze's side. Tukhachevsky was fervently committed to the offense. Fortified positions had little value, he argued. The loss or gain of territory was more important. By taking land an opponent would be weakened. Furthermore, Tukhachevsky maintained that the Red Army would be able to recruit new soldiers from the proletariat on the other side. To this end, the offense was critical. If anything, it would speed the end of the capitalist world—and strengthen the security of the Soviet state. Denying the importance of the class struggle in Soviet military doctrine meant denying the validity of the revolution itself.[24]

Trotsky used the Eleventh Party Congress to attack both Frunze and Klement Voroshilov.[25] In particular he blasted Frunze's selective use of history in constructing a unified military doctrine.

> What is the content of Comrade Frunze's military doctrine? It consists of an uncritical idealization of the past. Our heralds of military doctrine seek to deduce it from the class nature of the proletariat, and to render eternal that which characterized a certain period of the war.

This "idealization" of history would do nothing to solve the many problems facing the Red Army. "Please stop threatening to annihilate the enemy by throwing hats at him; let us instead learn the ABCs of military affairs from the enemy." Furthermore, Trotsky attacked Frunze's emphasis on the future role of the Red Army as an instrument of "revolutionary warfare." The idea of educating an army made up primarily of peasants in the spirit of revolutionary warfare made no sense. "With such abstract speeches we can never reach the moujik's heart. It is the surest way of ruining our military propaganda and our political agitation." Doctrinal statements should focus on the defense of the Soviet state, something to which peasants could relate.[26]

Turning to operational matters, Trotsky agreed that there was nothing wrong with the idea of the offense. "Annihilation is impossible without the offensive. The stronger will is revealed by him who creates the most favorable conditions for the offensive and utilizes them to the very end." The issue, according to Trotsky, was to know when to rely on the offensive and when to turn to the defense. "If the material conditions of mobilization militate against it, then I would be a hopeless formalist and dunderhead to build my plan on the notion that I must be the first to take the offensive." The problem with the approach advocated by Frunze and Voroshilov was that it could lead to major mistakes on the part of senior Soviet officers.

> If we hammer into the minds of our commanding personnel that revolutionary nature and "strong will" demand that you be the *first* to attack

then the very first period of our operations in the West can lead our commanding staff astray because conditions may impose upon us, and in all likelihood will impose upon us an initial period of flexible defense and maneuverist retreat.

Furthermore, an offensive strategy presupposed an excellent transportation and communication system in order to ensure that all resources were mobilized and the maximum amount of force was massed at the critical point at the correct time. The problem was that the Soviet Union faced major problems in all these areas, a situation made worse by its geographical expanses and population distribution. Likewise, an offensive strategy assumed a high degree of expertise on the part of commanders. Unfortunately, middle-level commanders were not sufficiently prepared for their task, while lower ranks were even weaker. As a result, Trotsky argued that the Red Army would have to rely on a defensive strategy during the early stages of a conflict.

> What conclusion, then, follows from this? It is this, that our strategic plan—not an abstract plan, but one calculated for a concrete situation and concrete conditions—must envisage during the first period of the war not the offense but the defense. Its aim is to gain time for the unfolding of mobilization. . . . having space and numbers in our favor, we calmly and confidently fix the limit where our mobilization, secured by our flexible defense, shall have prepared a sufficient fist to enable us to go over to the counteroffensive.

Flexibility would be all-important. Given the hostility of the peasants, the probability that the wave of world revolution was receding in Europe, and the technical deficiencies facing the Red Army, emphasis should be placed, not on ideology, but on pragmatism and adaptability. Thus, from a doctrinal standpoint, rather than emphasizing only one aspect of strategy—the offense—it was important "to start thinking . . . about concrete conditions," and with an open, unbiased eye toward the past, to devise a strategy to fit those conditions.[27]

Throughout the 1920s, Svechin was the most influential and articulate voice of the professional military on military doctrine. A strategy of destruction (*sokrushenie*, or the offense) focused everything on one goal: "Everything is subordinated to the interests of the general operation, and in a general operation everything depends on a decisive point." As a consequence, he maintained,

> The idea of destruction forces the commander to consider all secondary interests, directions, and geographical objectives meaningless. Pauses in the development of military operations contradict the idea of destruction.

In short, everything hinged on creating a breakthrough, and then keeping the offense going regardless of the costs involved. The idea was to knock the enemy out in one blow. The problem with such a strategy for the USSR was that it assumed a high degree of industrialization and technology. In fact, the Soviet economy would not be in a position to ensure the army's ability to carry out such an operation for many years to come, he argued.[28]

A strategy of attrition (*Izmor*, or the defense), on the other hand, was better suited to Russian conditions, Svechin believed.[29] To begin with, it placed less reliance on technology, because it called for the creation of a system of strategic defenses. This was especially important in the USSR, with its vast expanses, its forests and swamps. The establishment of several lines of fortifications, well placed to take advantage of geographical obstacles, would significantly raise the costs to an attacker. By constantly banging his head against such fortifications, the attacker would soon find his forces depleted, his troops exhausted, his equipment destroyed. Such a doctrine would also better accommodate a force structure based on a mixed militia-regular army.[30] Furthermore, Svechin maintained that a defensive strategy was as much a plan for victory as a war of destruction. "Like a strategy of destruction, a strategy of attrition constitutes a search for material superiority and the fight for it, but this search is not limited solely to the desire to deploy superior forces in a decisive sector." Instead, it was characterized by "limited goals," something he believed was more appropriate to the new Soviet state. Svechin argued that a strategy based on strategic defenses required fewer personnel and equipment. "In general, the pursuit of negative goals, that is, fighting for the complete or partial maintenance of the status quo, requires less expenditure of forces or resources than the pursuit of positive goals, namely fighting for conquest and forward movement. It is easier to keep what you have than get something new."[31]

Svechin did not believe in a static form of defense. As he saw it, history showed that both the offense and the defense must be integral parts of a Soviet strategy. The Soviet side might initially fight a defensive war, but once the enemy began to weaken, the Red Army would go over to the counteroffensive. To quote him, "If we must wage defensive warfare, then the thinking of a strategist should primarily dwell on the position in time and space at which one could count on changing the course of a war, causing a crisis and switching from negative goals to positive goals." Thus, for Svechin the counteroffensive—or as he called it, the counterattack—was a key part of military strategy.[32]

The second issue of concern to Svechin was parity. While parity did not play a major role in his book on strategy (it focused more on how to fight a war, rather than on questions such as the balance of power), he made it clear that he considered parity important from a military point of view. As he put it in *Strategiya*, "Military parity . . . leads to the renunciation of a destructive strike." Thus, from his point of view, the greater the degree to which the USSR had parity with its opponent(s), the greater the likelihood that the other side would be dissuaded from using military force.[33]

Both Trotsky and Svechin were correct from a military standpoint. An open-ended military doctrine that took into account both the possibility of offensive and defensive strategies, one that would be based on the specific situation existing at the time, was most appropriate. In the event of a war, it would enable the military leadership to consider carefully the situation at hand and decide on a strategy. As one observer described Svechin's view on this issue, "Given the unpredictability of war, it was dangerous to focus on one plan to the exclusion of other alternatives. Should the initial attack fail, the absence of any fall-back plan would leave troops in an extremely vulnerable position." To illustrate his point, Svechin cited the Schlieffen Plan, the German surprise attack into France via Belgium during World War I. It represented "a preoccupation with a specific strategy without due regard for secondary circumstances and avenues of advance." However, military considerations were only one part of the equation. Indeed, this discussion was also influenced by the struggle between Trotsky and Stalin, as well as by the emotions and self-interest of the individuals most directly concerned—the new Communist officers. For them, a defensive doctrine remained unacceptable.[34] As Fedotoff-White put it,

> A defensive doctrine would hardly have suited the leaders of Moslems in the first century of the Hegira. There was a fanatical belief in their right-ness, in their having a mission to fulfill. The same was true of the Russian Communists. . . . A defensive military doctrine, or any military doctrine short of a definitely offensive one, did not correspond to their emotional *Gestalt*, it was out of place in their viewpoint.[35]

This was *not* the time for a cold, rational, dispassionate discussion of this issue.

### The Offense Becomes Soviet Doctrine

By the mid-1920s Trotsky's star was in decline. He was not only ill, he was becoming increasingly isolated within the party. When in December 1923 he wrote a letter to the Central Committee attacking the growth of bureaucracy in the USSR, he was greeted with angry denunciations. He was even accused of treason by Zinoviev, who called for his arrest. To make matters worse, since June 1923, the Central Control Commission—dominated by Trotsky's opponents—had been conducting a full-scale inquiry into the state of the Soviet military. The report to the Central Committee accused Trotsky of mismanaging the armed forces. At the same time, Trotsky's deputy—

Sklyansky—was removed from his position to be replaced by Frunze. In addition, Klement Voroshilov was named commander of the vitally important Moscow Military District. These latter actions—combined with the fact that Trotsky had gone to the Caucasus for medical reasons—made Frunze the chief of the Red Army. A number of Stalin's allies were also appointed to the Revolutionary Military Council, and by the middle of the year Tukhachevsky was named as Frunze's deputy. In short, the military was effectively penetrated when it came to doctrine.

With Trotsky removed from military affairs, the center position in the debate disappeared. On one extreme was Voroshilov and those closely associated with Stalin, who favored politicizing Soviet military doctrine. A somewhat more moderate version of this position was articulated by Tukhachevsky, who argued for a proletarian doctrine, but who claimed that it would only succeed if the USSR overcame its technical deficiencies. At the other end of the continuum were the professional military officers, led by Svechin, who resented civilian interference in their affairs and continued to argue for a defensive strategy.[36]

Because of these disagreements, the Red Army still lacked a clearly articulated military doctrine when Frunze took over. To a large degree, this was a result of the absence of a unified structure. As a consequence, the army staff began work on a new structural basis for the Red Army, one which would enshrine the maneuverist principle. The most important action during 1925 was the issuance of *Provisional Field Service Regulations*. In contrast to the West, where regulations often serve primarily as tactical directives, in the Red Army there was a direct tie between such regulations and military strategy at the highest level. Indeed, these regulations provided officers and commanders with the wherewithal to implement the prevailing strategy. Consequently, what went into them had a major impact on both the country's strategy and its force structure.[37]

The *Provisional Field Service Regulations* were written by a commission headed by Tukhachevsky. He used these regulations to take sharp issue with those in the Red Army, most prominent being Voroshilov, who argued that because of the backwardness of Russian industry, the Soviet military could not compete with its more modern Western opponents. Instead, it would have to depend on revolutionary enthusiasm to make up for its industrial backwardness.[38]

In his introduction to the *Regulations*, Tukhachevsky attacked the Voroshilov line, calling this approach, "foolish chatter which helps counterrevolution." To be sure, technological progress would be needed to compete with the West. As he put it, "the superior technique of imperialist armies must be overcome by the Red Army's evolution and mastery of still more powerful technique." The *Regulations* themselves attempted "to detail the lessons of the Civil War into operational ideas and principles." These principles included: (1) the importance of close cooperation of all military forces; (2) the significance of initiative and the danger of "passivity"; and (3) a recognition of the supreme importance of the offensive as the most important form of combat. The defense was mentioned, but only as a means of winning time while the Red Army prepared its forces for the offensive.[39]

Svechin responded with the second edition of his book *Strategiya*, in which he reiterated his argument in favor of a strategy of attrition. Svechin's argument was a paradigm of Thomistic logic. He carefully constructed a set of assumptions on which he subsequently based his argument. In this case, he maintained that since the USSR would be unable to mount an initial decisive blow against an enemy, and since it was not vulnerable to a lightning blow—the kind which could and would annihilate a smaller state—a strategy of attrition made sense. At the same time, he maintained, the country's ability to conduct offensive operations should be improved.[40]

The key to Svechin's approach was trading space for time. For such a strategy to succeed, however, the front would have to be united with the rear "through the planned mobilization of the entire 'state rear,' by which he meant the national economy, for the purpose of supporting front operations." Svechin's effort to conduct a rational dialogue on the issue of a defensive/offensive strategy was to no avail. Not only was it opposed by Tukhachevsky, it was flying in the face of Stalin's "revolution from above," and his attack on all aspects of military autonomy.

As long as Svechin's defensive strategy was opposed only by the Red Commanders, he was able to make his points in an open debate. Now, however, the issue was politicized. One writer, for example, suggested that a defensive strategy was a recipe for defeatism. Indeed, support for a defensive strategy would become synonymous with betrayal of the revolution and eventually led to Svechin's arrest and subsequent death.[41]

Despite their disagreement on other points, Svechin and Tukhachevsky were in agreement in one area; an offensive strategy required the complete mechanization of the Soviet Army and the economy on which it was based. Tukhachevsky argued in 1927 that the only hope for the Red Army was the complete militarization of the Soviet economy. Indeed, according to G. Isserson, one of Tukhachevsky's closet collaborators during the 1920s, Tukhachevsky came up with a master plan for mechanizing the Soviet Army in 1927, at the height of the war scare. The country's political leadership rejected it.[42] In spite of his more ideological orientation and his penchant for the offense, Tukhachevsky shared Svechin's contempt for civilian party officials who tried to interfere with military doctrine. This put him in direct conflict with Voroshilov, a man who knew little about military affairs and whose every action was aimed at pleasing Stalin. As a consequence, conflict between the two men was inevitable. The matter came to head in July 1927 when "Yakir, Putna and several other high ranking officers closely identified with Tukhachevsky . . . sent a secret report to the Politburo, contending that Voroshilov was incompetent and unfit to direct the Soviet war machine." Since Voroshilov was Stalin's man, his position was secure. On the other hand, Stalin particularly disliked Tukhachevsky. As a result, Stalin demoted him to commander of the Leningrad Military District.[43]

Despite the work that had been done in preparing the *Field Service Regulations*, Voroshilov claimed that the Soviet Union lacked a comprehensive war plan. In practical terms, this meant that the USSR had done little in the way of long-term strategic planning. As a consequence, the final form the Soviet armed forces would take was still up for grabs. The problem, Erickson suggests, was that the solution of the military problem had to await the outcome of the political-ideological struggle "which sought to determine the main direction in which Soviet effort should move—towards expanding revolution or into a defence of the single Socialist bastion."[44]

Tukhachevsky's replacement as chief of staff was Boris Shaposhnikov, another former Tsarist officer. The contrast between the two was striking. Where Tukhachevsky was strong-willed, outspoken, and combative, Shaposhnikov was much more circumspect and more willing to compromise with political authorities. This difference in personalities led Tukhachevsky's sister-in-law to describe the two rival generals as "The Volcano and the Iceberg."[45]

Shaposhnikov's ideas were most clearly articulated in a three-volume book he published beginning in 1927 entitled *Brain of the Army*. In this work, he argued that since future wars would take place on a massive scale, a general staff should be created to control the military. At the same time, Shaposhnikov maintained that since war on such a scale would involve the whole country, it was critical that the state act in a unified manner. In accordance with the Clausewitzean dictum that war is the continuation of politics, Shaposhnikov believed the General Staff must be fully subordinate to the political leadership.[46]

Tukhachevsky reentered the debate with an article in 1928. He agreed that the military leadership should be subordinate to the country's political authorities. "Politics directs war," he stated. However, he also maintained that in the area of military operations the armed forces should be given a free hand to fight the war. Furthermore, citing Engels, he argued that to be effective the country's military forces must reflect the level of the country's economy. It made little sense to construct a military force requiring military equipment or weapons the country could not produce. Thus, the country's economy and its war plans must be carefully integrated; a recipe for the militarization of the Soviet economy.[47]

From an operational standpoint, Tukhachevsky was showing greater flexibility than he had with his earlier insistence on the offense. He admitted, for example, that the weapons available to the infantry at the time (1928) provided the defense with distinct advantages—although he was careful to qualify his statement by noting that weapons such as tanks and aviation were changing the situation. Nevertheless, he agreed that some degree of positional warfare was inevitable. "Given the dependence of goals and the course of the war with respect to territory, wars may be offensive and defensive, and can also combine both types of wars—offensive and defensive." Indeed, Tukhachevsky argued, there was no simple answer to determine the country's strategy. "The most appropriate and strongest will be those forms which most completely correspond to the political goals of the wars and the securing of its economic basis." Despite this seemingly more flexible position, Tukhachevsky remained committed emotionally to the offense. As Fedotoff-White put it, "On the whole Tukhachevsky, in giving lip service to the flexibility of forms of future war, still has his heart set on a crushing offensive and does not expect to obtain the best results by a war of attrition." For Tukhachevsky, the bottom line was that one could not win by defensive operations.[48]

It is one of the ironies of history that after having sternly opposed any suggestions that the Soviet military could not hope to fight a modern war without the necessary industrial infrastructure, in 1928 Stalin reversed his course and launched an industrialization campaign. This was good news for the military because as late as 1928 the Soviet Army lacked a meaningful industrial base, which in turn resulted in an army in which "up to 1929, these few dozen tanks had to serve as models for the whole Red Army to receive its training and education. We exhibited these tanks in our parades and they naturally raised smiles from the foreign attaches. . . . But there was no smile on *our* faces." The industrialization campaign launched in 1928 under the first Five-Year Plan had as its goal the "build up of heavy industry, at the expense of any other consideration; at the center of preoccupation was the intention to establish a powerful armaments industry, which resulted in 85 percent . . . being invested in this undertaking out of the whole Soviet industrial investment plan from 1929 to July 1, 1941." By the mid-1930s significant progress had been made in modernizing the Soviet armed forces.[49]

In 1929 the military leadership introduced a new version of the *Field Service Regulations*. Its publication marked the first formal codification of Soviet views on military strategy, and it represented a victory for the Frunze/Voroshilov school of thought. The *Regulations* enshrined the concept of the offensive, arguing that "defense can only weaken an enemy, but not destroy him." To destroy an enemy, Soviet commanders were told to master the maneuver principle. The task of the commander was to outflank his enemy, envelop him, and destroy his forces. The key to such an operation was close coordination of all branches and types of forces. By 1929 the debate over doctrine was over.[50]

Svechin was in disgrace. A symposium was held at which Tukhachevsky attacked him "because he did not believe in the possibility of decisive operations but defended the idea of limited war." From a personal and moral standpoint, this was not one of Tukhachevsky's finest moments. He called individuals who favored wars of attrition, "class enemies," about the worst thing one could call a person at that time. This attack represented not only the end of the debate over the offense and defense, it silenced the pen of one of the USSR's most brilliant military theoreticians. In 1931 Svechin was arrested as an enemy of the people. He was released a year later and returned to the General Staff Academy, where he continued to teach and write articles. His last article was published in 1937; he was re-arrested and shot in 1938.[51]

## Conclusion

If one looks upon Svechin and some of his colleagues as representatives of the professional military, then there is no doubt that the old-line generals saw themselves as members of an interest group—the armed forces. While they accepted the idea of civilian control of the military, they deeply resented what they considered interference by amateurs in an area as critical as military doctrine. In the end, however, they were defeated. As Kolkowicz suggested, the party—in the form of Stalin—could not stand the idea of an autonomous military. If the generals had been able to determine something as central as doctrine, they would have had a major impact on a whole number of societal issues—from the economy to political socialization.

Likewise, the professional military also resented the involvement of civilians in an area as complex as military technology. Their concern was not so much that they believed that the military was becoming too technological—one of Kolkowicz's key assumptions—but they felt that Frunze's and Stalin's efforts to politicize all areas of military doctrine was a recipe for military disaster. They feared that such politicization would upset the country's entire military structure and threaten the country's security.

Odom's model had little relevance for the 1920s. The entire period was marked by conflict. Similarly, while Colton's paradigm could have been useful because it would have helped chart the decrease in military autonomy in the area of doctrine, it would not have explained the nature of the overall relationship at this time.

# *II*

# DECIDING ON A FORCE STRUCTURE
## DEBATE ABOUT A MILITIA

> In the condition of this modern class state, a militia can only play a second-class subordinate role.
>
> Franz Mehring

> The introduction of a militia system would mean the crucification of the Soviet republic.
>
> Marshal Mikhail Tukhachevsky

### The Problem

Few issues related to the creation of an armed forces in the new Soviet state caused greater controversy than the debate over a militia system. Professional military officers wanted no part of this "amateurish" approach to military affairs. They preferred to rely on a large, standing army. Many Bolsheviks, however, strongly favored reliance on militias; indeed, there were some who argued that for ideological reasons regular military forces should be disbanded in favor of militias. A clash between the two sides was inevitable.

### The Basis of the Debate

The militia, a favorite institution of nineteenth-century liberals, was characterized by short-term universal service. It was viewed as an alternative to mercenary or standing armies, which in the eyes of the liberals of that period had been and would continue to be tools of reaction and absolutism. In standing armies both officers and men served for long periods of time and were commanded by professional officers, who shared a common ethos, and owed their allegiance to the existing regimes.[1]

Where the professional military was made up of experts, subject to rigorous discipline, the militia system assumed that numbers and spirit would make up for a lack of training, discipline, and knowledge. Historically, proponents of a militia argued, the effectiveness of this approach was evident during the wars of national liberation against Napoleon. Furthermore, they believed, the absence of a professional military would help ensure that the nation's armed forces would never be used against the lower classes. Supporters of this approach believed that it would be better to have a politically reliable, albeit less competent military force.[2]

Others, however, argued that a militia—however desirable from an ideological point of view—would not solve the state's security problems. Quoting Napoleon, one author argued that "it is possible to win a brilliant victory with a militia, but it is not possible to carry out a lengthy and well-thought-out military campaign with a militia."[3] Lacking the necessary discipline, and technical training, such units had limited military value.

Unfortunately, neither Marx nor Engels was much help in resolving this problem. Engels, who was the military expert of the two, was at best ambivalent. In his early writings—and this was the case with Marx as well—he expressed a preference for "popular enthusiasm toward militias." By 1851, however, Engels had begun to reevaluate the relationship between the two and, according to one expert, had decided that a standing army was essential to military success. As a consequence, he began to doubt the value of "a system that relied on spontaneity and spirit as substitutes for order, and after 1851 he considered militias virtually useless under existing conditions."[4]

This lack of clear ideological guidance placed Bolshevik theorists in a difficult position. All agreed that a successful seizure of power depended upon the destruction of the old "bourgeois" army. But what would replace it? From an emotional standpoint, there was a desire to create a "new" type of army and if a choice had to be made between a militia and a professional force, they preferred the former. A professional military was too similar to the army they had just succeeded in destroying. The real problem, however, lay in determining what was meant by the term "militia."

According to one Soviet writer, as understood by the Bolsheviks in 1917, the term "militia" referred to an organization in which universal military service was the rule. In order not to damage production,individuals would be called up for training where they worked or lived for short periods of time. A small cadre of military officers would be maintained as instructors and to man skeleton staffs. In the event of an attack, these militias would be mobilized to defend the country. Thus, while conscription would not have been the first choice for many Bolsheviks, using it to staff a militia was certainly preferable to creating a professional military.[5]

For his part, Lenin's position on this issue was as ambivalent, changing, and pragmatic as it was on most other topics. At the time of the Bolshevik seizure of power, Lenin favored a militia. For example, he argued at the Seventh Party Congress in April 1917 that the Treaty of Brest-Litovsk, which had just been signed with the Germans, provided a breathing space during which the old army could be demobilized, the masses given military training, and a new force structure created.

The events of 1917 did little to shake his faith in militias. "Our Task, which we cannot overlook for a minute, is the universal arming of the people and the abolishment of a standing army."[6] By the beginning of 1918, the General Staff was told to prepare plans for the creation of "a powerful armed forces on the principles of a socialist militia," and the general arming of workers and peasants. Reality, however, soon forced the Bolsheviks to change plans.[7]

### The Controversy over the Creation of a Regular Army

The new Soviet state found itself in a precarious position. The threat of a resumption of hostilities by the Germans was real. And given the sorry state of the Imperial Army (a nonexistent army for practical purposes), the only military force available to the Bolsheviks was a combination of Red Guard formations and units such as the Latvian Riflemen or the Baltic sailors.[8] Furthermore, the danger of a civil war loomed on the horizon. In short, something had to be done immediately. There was no time to work out a program that would be ideologically acceptable to all segments of the Communist party. As a consequence, Lenin adopted a two-part program. First, he came out in favor of a regular army. Second, he made a concession to those who favored the militia approach by suggesting the implementation of compulsory military service—the long term aim of which was the construction of a militia. The military specialists, who were told to come up with such a plan, had no experience with or sympathy for the idea of a militia. As a result they concentrated on building a new Red Army, leaving work on a militia to *Vsevobuch* (the Administration for Universal Training), which was staffed by militia supporters. Vsevobuch's primary task at that time was to provide large numbers of people with military training.

In March 1918 military specialists proposed dividing the military into three components: operational forces, garrison troops, and instructional units for training the masses in basic military skills. With an eye on the past, they recommended that the structure of the armed forces follow that used in the Imperial Army: companies, battalions, regiments, divisions, corps, and armies. They also advocated the adoption of compulsory military service, but it was rejected for the time being.

The first major problem, however, was how to obtain qualified officers. It was clear to the political leadership that without military expertise, especially on the part of those in command positions, the army faced a dismal future. Meanwhile, there were not enough politically reliable workers or peasants who were also competent in military affairs. As one observer put it, "the Bolshevik rulers were on the horns of a dilemma . . . they could not count on the faithful devotion of the old officers. . . . On the other hand, they could not dispense with their services."[9] The Bolsheviks reacted by accepting officers from the Imperial Army into the ranks of the Red Army.

Given the problems facing the new state—foreign intervention and civil war were only a month or two in the future—there was no alternative but to utilize officers from the Tsarist Army. As Lenin himself noted, "If we had not accepted them into the service, we would not have been able to create an army."[10]

Rank-and-file party members were outraged. Bolshevik propaganda had worked long and hard to drive a wedge between the officers and men of the Imperial Armed Forces—to the point where the mere word "officer" evoked emotions of hatred and bitterness. These representatives of the old regime typified everything the average sailor or soldier had fought against only a year or two earlier. Opponents claimed that "the 'new army' was sliding into odious bourgeois orthodoxy with its noxious discipline, alien specialists and dangerous centralization."[11] Opposition was so strong that there were instances of violence against these former Imperial officers. Erickson reports that "on the Northern Front Red regiments shot their new officers, with the result that capable Red privates or NCOs took over effective command and the ex-officers were withdrawn."[12]

With the beginning of the Civil War, the Bolsheviks were forced to abandon voluntary recruitment in favor of conscription. Again the problem of where to obtain officers emerged. Some former Imperial officers—those who had volunteered and whose actions indicated they would be reliable—were admitted into the Red Army. However, by the middle of 1918 it was clear that their numbers were insufficient. For example, a report from the All-Russian Main Staff stated that the Red Army was short 55,000 officers in command positions. As a consequence, the Bolsheviks decided to draft officers from the former Imperial Army into the Red Army. To give this decision political legitimacy, the Fifth All-Russian Congress of Soviets passed a resolution, "On the Organization of the Red Army," noting the need to make full use of the expertise of these individuals.[13]

Concurrent with the construction of a new, regular army, the government also began work on a militia-type organization. The problem was that there was almost no historical precedent for such an organization. The only "new" type of military force that had been created was the Red Guards, which were loosely organized units under the control of local officials. This arrangement clashed with the desire on the part of the Kremlin's leaders for a more centralized structure.[14]

In April 1918 a law was passed making participation in paramilitary training obligatory for all workers and peasants between the ages of eighteen and forty. The law called for training to be carried out over a period of eight weeks, with at least twelve hours a week devoted to military instruction. To administer this organization, a completely new bureaucracy was established. In many cases this led to a duplication of effort between Vsevobuch and the Military Commissariats. The latter's role was to provide soldiers for the regular military. This led to confusion and conflict as both organizations often tried to recruit the same individual. The problem was solved by subordinating Vsevobuch to the Military Commissariats. Eventually, Vsevobuch focused its attention on preparing young men for military service.[15]

Resentment over the idea of a regular army refused to go away. In April 1918 Sergey Gusev, a Bolshevik military organizer who would later switch sides in this debate, wrote an article in favor of a militia approach. A military organization should be built "from below on the basis of voluntarily chosen centralism." Furthermore, Gusev argued, military technology could be easily learned at the workplace. Paraphrasing Lenin, he stated that "creating an army by transforming illiterate 'peasants' into 'half-officers' is no more a dream than putting cooks in charge of the state."[16]

In November 1919 two critics published an article charging that former Tsarist generals were now running the new Red Army. Then in December, one of these critics claimed that military specialists were counterrevolutionaries, that their continued use would lead to the resurrection of a professional army like that which existed prior to the revolution and called on the party to get rid of them.[17]

The Eighth Party Congress, held in March 1919, at the height of the Civil War, debated this issue. Proponents of the militia plan argued that the Red Army was out of control, that discipline was too harsh, that too much power had been delegated to the military specialists, that greater control should be given to military commissars and local party officials, that commanders should be elected; and they maintained that more attention should be given to creating a militia-type military. Lenin, in his speech to the Congress, was defensive, attempting to justify the current policy by arguing that the party was traveling unchartered territory and that it had no alternative to the creation of a regular army employing military specialists. The country and the party were in the midst of a vicious civil war. Without a highly disciplined and well-trained army, staffed by officers who knew what they were doing, the revolution would collapse. Indeed, as one speaker put it, military specialists were key to success on the battlefield.[18]

Criticism by those favoring the militia approach struck a sensitive nerve. This was evident in the final resolution of the Eighth Party Congress, which stated that "the recent rejection of the so-called universal character of the militia as it is stated in our party program does not mean that we have in any way deviated from the Program." It was a matter of expediency. The regular army would be based on "obligatory training in military affairs outside military bases, where possible close to work places."[19] Militia-type units would be formed, but only as reserve battalions. For practical purposes, Vsevobuch would administer the militia-oriented units. In addition, the Party Congress focused attention on the role of commissars, called for increased emphasis on discipline, and rejected a proposal for the election of officers. In short, the structure of the Red Army was provisional. This gave opponents (known as the Military Opposition) hope that they could get approval for movement toward the militia concept as soon as the Civil War ended and the situation normalized. However, the congress made the idea of transforming the army into a militia dependent on "the military and international-diplomatic situation." The "defense capability" must be kept at "the necessary level."[20] Professional military officers constantly utilized this linkage to the international situation to counter those favoring a militia system.

In an effort to build up the armed forces, the military leadership had drawn up a plan the preceding year calling for the creation of 131 divisions. However, it was already clear by the end of 1918 that such a plan went far beyond the resources available to the Soviet government. A single division, which was made up of 26,972 soldiers, required 288 machine guns, 68 field guns, and 10,048 horses. Thus 131 divisions required 3.5 million soldiers, 22,028 machine guns, 8,908 field guns and 1.3 million horses. As a result, a more modest plan, which called for a number of regiments to be formed in most of the major cities, was adopted. Even this turned out to be too expensive, however, and on January 10, 1919, a directive was issued calling for a halt in the formation of such units while the Civil War continued.

The end of the Civil War again brought the question of a militia versus a professional military to the fore. Without a standing army, the country would be defenseless, thus creating the need for some kind of organized military structure. As a result, the Revolutionary Military Council (*Revvoensovet*) called on the All-Russian Main Staff (*Vseroglavshtab*) to formulate a plan that would provide for the demobilization of troops and transfer to a militia-type system. The Revvoensovet ordered the Vseroglavshtab to keep officers from the regular Red Army on active duty and to use them to form the core of the military units, which were to be raised and used as militia-type units under the direction of Vsevobuch. Such an order was in effect "a prescription for a militia-based defense system." As a consequence, major cuts were made in the size of the military staffs in the regular army.[21]

In compliance with these orders, officers on the All-Russian Main Staff proposed a plan, which also drew in part on past Imperial Army structure. According to this plan, the military would be divided into four types of units. The first would be engaged in garrison and guard duties, the second in maintaining internal order, the third in guarding the country's borders, and the fourth in training the civilian population. The plan called for these tasks to be carried out by internal security forces working together with troops controlled by Vsevobuch. The remainder of the Red Army would be disbanded, thereby giving the armed forces a peacetime size of 342,500 officers and men. The Revvoensovet rejected this proposal.

Trotsky came out strongly in support of a militia system in August 1919. Writing in *Voennoe delo,* he argued that together with the regular army, a militia was an indispensable tool for ensuring the country's security. He criticized Svechin—who opposed a militia system—for ignoring both the changes that had occurred in the Communist party's attitude toward military affairs since the beginning of the Civil War, and the significance of the Civil War experience itself. It was not true to suggest—as Svechin had—that a militia army was only capable of fighting a civil war. Furthermore, the same level of discipline that was inculcated in a barracks could also be achieved by a militia. Indeed, universal military training—the key to a militia system—would not only provide the Soviet state with well-qualified officers and men, it would also tap the country's most important resource—the ideological enthusiasm of its workers and peasants. The USSR would be able to substitute—at least in part—"Communist unity and education" for the "barracks" environment. All the latter needed was military expertise. They could obtain this expertise through short training courses. Predicting the future was difficult, Trotsky argued; the course of history was anything but straight. In two or three years American or Japanese capital could again attack the USSR. To defend the country, more than a regular army would be necessary. A "new system of armed forces—the militia army—must be created."[22]

Nikolay Podvoysky, who was in charge of Vsevobuch, followed up on Trotsky's call for a militia in December, when he recommended that the best elements of the Red Army should be use to build a militia army, while the remainder could be utilized as a reserve of organized labor to assist in overcoming the country's serious economic problems. Meanwhile, Ioakim Vatsetis, who had until recently been commander in chief of the Red Army, responded by arguing that given the current international situation, it was essential to maintain a powerful military force capable of responding immediately to any threats that might arise. "Current military conditions demand constant military preparedness. This can only be guaranteed by a standing army." To be effective, Vatsetis argued that at least twenty full-strength divisions were required. Ten of these divisions would form the core of the armed forces, with the other ten to be brought up to strength in the event of a conflict.[23]

The plan proposed in January 1920 by the then commander in chief of the armed forces, Sergei Kamenev, followed Vatsetis's proposal. It would split the Red Army into two parts; the first would be held in a state of constant readiness, while the second would be used to train and staff the militias. The regular military would be even larger than that envisaged by Vatsetis; 66 rifle divisions and 15 cavalry divisions divided into two parts: 21 rifle and 9 cavalry fully mobilized divisions and 45 rifle and 6 cavalry cadre divisions to be held in reserve. To staff this military, it was estimated that 900,000 troops would be needed.[24]

Despite the calls for a militia from individuals such as Trotsky and Podvoysky, professional military officers, led by Svechin, remained adamantly opposed. Writing in *Voennoe delo* in April 1919, for example, Svechin ridiculed Trotsky's concept of a militia. Svechin argued that a "regular and standing army" was of more military value and would gain greater respect than a militia. Emphasizing the importance of military efficiency, Svechin argued that history had shown that a militia force—"a nation in arms"— would not be able to successfully fight a modern war. Indeed, he suggested, from a military-historical point of view, such a force was "nonsense."

> An army can be white, or gray, or red, it depends on the preferences of those who build it. However, the durability and quality of its color is exclusively dependent on the number of barracks, through whose network pass recruits; real barracks, not a charitable institution. A militia cannot have a definite color because the color of a militia is the color of a mirror which reflects all of the political whirlwinds that take place in a country. The Red Army is an expression of a definite color. The Red Militia is nonsense—like red bread!

Only a professional military staffed by experts trained in the art of modern warfare could defend the Soviet state.[25]

These plans and counter-plans resulted in a deadlock. Professional soldiers were prepared to compromise to the point of permitting the establishment of a militia (or reserve system) that would serve as the basis for a professional standing army, but that was not acceptable to Podvoysky and his allies, who wanted no part of a regular military—even in its modified form.[26] In any case, by the end of April 1920 the Red Army was fighting the Poles, a situation that focused national attention on the need for regular army units to fight against Warsaw.

Supporters of the militia option won a partial victory at the Ninth Party Congress, which was held from March 29 to April 5, 1920. The resolution adopted at this congress (entitled "On the Transition to a Militia System"), not only supported the idea of a regular military, it also introduced a new factor into the debate. The resolution called for the introduction of a territorial-based militia. This militia would also include a number of regular Red Army units to ensure the country's ability to respond immediately to military threats. These militia units would be set up near industrial and agricultural enterprises to ensure close collaboration between the militia and those parts of the populace considered most reliable. A factory manager or a trade union official could become a regimental or company commander. In practice, this resolution had little effect because it was again carefully qualified by making the transition gradual and relating it to the international situation.[27]

Despite the qualifications included in the Ninth Party Congress resolution, the need to demobilize hundreds of thousands of soldiers after the end of the Polish and Civil wars, as well as pressure to come up with a new military structure, continued to focus attention on the militia-professional controversy. In February 1920 a commission, under the direction of P. S. Baluyev, suggested the unification of the army and the navy in a People's Commissariat for the Army and Navy. Control over the armed forces would be vested in a Central Executive Committee while the direction of day-to-day operations would be lodged in an All-Russian Army-Navy Main Staff. Such a structure would increase centralization and provide for the unified command favored by the professionals. Then in October, another commission, this one under the chairmanship of General Aleksey Brusilov, was tasked with the job of coming up with an administrative structure to combine the two. This commission fared no better than the others. It suggested the creation of twenty-five divisional districts, with three divisions to be assigned to each district. The key problem, however, which they were not able to resolve, was how to further subdivide the brigades, regiments, and battalions. Such structures would have disrupted the country's administrative map.[28]

Militia proponents struck back at town meetings in October and November. They argued that Vsevobuch should be responsible for the militia, and that it should be staffed by Vsevobuch officers (thus making the professionals superfluous). Podvoysky followed up with a letter to the Central Committee reiterating the statements made at public meetings and called for the creation of a Main Staff for Militia Troops, which would be subordinated, not to the regular army, but to the Revvoensovet.[29]

Meanwhile, to further complicate the situation, Revvoensovet ordered the Red Army staff to come up with a plan to deal with demobilization. The plan, which was submitted on December 5, argued that the Red Army should be strengthened. According to this plan the size of the regular army would be 1,489,000. Overall troop strength, including administrative, personnel, internal security forces, support, and reserve troops as well as Vsevobuch would be 3.3 million—a cut of some 1.7 million.[30]

As usual, Trotsky's position at this time was somewhere between the two sides. Trotsky's primary concern was the reconstruction of the Soviet economy and, as a consequence, he argued that the transition to a militia system should be made contingent upon the "militarization of labor." Trotsky suggested that rather than demobilizing large numbers of soldiers, they should be turned into "labor armies" to help out on the economic front. After all, he maintained, it should be clear to everyone that military power was based on a strong economy. Insofar as a militia system was concerned, it could help in the transition to a regular army. As he put it, "We want to create a direct contradiction; a regular army based on a militia system." While the country needed a large army to protect it, it would not be possible to take thousands of individuals out of the "productive process" for three to five years. The only way to achieve such an end (he mentioned creating seventy-five divisions) was to "locate regiments near fields, near factories, near neighborhoods." This new type of army, Trotsky suggested, would exist for five to eight years while the economic basis for a modern, regular army was created. Over the short run, officers could be selected from those who were being demobilized. Over the long run, they would be trained in special schools. Once the appropriate preconditions were established, the transition to a regular army would occur.[31]

The issue came to a head in December 1920 at the Second All-Russian Meeting of Political Workers of the Red Army and Fleet. Fedor Dan, a well-known Menshevik leader, demanded the immediate liquidation of the regular army and the transfer to a militia system. Others, citing the resolutions adopted by the Eighth and Ninth Party congresses, expressed similar views. Participants also freely cited Marx and Engels. The latter, for example, had stated in 1845 that "in a Communist society it would not dawn on any one to think of a regular army."[32] As a consequence, a number of speakers argued that "the most effective form of organization for an armed forces during a period of the dictatorship of the proletariat is a militia."[33]

Sergey Gusev, a close ally of Frunze, who had previously supported a militia system, reversed himself. He argued that creation of a such a structure, which would inevitably be based on peasants who were suffering considerable hardships, even starvation, and would encourage anti-Soviet activities in the countryside. A high level of discipline—which would ensure that all forces remained under Moscow's strict control—was the only approach compatible with a regular army. Furthermore, Gusev stated, the low literacy rate among the peasantry meant that it would be difficult to turn them into qualified soldiers.[34]

In the end the assembly passed a resolution agreeing with Gusev. The resolution stated that "the most efficient form of an army for the RSFSR at the present time is a regular army, made up of young men, not especially large in number, but well trained in military matters and politically prepared."[35] Then, two days later at a meeting of the Revvoensovet, the idea of a regular military again won the day. Despite the storminess of these meetings, and the serious economic hardships facing the country, the majority was against moving to a militia system. Thus, when it came to the question of where to get cadres for a militia system, the majority voted in favor of the Red Army—not Vsevobuch. In addition, those present recommended that Vsevobuch be subordinated to the regular military and rejected the idea of two staffs—one for the Red Army and one for Vsevobuch.

Intellectual ammunition for militia opponents was provided by

Tukhachevsky. In making his case against a militia, Tukhachevsky argued that wars were an unavoidable aspect of life. In addition, he maintained, history demonstrated that the offense always has been superior to defense and that the key to an effective offense has been mobility. In order for a militia to conduct mobile offensive operations, it would have to: be well trained; have a good transportation and mobilization system; and be equipped with the most modern technology and supply system. Given the backward nature of Soviet industry and the other problems facing the USSR, Tukhachevsky argued that the creation of a militia would be the equivalent of the USSR committing suicide. Focusing on the question of cadre, Tukhachevsky maintained that just because an individual was a good foreman in a factory it did not follow that he would be an effective military officer. The only alternative was the creation of a regular military. This would permit the country to spend its limited resources on training and equipping a smaller force structure, but one that would be qualitatively better. It would also put less strain on the country's transportation system.[36]

Gusev and Frunze supported Tukhachevsky's position in the sixteenth of the twenty-one theses they had prepared for the Tenth Party Congress. They argued that the introduction of a militia "in the current difficult period of the proletarian dictatorship is fraught with tremendous dangers," and must be approached with considerable care. Their reasoning was simple. First, such a force would be unable to protect the country. Second, recognizing the problems that would later develop with the creation of national formations, they argued that there was a danger that such forces would be more concerned with local rather than national interests. For that reason, they continued, new units should be limited to "the proletarian and half-proletarian masses living in cities and villages," and subordinated to the Red Army's High Command. To ensure political reliability, such units should also have very close ties to party and territorial administrative centers.[37]

The Tenth Party Congress, held in March 1921, was a watershed in the militia–standing army controversy. The Civil War had ended, and the party was planning to carry out a major reduction in force. Given the magnitude of the reductions that were being planned (figures of 2-4.3 million were mentioned), a major reorganization of the military was vital. The time for talk was over. A new plan had to be decided upon and put into effect *now*. As he had in the past, Podvoysky again put forth a proposal calling the militia the only genuinely socialist form of military organization. His preferred option, of course, was a massive militia system to be led by Vsevobuch. Trotsky, meanwhile, called for the introduction of militia units in at least three military districts on an experimental basis.

The Tenth Party Congress had hardly begun when sailors at Kronstadt, irritated over the poor state of the country's economy, the party's continued insistence on strict discipline and the use of military specialists, mutinied. Shortly thereafter, an uprising of anti-Soviet forces in Tambov was put down by the Red Army. In effect, these two developments destroyed any chance for the adoption of the militia approach. As Gusev put it,

> The events of the spring of 1921 showed there cannot be any discussion of a general transition to a militia system in the present stage of Russian revolution, because in fact the development of a militia system could result in providing military forms of organization for petit-bourgeois, anarchic, counterrevolutionaries.[38]

Ivar Smilga, formerly head of the Main Political Directorate, adopted a similar position, arguing that "given the numerically weak proletariat in Russia, we will not be able to ensure proletarian guidance in these units."[39] The message from Kronstadt was clear. The country was passing through very difficult economic times. The situation would probably get worse before it got better. Other segments of the populace were also upset at the party's handling of matters. What was to prevent the masses from following a path similar to that trod by the sailors at Kronstadt? Arming them would make the situation even worse. The only alternative was to ensure that the country's military forces possessed a strong organizational infrastructure through which firm discipline could be maintained.

Faced with a deteriorating domestic situation and recognizing the need for a strong military to protect the country, the congress reversed the plans adopted by the Ninth Party Congress. It agreed to a resolution calling for the establishment of a regular, standing army. "During the immediate future, the basis for our armed forces will be the current Red Army." Furthermore, in discussing the idea of a militia, the congress stated that "agitation on the part of some comrades for the practical liquidation of the Red Army and the immediate transition to militia is incorrect and dangerous." Any future transition to a militia would be dependent on "international and internal conditions, on the length of any breathing-space (*peredyshka*), the relationship between cities and villages, and other factors." The only positive mention of a militia was the statement that such structures would be created in areas with a large proletarian population such as Moscow, Petrograd, and the Urals.[40] For practical purposes, the militia question was now settled. As Frunze put it in an article published toward the end of 1921, "For the foreseeable future, the basic form of our armed forces can only be a standing army."[41] The transition to a militia system—based on Vsevobuch—would only occur once the country's economy permitted and the army's capabilities were at the necessary level.

Having decided in favor of a regular army, the Tenth Party Congress also passed a number of resolutions on how to improve the quality of this army. In order to ensure its political reliability (an important consideration in the aftermath of the events in Kronstadt), the congress called on military authorities to strengthen the proletarian element in the armed forces, and to intensify efforts at politicizing it. Recognizing the technical problems it faced, the congress demanded that the military devote special attention to technical units (i.e., artillery, machine gun, armored vehicles [*avtobronenye*], aviation, engineering, and armored train formations). In addition, the congress called for the construction of a Soviet Navy, for improving the standard of living of officers and men, and for the gradual replacement of military specialists with convinced Communists as soon as they had the requisite military knowledge.[42]

While all of these changes were occurring, the size of the armed forces was also shrinking. By the end of the Civil War the Soviet Union had some 5.3 million men under arms. In December 1920 the Eighth All-Russian Congress of Soviets adopted a resolution ordering a reduction in the army. The reductions were to be carried out in phases. During the first period (December 1920 to December 1921), the size of the armed forces shrank from 5.3 million to 1.6 million men. During the second period (May to October 1922), it was cut further to 800,000. Finally, it was to drop to a total of 600,000 men by February 1, 1923.[43]

## The Transition to a Mixed System

Militarily, the idea of a regular military made much more sense than a militia, as Frunze himself noted in 1925, "Naturally, if we had the choice between a 1.5–2 million man cadre army and the current mixed system, from a military point of view all of the data was in favor of the former. But we did not have that choice."[44] The fact was that by mid-1923, the Red Army stood at 562,000. Such an army could not effectively defend the country, as Frunze noted: "Obviously a cadre army of 562,000 men could not carry out those tasks which must be resolved by the country's military system."[45] Some combination of a militia/reserve force was indispensable. Thus it was not ideological preference which dominated the debate over a regular or militia army in the 1920s. It was a combination of economic necessity and military expediency that were the primary concerns. Given the country's economic problems, an effective military system could only be built on "a combination of a cadre army with a militia system."[46] Since individuals served for four months, a militia system would provide additional numbers of trained soldiers who could be called up in an emergency. "A territorial-militia division could prepare three times more recruits than a regular army division in the same amount of time."[47] Furthermore, since a militia division possessed two to three times fewer regular personnel, it was cheaper to maintain and because the recruits served for short time periods, there was less impact on the civilian economy. The problem, however, was that there was little order in the transition process, the blame for which Soviet analysts have traditionally assigned to Trotsky. It was clear that to be effective, the process of demobilizing had to be rationalized.

Despite its lesser financial cost, reliance on militia units as a mobilization reserve carried with it serious problems. To begin with, such soldiers were not as well trained as regular personnel. Their discipline and political reliability was not as high. The fact that these various militias were scattered around the country meant that some time would elapse before they could be mobilized and moved to where they were needed in a crisis. The short periods of time they spent on active duty meant that they were not sufficiently trained to handle the increasingly more complex technical equipment.

During January and February 1923, ten divisions were converted to a militia status. Each division was to have a regular core of 1,607 men and a total strength of 10,959 in the event of mobilization. To this point the only "mixed" unit was located in Petrograd. By the summer, however, the process had been completed, and on August 8, 1923, conditions of service were laid down. Officers serving as the cadre for these divisions were subject to the same conditions then prevailing in the regular armed forces. Each year all members of the militia would undergo three months of training and were subject to an annual mobilization. They were obligated to serve four years. The first mobilization of militia units occurred in the autumn of 1923. While problems were evident, (desertions, banditry), in John Erickson's words, they "passed the test." The period of stagnation was now over.[48]

Partly as a result of the chaotic situation in which the Red Army found itself, and partly as a consequence of the political struggle between Trotsky and Stalin, a commission was created in mid-1923 to investigate conditions in the military. The commission's report, which had as one of its major goals to show that Trotsky had mismanaged the Red Army, stated among other things that the regular army-militia arrangement was not working. In some instances there was a 50 percent shortage of officers in militia formations. There were also major deficiencies in weapons, equipment, and the qualifications of officer cadre. To make matters worse, personnel turnover was too high. "The majority of units changed their personnel in 1923 several times."[49]

On February 3, 1924, Gusev, speaking at the plenum on behalf of the commission, delivered a blistering attack on the army's condition, arguing that "in its current state the Red Army is not combat capable." Shortcomings and deficiencies were evident at every level. Frunze, for example, complained that personnel problems and supply difficulties showed "that we are not ready for a major war." The result of this power-play/investigation was that Trotsky's deputy was removed from his position and replaced by Frunze while Voroshilov was named commander of the Moscow Military District, a critical post.[50]

With the appointment of Frunze to this position, work on reorganization of the Red Army intensified. On February 4, the Revvoensovet gave Frunze power to draw up a reform plan. The plan drawn up by the commission, headed by Frunze, called for "strengthening and improving territorial (i.e., militia) units," as well as for improving conditions in the regular military.[51]

By 1924 the militia forces were playing an increasingly important role in Soviet security policy. As of October 1, 1924, for example, there were 43 infantry divisions, which accounted for 52.4 percent of the infantry strength of the Red Army. Berkhin placed the size of cadre elements in militia divisions at 16 percent.[52]

Recognizing the seriousness of the problems inherent in the creation of a militia-type system outlined above, a plenum meeting in November/December 1924 called on the regular military to work more closely with the militia formations. In addition, the Revvoensovet issued an order forbidding any reduction in the number of regular officers in a division. Pressure also was placed on local civilian institutions to help in training and equipping units located in their areas (e.g., by helping wipe out illiteracy on the part of Red Army personnel).

In order to intensify this effort to improve the functioning of the militia units, the third All-Russian Conference adopted a resolution in 1925 which stated that in the USSR infantry would consist of 77 divisions—31 cadre and 46 militia/territorial; one division out of every 11 divisions and 8 brigades would be militia; and artillery and special technical services would be made up almost entirely of regular army personnel. In addition, in recognition of the problems involved in mastering modern technology, almost all of the personnel assigned to militia units were placed in the infantry. However, since they were located near industrial sites, they were not evenly distributed around the country. For example, in the Moscow Military District there were thirteen divisions, but only one in Siberia. In general, personnel from a particular district (*raion*) were assigned to the unit located in that district.[53]

There were three types of militia units: front-line divisions with a large staff of regular personnel (2,400), second-line divisions with fewer regulars (604-622), and skeleton divisions having only 190 regular army personnel assigned to them. There were 28 first-line divisions, 16 second-line divisions, and 14 skeleton divisions.[54] The military mobilized these units once a year for training purposes. The first mobilization occurred as early as 1923 and appears to have been chaotic. Indeed, there were even reports that some units engaged in banditry—a result in large measure of the increasing alienation of peasants from the central government. To deal with this situation, the leadership introduced a program of pre-mobilization political indoctrination as well as modifications in supply procedures. Local party organizations were ordered to assist in this effort—to the point of being required to submit a yearly report concerning their involvement in the preparation and carrying-out of these mobilization exercises.[55] As a result, the exercises conducted in 1924 were "better organized with better results."[56] By 1927 the situation had improved to the point that Voroshilov stated in his report to the Fourth All-Union Meeting of Soviets that "the

Fall maneuvers carried out the preceding year in a number of districts' territorial units were able to carry out the tasks assigned to them under conditions closely resembling that which exists in combat."[57]

## Conclusion

While the battle over a militia was not as bitter as was the case with doctrine, there were clearly major areas of disagreement, as the Kolkowicz model predicted. The concern for military efficiency clashed with the desire for ideological purity. Military officers took umbrage at this attempt by civilians to dictate the country's force structure. What made things even worse from the military standpoint was that the individuals concerned knew little about the technical aspects of military affairs. They were not qualified to suggest a force structure that would deal with the problems facing the High Command. Podvoysky might have the best intentions, but there was general agreement among the generals that his militia idea would destroy the Red Army as an effective fighting force.

From a methodological standpoint, this issue fits well with the Kolkowicz model. The High Command resented civilian meddling in military affairs and believed that because of their specialized training the generals understood force structure better than the civilians.

At the same time, it is important to stress that the battle lines were not as clearly drawn as Kolkowicz suggested. The relationship between the military and civilian worlds was not as dichotomous as Kolkowicz assumed. This is evident from the fact that while certain party officials pushed the militia idea, other senior political officials, e.g., Lenin himself, sided with the generals. They acted this way not so much because they identified with the military, but because they believed the generals were right. The country could not be defended if it placed primary reliance on a militia.

Odom's paradigm does not fit the militia issue any more than it did the question of doctrine. Professional soldiers such as Svechin were more than prepared to take on civilian party officials, who were pushing the militia idea—as long as the debate remained open and they were able to do so. For individuals like Svechin, there was too much at stake for the generals blithely to agree to plans for a militia. The result was more conflict than Odom's model predicted.

Colton's model was probably the most useful in understanding the battle over a militia. Looked at from his vantage point, it was clear that military participation in resolving this issue was significant. Indeed, one could argue that military participation grew as the debate continued. While there was agreement that the military should not have the final say about doctrine, there was general agreement by Lenin and his allies that this was an area where the generals should have the final say—even if they had to make some concessions to the politicians along the way.

# III

## HOW TO DEAL WITH NON-RUSSIANS
### THE QUESTION OF NATIONAL ARMIES

> The Necessary Condition for the success of
> these troops is the unified command of all
> units of the Red Army and the strict
> centralization in the command of all forces
> and resources of the socialist republic.
>
> V. I. Lenin

### The Problem

The question of what to do with the large number of non-Russians under
Soviet control, who did not speak Russian and often felt antipathy toward
the new regime, was closely tied to the professional-militia issue. Should
they be permitted to join the Red Army? From the standpoint of the regular
officers, the answer was clear. Units made up of potentially unreliable soldiers who barely spoke Russian would have little utility. Non-Russians might
be utilized, but only in units in which the more reliable, technically competent Russians were a majority. The situation within the party leadership was
somewhat different. Aside from those who saw national units as an exten-
sion of the militia concept, the party leadership fully understood the concerns expressed by the regular military, but they saw these units as a means
of securing additional manpower, as well as a tool for socializing hundreds
of thousands of non-Russians. If nothing else, they could be indoctrinated
with the new ideology and would learn to read and write Russian.

The one point that both military and civilian officials agreed upon, however, was that these units must be under the Kremlin's complete control.
Furthermore, given Bolshevik concerns over the military's reliability in
general, Moscow also wanted to make certain that the military leadership
would never be in a position to exert direct control over these units. Both

the regular military, as well as national units, must be fully penetrated by the party.

From a historical standpoint this was not a new issue. Some non-Russians—especially those from Central Asia—were banned from serving in the Imperial Army, while others were permitted to serve, but with certain restrictions. For example, non-Russians were limited to 25 percent in any unit of the Imperial Army. This situation often forced Russian recruits to travel outside of their home areas to complete their military service.[1]

## The Need for National Formations

For the Bolsheviks, reliance on non-Russians was a military necessity. In order to defend the country Moscow had to exploit all of the USSR's manpower resources. As one Soviet source put it, "The difficult battles, which occurred on all fronts during the Civil War, made it necessary to unify military and material resources of the Soviet Republic, they required the complete unity of their operations."[2]

Having exhausted its reserves of troops with a proletarian background (those believed by the Soviets to be the most reliable), the Red Army soon found it necessary to draft not only peasants and officers from the former Tsarist Army, but to turn to non-Russians as well in their battle against the Whites. In addition to their military value, these troops served important political purposes. For example, their presence demonstrated that unlike their Tsarist predecessors the Communists were serious about their nationality policy, and that they intended to treat non-Russian nationalities fairly and equally. Furthermore, this policy helped raise the country's international prestige, and finally, the allegiance of national formations helped deny the regions from which they came to the Whites. The presence of non-Russians in the Red Army also provided the Kremlin with an opportunity to socialize them, to inculcate in them values and attitudes sympathetic to the Soviet state.[3]

The question of how to handle non-Russian troops was probably the only area in which the Bolsheviks and military specialists agreed. Both realized that they would have to employ many of the same controls utilized by the Imperial Army if Moscow hoped to maintain control of these forces and fight provincial nationalism. While the Bolsheviks were ready to expand the role played by non-Russians beyond what it had been in the Imperial Army, they were also deeply suspicious of these forces, and believed that to be useful they had to be under Moscow's control.

Reliance on non-Russian nationalities was complicated by the success of the Whites in making use of them during the Civil War. In order to lessen the likelihood that they would betray the Soviet state, the Kremlin introduced restrictions which permitted the formation of national groupings *only* as part of larger Russian-dominated military units. This policy was authorized by the People's Commissariat for National Affairs of the RSFSR on November 17, 1917. Unfortunately, local authorities tried to take advantage of the situation by utilizing such units for their own purposes. As a result, Lenin found it necessary to call a temporary halt to the creation of non-Russian units.

Faced with the intense pressure for more troops, however, Moscow soon relented and the idea of national formations was resurrected. In May 1918 the Sovnarkom issued a directive authorizing the creation of these formations. Recognizing the continuing danger of ethnic nationalism, however, the Sovnarkom made their formation subject to a number of strict political criteria. These units had to be politically reliable, committed to the Soviet regime, and supervised by local party organs—which were held responsible for their conduct. Moscow also made sure that these units were centrally controlled. To further strengthen central control, and ensure their reliability, the party ordered Communists (in some cases where ethnic minorities were not available, the Kremlin utilized ethnic Russians) to join these units. In addition, the leadership often intermixed them with Russian formations to ensure their reliability. In short, Moscow worked to make certain that these formations were fully penetrated.[4]

By the summer of 1918, a number of national units began to appear. By mid-1918 the list included the First Tatar-Bashkir division, the First Free Bashkir Regiment, the Muslim-Soviet Regiment, the Orsk Volunteer Muslim Combat Unit, the Orenburg Muslim Regiment, the Muslim Regiment, the Ural Tatar Battalion of Red Communists and the 21st Muslim Regiment. In addition, there were Ukrainian (five armies), White Russian (two armies), a Latvian Infantry Regiment, as well as the Estonian Red Regiment. In areas where there were not enough individuals of a specific ethnic background to justify creating separate units, the various groups were combined into multinational formations. This is what happened in Turkestan.[5]

Recognizing the need for additional steps to counter non-Soviet influences, Moscow issued a directive on May 7, 1918, first, calling for the formation of units *only* on the territory inhabited by such ethnic groups (i.e., Ukrainian units could only be established in Ukraine), and, second, ordering that those units made up of deserters from the other side, or nationalities from outside the USSR (e.g., Poles) get special attention from both the party and the National Commissariat for Nationalities. In addition, on June 1, 1919, a directive was issued outlining the need for closer cooperation and coordination of the actions of all units—including national formations. The directive cited the danger presented by "monarchist" and "capitalist" forces, and stated that such a situation "demands . . . close unification of all combat forces, the centralization of the leadership in the battle for life and death." As a consequence, the directive called for a unified military organization and command. This led to the combining of a number of ethnic units into larger formations under central command. Thus Moscow incorporated the First and Third Ukrainian Armies into the 12th Western Front, while the Kremlin made the Second and Fourteenth armies part of the Southern Front.[6]

The combat record of these national units during the Civil War was mixed. In the Transcaucasus national units tended to side with the Whites. Similarly, in Moldavia, many of the ethnic Rumanians enlisted to fight on the Soviet side went over to the Rumanian nationalists who wanted to win the province back for Rumania. In European parts of the USSR, the situation was somewhat better. Once the Germans had withdrawn, national units were formed in areas such as the Baltics, Byelorussia, and Ukraine. These units were subordinate to the Revvoensovet.

The situation in Central Asia was somewhat different. Because of their assumed unreliability, Muslims were not permitted to join the Imperial Army.[7] As a result, they lacked a tradition of military service. There were also problems with language (most did not know Russian), a lack of a native cadre, and strong anti-Soviet/Russian attitudes. Despite these obstacles, the Reds had some success. For example, one source estimates that by 1920 as many as 50,000 Muslims were fighting on the Soviet side on the Eastern and Turkestan fronts.[8]

Despite all of the efforts by the central government to ensure the political reliability of national formations, it was clear by the end of the Civil War that the tendency to place the interests of a particular ethnic group above that of the union—the sin of separateness or national chauvinism— was still strong. In 1920, for example, Frunze warned that there were sections of the country "which show a tendency toward the transformation of national formations into the nucleus of national armies."[9] Similarly, Vatsetis, the commander of Soviet forces at the time, had warned a year earlier of the danger of separatism in these units, leading Lenin to order him to issue a directive and publish a number of articles in the press stressing the importance of national unity. The text of this order, which was confirmed by the Central Committee on May 4, 1919, stated that "the violation of the unity of command and control, and the fragmentation of national armies will lead to ethnic conflict among units of Red Soldiers themselves and is a certain path to the destruction of the army." The following day, the Politburo issued a directive calling for a reorganization of all national armies.[10]

Despite their propaganda value, these national formations did not play a major military role during the Civil War. It was the Russian-manned and Russian-led Red Army that was primarily responsible for expelling the Whites from the Soviet Union. Indeed, according to one set of Soviet figures, the Red Army was overwhelmingly Russian: 77.6 percent Russian, 13.7 percent Ukrainian, 4 percent Byelorussian, and 4.6 percent others. Furthermore, according to Berkhin, "The experience of the Civil War demonstrated that territorial units were not justified; the soldiers deserted during attacks and retreats and did not want to leave their homes." Not surprisingly, the majority of these national units were either disbanded or attached to regular Red Army units in the aftermath of the Civil War.[11]

## Setting Up National Formations

In reorganizing the Soviet Armed Forces during the mid-1920s, Frunze faced a dilemma. From the standpoint of linguistic capability and political reliability, it was clear that primary reliance should be placed on Russian units—whether regular or territorial. From a political point of view, however, Soviet nationality policy called for an effort to reach out to non-Russians in order to integrate them into the new state. After all, despite all of the problems inherent in national units, they had several advantages. To begin with, they increased the country's mobilization potential in the event of a war. In addition, from a political perspective, Moscow also could use them to socialize large numbers of non-Russians.

The first major move toward the creation of national formations in the aftermath of the Civil War occurred at the Twelfth Party Congress in April 1923. In this regard, the congress made two important decisions. First, it called for their creation. Second, with an eye on the problems experienced in the past in integrating non-Russian nationalities into the USSR, it called for a further penetration of these forces through educational work by party members. The latter was to be done "in a spirit of propagating the idea of brotherhood and the solidarity of the people of the Union."[12] In fact, political education became one of the primary functions in such units. "National military formations were intended (and in fact utilized) first and foremost as an important vehicle for political education, and as an important lever for raising the educational and cultural level of those peoples who had earlier been under the yoke of Tsarism, and as a distinctive 'educational enterprise' for training national cadres."[13] This work was especially important in educating peasants. To quote Bubnov, "Through the Red Army we must carry out education in the country-side; through education and a strengthening of the economy in the country-side we will strengthen and raise the military power of our Red Army."[14]

On May 13, 1923, the Main Staff issued a directive laying out procedures for a transition to a national army. According to this directive, "all work in preparing for receiving the temporary staff of territorial units shall be completed by August 1." The summer period was devoted to training cadre and making sure that all of the necessary artillery, engineering, and quartermaster supplies were on hand. By October 1923 all national units were to be capable of full mobilization in a crisis. The size of a national division was set at 12,566. Of this number, 1,607 were to be regular officers, while the remaining 10,959 were individuals serving for limited periods.[15]

Unlike other areas, differences between Trotsky and Frunze over this issue were more of nuance than substance. Trotsky favored the creation of such units, but gradually. Writing in 1922, for example, he stated that "we must now begin to prepare the conditions for the creation of national units and armies." This would be "a lengthy process," requiring extensive work in all areas (i.e., educational, political, military), he added. These units would not only help to overcome national antagonisms, they also "will provide an opportunity to establish a complete and unbreakable tie between the army and the people in all their national characteristics." For the present, Trotsky argued, Moscow should focus its attention on setting up a net of military educational institutions to train non-Russian officers. This would provide the USSR with qualified non-Russian officers when a decision was made to establish such units.[16]

Frunze wanted to move more quickly in creating such units.

> For us national formations are not merely an amusement, not a game for satisfaction for the national egos of different peoples of the Union. It is a serious task, flowing from the very character of our state and determining the basic principle of our internal and international national policies.

Given the situation in the country, there was, as Frunze put it, "no other way to build an army."[17] Frunze won the day and work on the creation of these formations began. By the end of 1924 each of the republics in the Transcacasus possessed a national division, manned mostly by local personnel. Thus 95 percent of enlisted personnel in the Armenian division were Armenians, while in the Georgian division the breakdown was a follows: 85 percent Georgian, 7 percent Armenian, 5 percent Russians, and 3 percent Osetin. These units operated under the same regulations as the Red Army.[18]

The greatest success was achieved in areas such as Ukraine, Byelorussia, and the Caucasus. These areas had the highest levels of industrialization, the strongest commitment to the new regime, the most literate populace, and the longest tradition of service in the Russian armed forces. Even in areas such as the Caucasus, however, there were serious problems. For example, it was difficult to find qualified officers with the appropriate ethnic background. In Azerbaijan there were very few who had served in the Tsarist Army. There were some with military experience in Georgia, but the vast majority were strongly opposed to the new Soviet state. The situation was somewhat better in Armenia, but here too it was not satisfactory. As a consequence, it was necessary to create military training schools for all three nationalities, and instruction was in the native language.

The situation in Central Asia was more difficult. Illiteracy was much higher and the populace had no tradition of military service. By 1923 the only significant national military formation was in Bukhara. To train cadre for these units, the Main Directorate for Military Educational Instruction opened four national military educational institutions to prepare officers for mid-level assignments.

In an effort to get matters moving, a Central Committee Conference held in June 1923 called "for the creation of national schools in Republics and Districts for the production in significant numbers of command cadre from the local populace." In those areas where there were officers from the old army, the declaration continued, regiments could be formed immediately. And there were instances where these units were quickly set up.[19]

A directive entitled "Concerning the Organization of Territorial Military Units and the Carrying Out of Military Training of Workers" provided these units legal status. This directive expanded on the one issued in May, calling for such units to be at the same level of combat readiness as those in the regular army. The directive also set up the basic organizational structure in these units. To begin with, it defined the types of regular and temporary personnel who were mentioned in the May directive. On the one hand, it would include permanent (regular) officers who were defined as all higher, senior mid-level, and junior regular and political officers, administrative, medical, and veterinary personnel as well as some Red Army officers necessary for staffing the schools training junior officers. The second category included individuals from the local region who, after completing a three-month basic training course, would serve for four years. Active service was limited to a yearly training course which could not exceed five months in a four-year period or two months during any one year. To further enhance the qualifications of recruits, a system of pre-military training was set up. Turning to the location of such units, the directive stated that preference should be given to creating units in areas that were completely reliable from a social-political perspective. In practice, this meant areas where at least 10 percent of the recruits were from the working class. In addition, the directive stated that the party must establish an effective party structure in the region. In addition, it noted that all male citizens who did not serve in the Red Army would be required to serve in national formations.[20]

A plan for creating national formations was drawn up in November and adopted by the Central Committee in December 1923. The problem, however, was that in spite of Moscow's good intentions there were still insufficient cadre and material resources to implement the program at that time. Frunze admitted as much in 1924, when he stated that the program adopted the previous year "could not be fully implemented because of the very difficult situation in which the Red Army found itself this year."[21] That this view was shared by others is evident from a comment by Bubnov: "It is necessary to say that in this question, we have achieved some results, but the majority of work is still ahead of us."[22] Recognizing the need for a longer-term solution, Frunze came up with a new plan for the creation of national units. According to this plan:

1. all Soviet citizens would be obligated to perform military service (in either national or Red Army units);

2. in areas where there were small national minorities, special units for training purposes could be set up;

3. nationalities with previous military experience (e.g., Ukrainians, Byelorussians, Tartars) would be immediately formed into national units;

4. in those nationalities without a military tradition (e.g., Kirgiz, Uzbeks, Tadziks), national units would be formed gradually, beginning with the training of appropriate cadre;

5. officer training schools would be created for the various nationalities; and

6. as national units were created, ethnic data was to be collected and utilized as the basis for determining what types of units (infantry, cavalry, mountain troops) should be formed and how they could be most effectively utilized.[23]

To ensure the political reliability of these new units, the Kremlin created the appropriate political structures. Moscow assigned political officers who spoke the local languages and dialects to these new formations, while at the same time it established military newspapers in the local languages. In addition, in many units Moscow ordered Communists to join as a way of ensuring the formation's loyalty. National units would be of little use if persons with anti-Soviet attitudes were permitted to serve in them. Indeed, a Central Committee Plenum held in April 1924 called for even greater efforts in this regard. "The Plenum considers it necessary to further broaden and deepen this work in the spirit created by the Twelfth Congress of the party."[24] This view was repeated at the Thirteenth Party Congress. The resolution adopted by that body stated that "in those areas where there are territorial units, their cadre should be utilized as a new means for tying the Soviet state and party to the peasants."[25]

To increase public support for these units, national formations mirrored the country's administrative structure. "For example, a division was organized in a province, a regiment or battalion in a district, and a company in a county." To further facilitate better contact between the local populace and these units, "provincial and district military commissariats were abolished or more precisely they were changed into corps (divisional) territorial headquarters, and were placed under the commanders of the territorial formations."[26]

## Implementing the Plan

By the fall of 1924 Moscow had made some progress in creating these units. For example: in the Transcaucasus, the first and second rifle divisions had been established in Georgia, while one division had also been set up in

Armenia and in Azerbaijan; one rifle division had been created in Byelorussia with an additional four divisions in Ukraine; and similar units had been established in the RSFSR, in Bukhara, and in the Khorezmskiy SSR. The greatest degree of success occurred in areas like Ukraine, the Transcaucasus, and Byelorussia; Central Asia remained a problem.[27]

A plenum of the Revolutionary Military Council held in December 1924 adopted a five-year plan dealing with the development of national formations. Noting that a number of "obstacles and deficiencies" existed, the two-and-a-half page resolution adopted by the council was sharply critical of the current situation and called for greater attention by party and union organizations to help with the national formations. To be effective, the resolution stipulated that the actions taken depended on the local situation. In areas such as Ukraine, Byelorussia, Georgia, and Armenia, which had already achieved considerable success, national units were created from units of the Red Army stationed on their territory by including local personnel regardless of whether they were in command, political, or enlisted positions. In other areas (e.g., Central Asia) Moscow adopted a more gradualistic approach. Only after the military had trained a sufficient number of officers, pre-military training programs had been carried out, and the populace sufficiently politically indoctrinated would it be possible to consider actually setting up national units. Indeed, unlike areas such as Ukraine or the RSFSR, where a draft was utilized, in regions such as Central Asia the initial approach was to rely on volunteers. In practice this meant that the military created cadre units rather than fully staffed, national formations.[28] One thing was clear: Moscow was tired of delays and expected action.

In drawing up the five-year plan the Soviet government was careful to ensure that the Kremlin would be in full control of these units. For example, there were individuals (including party members) in places such as Central Asia who advocated setting up armies independent of the Red Army. Frunze rejected such proposals out of hand. Such an approach would "not ensure the unity of military thought and carries with it the risk that all of our work would lead in different directions and create chaos in military affairs; something we cannot tolerate." The Kremlin worked to ensure that national unity was maintained by ordering all of the national units to follow the same procedures as the Red Army. To quote Frunze, unity would be guaranteed "first by a unified system of development; this means that we will not permit the existence of national armies in each individual district or republic: we will include national units in the over-all system of the Armed Forces of our Union." In practice this meant that a unified Red Army would outfit, structure, train, administer, and, most importantly, command these units. In addition, political lecturers repeatedly stressed the importance of national unity and the need to avoid any appearance of "national chauvinism." The idea of autonomous units was an anathema to Moscow. To be effective they must be under the Kremlin's complete control.[29]

Despite efforts to eliminate ethnic nationalism, problems remained. This led to the Kremlin's decision to hold up the introduction of some of the reforms that were being put into practice in the regular army at that time. Frunze reported, for example, that while Moscow was introducing the principle of unity of command (the supremacy of the regular officer over his political commissar) in the army, the Kremlin had decided to retain the old approach of equality between the commander and the commissar, which was retained in the navy and especially in national formations. "Here . . . a period of feverish organizational activity is continuing, which demands the immediate and maximum proximity of the party to work with the leadership." Once the army succeeded in overcoming this problem, he added, "the question of implementing unity of command can be considered."[30]

As a further vehicle for ensuring the political reliability of national units, Moscow decreed that most would have a proletarian background, and that the vast majority of them would be members of the Communist party. "In those areas where the proletarian basis is weak, the manning of such units must deviate from the general principle of military obligation. In those areas, the selection of politically proven elements through party, Komsomol or trade union organizations should be active." In addition, to ensure that these units would be useful militarily in the event of a conflict, the plenum stated that their combat readiness should equal that of the Red Army.[31]

From a military standpoint this approach meant carrying out training exercises, while ensuring that manuals were translated into the local language. It also required the senior command personnel to be fluent in Russian. While this approach did not require that junior personnel have a knowledge of Russian, it demanded that senior officers speak the language in the event of a conflict. All of these tasks would be especially difficult to carry out in the more backward regions of Central Asia. In the long run, the most important accomplishment of the December 1924 plenum was to make the central government's approach to the issue of national armies more systematic and better coordinated.

It was clear by the end of 1924 that the process of creating new units was being taken seriously and that the central government was allocating a considerable amount of resources to them. By this point, for example, there were "four Ukrainian divisions, one from Byelorussia, two Georgian, an Azerbaijani and an Armenian division. Others were beginning to be formed in other parts of the country."[32]

Looking at the question of ethnic military schools, for example, Moscow created three types. The first was a unified middle military school (to prepare platoon commanders in the infantry, squadron commanders for the cavalry, and battery commanders in the artillery), the second, military-political schools, and the third, special schools for junior commanders from areas that had been excluded from service in the pre-Communist Russian Army.[33]

Despite the opening of these schools, major problems plagued Soviet efforts to educate and train national officials. Among the more serious were: an insufficient command of the local language; the nonavailability of military regulations and literature in Russian in local languages (in many cases there was no local equivalent for the Russian military terms); and the low educational level of most of the officer candidates. In 1924, for example, around 94 percent of all the officer candidates were either educated at home or had only a primary education.[34] This educational deficiency seriously limited the type of subjects that could be taught and meant that instead of the three-year courses offered at regular military schools, students had to spend four to five years so they could learn basic subjects such as reading, writing, and arithmetic.

To make matters worse, the military often found it difficult to recruit students for these schools. Local officials sometimes had to resort to coercion to get cadets with the appropriate educational and political backgrounds. In some cases, Communists were simply ordered to join national units in order to fill a quota. Furthermore, national formations were given second priority in this area, as Frunze himself admitted when, in discussing efforts to supply sufficient educational supplies and equipment, he stated in April 1925 that "we have not completely overcome this problem in national formations."[35] He reiterated this position in a speech the next month.[36] Indeed, he went so far as to call for even closer cooperation between military, state, societal, and trade union organizations. Frunze was especially concerned about areas such as education (e.g., cultural, literacy, and military training), the procurement of items such as horses, and help to convince the average Soviet citizen that they had an obligation to serve in the armed forces. Two months later, Frunze published an article aimed directly at the selection of political officers for territorial units, in which he argued that "the further strengthening of the bond between the working and peasant classes depends on the correct political approach to selecting officers for our territorial units."[37]

The adoption in 1925 of the Law on Universal Service strengthened national formations. As a result of this law for the first time conscription was introduced in the Karelian, Buryat-Mongolian, and Yakut ASSRs and in the Georgian RSFSR. It was delayed in some areas such as Azerbaijan until 1927, but the message was clear. The local population had the choice of either serving in the Red Army or becoming part of local units. Many of them chose the latter.

By 1925 national formations began to appear even in the Central Asian regions of the USSR. The units were much smaller than in other parts of the country, but it was clear that Moscow was making progress. In the Uzbek SSR, for example, there was a rifle battalion, several infantry regiments, and segments of a cavalry division.[38] National formations were beginning to play a more important role. According to one Soviet source, by the fall of 1925 they made up 10 percent of all Soviet troops.[39] Six months later another source reported that national forces had increased to the point where the USSR now possessed thirty-three first-line fully staffed, and three first-line partially staffed infantry divisions (vs. twenty-eight first-line in October 1925), and twelve second-line infantry divisions (vs. eleven six months earlier).[40]

Central authorities continued to worry about political reliability. In September 1925 the Central Committee issued a directive stating that one of the basic tasks in the formation and manning of national units was the assignment of a sufficient cadre of political workers. To this end, the Central Committee ordered, first, an immediate halt to the release of party workers from the military without the express approval of the Central Committee and, second, it instructed party committees in the national republics and regions to assist political organs in the Red Army in locating political workers for the national units.[41]

Looking at the situation with respect to national armies in 1927, Voroshilov commented in his report to the Fourth All-Union Meeting of Soviets that "in all of the republics in which national military units were created, these units qualitatively resemble units of the workers and peasants' Red Army." "In spite of a whole list of problems," he continued, "new situations, insufficient national command and political personnel, the absence up until recently of national regulations and military literature, the construction of national units in the aforementioned republics has not run into insurmountable obstacles and is moving smoothly." This was true, Voroshilov argued, even in the republics of Central Asia.

> We have already begun to implement the program of national units in Uzbekistan, Turkmenistan, and Kazakhstan; the first national units have been established in the Dagestan ASSR, the Yakut ASSR, the Buryato-Mongolian ASSR, the Karelian ASSR and the Autonomous Region of the Northern Caucasus.[42]

Support for Voroshilov's comments on the improvement of the situation in Central Asia came in an article written at the time which noted that "already today, we have a situation, where with the exception of artillery, all command positions at the platoon level in national units are manned by officers of the indigenous population."[43]

Gradually, the quality of national cadres began to improve. Teachers who were literate in the local language were hired for the military schools. A number of the local civilian pedagogical schools opened military departments, while Moscow sent some of the officers from the national armies to Soviet military academies. Problems remained, however, with the overall educational level of the local populace. In 1927 Voroshilov reported that 12.4 percent of those drafted into the Red Army were illiterate, while in 1928 another source noted that in the North Caucasus 75.9 percent of those drafted were illiterate. For Kazakhs the figure was 70.8 percent, while among those volunteering from Central Asia as a whole 61 percent were unable to read and write.[44]

By 1927 the government was providing more financial support for the national formations. Voroshilov reported that while in 1926 it was necessary to curtail training exercises, the financial situation in 1927 was such that "we are not only carrying out the training of rifle units in accordance with the full letter of the law, but the method of organizing the training of troops has been significantly improved. The latter permits carrying them out with greater regularity." Despite these improvements, Voroshilov emphasized that more needed to be done. For example, he stated that

> a normal prerequisite for normal growth is on the one hand, the growth of a net of study rooms, sport clubs, pre-military training organizations in the area from which soldiers are recruited, and on the other, the existence of a material military basis (especially obtaining field training sites, firing ranges, camps and all kinds of educational materials).[45]

Another writer reporting on the status of national units in Uzbekistan strongly criticized the level of political work and, in particular, he took on political officers for their insufficient military knowledge, their weak political and general educational preparation, as well as their lack of commitment to the party.[46]

Looking at the status of national formations in 1929, Voroshilov singled out five areas where he felt that the creation of national units had strengthened the country. First, they had helped make the country's borders more secure (since most of them in Central Asia were located on the country's perimeter). Second, he argued that the ability to train these individuals in their native languages was especially important given the increasing level of military technology. Third, Voroshilov observed that they had contributed to better relations between nationalities, especially in those formations which were made up of different ethnic groups. Fourth, those who returned to civilian life after serving in national formations were not only literate, but they often took with them a greater commitment to the new regime. Fifth, he singled out the importance of these formations in helping convince national groups that they were no longer being exploited (as had been the case under the Tsars), but were now on an equal footing with other nationalities.[47]

## The 1930s

While most of the more dramatic actions involving national formations occurred during the 1920s, these units continued to exist until near the end of the 1930s. This was true even of Central Asia. For example, between 1926 and 1930 the Kremlin formed two Uzbek and two Turkmen regiments and a squadron of Kirghiz cavalry. The army eventually transformed the latter into a division. In 1930 the question was raised concerning the formation of a Karakalpak division of cavalry. Then in 1934 the military made units of Uzbek infantry into a regiment of mountain troops. Progress was also evident in other areas. For example, during the early 1930s the Kremlin formed a mixed brigade of Uzbek cavalry and artillery, and a Tadzhik brigade. And in 1935 the Red Army created a combined division of Turkmen, Uzbek, and Tadzhik mountain cavalry.[48]

In an effort to deal with the increasing modernization of the Red Army brought about by the first Five-Year Plan, which was launched in 1928, the military leadership introduced a directive "On Changes in the Territorial Forces of the RKKA." Citing the increasingly complex technological problems faced by the Red Army, the directive recognized the need to create special technical units within national formations. In addition, it called for paying certain officers bonuses (up to 25 percent), giving greater attention to military training for civilians, and providing better training for those serving in national units. Despite this effort to bring greater technical sophistication into national units, it soon became clear that such steps were insufficient. Because they only served for short periods of time, those assigned to national units were increasingly unable to deal with the demands of modern technology.[49]

In order to raise the level of their combat readiness, the military gradually increased the size of their full-time staff in national formations, while at the same time turning most of the rifle units in the Central Asian region into mountain troops. By 1938 one source reports that there were "a total of 17 national mountain-rifle and cavalry divisions, two separate regiments and a significant number of sub-units."[50] Furthermore, Soviet sources claim that most of these units performed well. For example, outside observers rated them as "good" and "outstanding" during maneuvers held by the Red Army in 1936-1937.[51] In terms of their overall numbers, one source claims that by 1932 there were a total of 193 national rifle regiments, 67 artillery regiments, as well as a number of other specialized units. "All in all, by the end of the first Five-Year Plan, national units composed 77 percent of the Red Army's divisions."[52]

The situation soon began to change, however. By 1935 the Kremlin had begun to move away from primary reliance on national divisions to greater emphasis on regular forces. For example, by the end of 1935 the relationship between national and cadre units had changed dramatically; 77 percent of the total divisions were regular while only 23 percent remained national.[53]

On March 7, 1938, a Central Committee directive transformed national units, formations, military schools, and training facilities into all-union forces.[54] They had served their function. The increased danger from Germany as well as the greater technical sophistication of most weapons systems placed a premium on a cadre system. The national formations were no longer able to carry out the tasks assigned to them. As Voroshilov put it in 1939, "The existence of separate small national military formations, permanently attached to their respective territories, contradicted the fundamental principles of the Stalin constitution, and the principle of extra territoriality in the recruitment of the army." As a consequence, Moscow converted national military facilities (e.g., units, schools) into union forces, thereby bringing the experiment with these types of forces to a temporary halt.[55]

## World War II

National formations were resurrected during World War II. The demands for manpower were even greater than they had been in the Civil War. The country could not afford to ignore the thousands of Soviet citizens who did not know Russian well enough to serve in the Red Army. As a result, a directive dated November 13, 1941, was issued authorizing the establishment of special units "for those who had a weak (or no) command of the Russian language."[56] Responsibility for equipping and feeding these units was laid on the Central Committee of the respective republic. By the end of November units were being established in Uzbekistan, Kazakhstan, Tadzhikistan, Turkmenistan, and Kirgizia. The lack of trained officers of the appropriate national background as well as an insufficient supply of technical specialists made it necessary for Moscow to assign Russian officers and specialists to many of these newly formed units. Indeed, the vast majority of officers assigned to these units were "Europeans." In an effort to deal with this problem, officer candidates from Central Asia were sent to short (i.e., three-month) schools, similar to those that had existed in the 1920s. In the meantime, such units utilized two different languages. The commander at the regimental or even squadron level spoke in Russian and then utilized an interpreter to translate his instructions into the local language. Unfortunately, the use of translators, many of whom "had been badly prepared," led to numerous mistranslations. The army tried to overcome this problem by holding Russian-language classes for all of the troops. In addition, it devoted considerable attention to political training. In some cases, because of the problem with language, political officers had to hold classes in the local language. One indication of the extent of the language problem was the fact that newspapers and journals were printed in some fifty-five languages during the war.[57]

The contribution of the non-Russian republics was significant. According to one source, Central Asia supplied fifteen infantry brigades and twenty cavalry divisions, while the other non-Russian republics (i.e., Georgia, Armenia, Azerbaijan, Latvia, Lithuania, and Estonia) provided a total of twenty-one divisions. The first national unit was the 21st Latvian Rifle Division, which was created on August 3, 1941.[58] Despite the delegation of responsibility for manning and supplying these units to the various republics, operational responsibility remained in the hands of the Soviet High Command. In practice, this meant that while the various republics were responsible for items such as transport, horses, shoes, harnesses, clothing, and food, only Moscow gave operational orders. It is worth noting that even though these were "national formations" many of the troops—as well as the officers—did not come from the local region. For example, only 30 to 35 percent of those in units from the Baltic republics were from that area, while in the rest of the country only 50-70 percent were from the local region. On February 1, 1944, the Supreme Soviet passed a law permitting the creation of national units in each republic.[59]

The units established during World War II continued to exist until the mid-1950s. The appearance of new and more complex types of weapons systems argued against their continued existence. In fact, by the end of the 1950s national forces had become useful only as training units for the less technical ground forces.

Despite all the problems with them, these units served a valuable purpose. In evaluating the significance of these units, Soviet writers have singled out four areas where they made an important contribution. First, from the political point of view, they served as an effective propaganda tool in the international arena. Frunze himself remarked on the international importance of these units when he stated in 1924,

> You can see how now each fact from the area of international relations speaks of the greater importance given to the actions of colonial peoples. You can see how with each day the national-revolutionary movement further expands and how the logic of that development leads to the conclusion that colonial peoples should tie their fate to that of the Soviet Union.

By building strong, effective national formations, Frunze continued, the USSR would increase its prestige throughout the colonial world.[60]

A second factor motivating the establishment of such units was to help improve understanding and relations between the various national groups in the country. As one source put it, "National units were a major means of overcoming international hostility and the creation of peaceful, fraternal relations between the multinational peoples of the Union."[61]

These units also were important militarily. They "significantly increased the army's mobilization capabilities," a development that was critical when the country was faced with the need to mobilize the population during

World War II—a semi-trained reservoir of men was available.[62] According to Trotsky, during the 1920s national formations together with militia formations made up 74 percent of the total forces of the Red Army.

Despite their military significance, it was clear from the beginning, however, that "they also had weak aspects. It was difficult to organize systematic and well supported combat training in the territorial units. In this regard, they were largely inferior to the regular units."[63] In the main, military factors played a secondary role in the creation of such units during the 1920s. To quote Frunze, "It is uncertain which would be better—to have ten divisions made up of Russians, well trained and disciplined, or to have only five good divisions and five weakly trained, qualitatively inferior, but national divisions. From the point of view of the broadest perspective it may very well be that the first would be preferable."[64]

These units also played an important economic role. Engels probably said it best when he noted that "nothing depends so much on economic conditions as the army and navy. The weapons, personnel, organization, tactics and strategy depend above all on the level of production and means of communication available at that time."[65] During the early 1920s the USSR did not have the wherewithal to fund a regular army. Just as the mixed formations discussed in chapter 2 helped deal with the problem, so did the existence of national forces. They were considerably cheaper. Voroshilov stated in 1927, for example, that a national division cost one million rubles less than a regular one. Furthermore, he added, "The cost of maintaining one territorial soldier for five years costs 54 percent of what is involved in maintaining one regular soldier for five years."[66] Another Soviet writer summed it up best when he said, "The territorial-cadre system for the development of the Red Army was the most efficient for that time."[67]

Finally, national formations played an important role in socializing and educating large numbers of illiterate peasants. Among those joining national units, the percentage of soldiers who were illiterate was as follows: Georgia, up to 35 percent; in Armenia, up to 45 percent; in Azerbaijan, up to 95 percent; and in Central Asia around 90 percent. "They returned from the army fully literate and politically educated citizens." In fact, from the Soviet perspective, this latter role was their most important function. "National Militaries were intended (and in fact utilized) above all as channels for political socialization, as an effective level for increasing the educational and cultural level of people previously under the yoke of Tsarism, as an original 'educational institution' for the training of national cadre."[68]

Regardless of the overall value of national formations, the Soviets believed that, given their disastrous economic situation at the time, they had little choice. As one Soviet officer put it, they "were a result of the concrete historical conditions existing in the life of the Soviet Union" at that time.[69]

## Conclusion

The lines between civilians and military professionals were not as clearly drawn in this area as with militias. On the one hand, the regular military officers did not place much value on national formations. If anything, they took resources away from the standing army. The professional soldiers objected to this outside interference by politicians who sought to tell them what kind of military formations they should create. It didn't matter if it was being done for solid political reasons—e.g., political socialization. The fact was that most of the generals believed they knew best in this area. In this sense Kolkowicz's model made some sense.

Kolkowicz's hypothesized relationship between technology and military corporateness also made sense—the generals were concerned about the inability of such units to master modern technology. However, Kolkowicz's assumption is misleading. In fact, most civilians agreed with the generals. These units were only of minimal military value. At the same time, they fulfilled important political and economic purposes. In any case, once these units had carried out the political and economic tasks assigned to them, they were disbanded.

Seen from another perspective, Odom's model makes sense. After all, while the High Command resented being forced to waste resources on these units, the generals understood the need for this type of political socialization. Furthermore, both civilians and generals agreed with the idea that these units had to be under firm control. In this sense, the relationship between the military and the civilian was more symbiotic, as Odom suggested.

# IV

## RED OR EXPERT
### PERSONNEL ISSUES

> You have heard about the glorious victories
> of the Red Army. Tens of thousands of
> former officers and colonels serve in it. If we
> had not accepted them and forced them to
> serve in the military, we would not have
> been able to create an army.
>
> Vladimir Lenin

> Every non-party commander of the Red
> Army should be aware that he is a com-
> mander of the army of the Soviet Republic,
> the army of workers and peasants. And he
> should draw the necessary conclusions from
> that.
>
> Mikhail Frunze

### The Problem

The question of where to find sufficient officers to staff the Red Army went
to the heart of the problem facing the Bolsheviks. On the one hand, there
was a clear difference in political and societal values between most of the
former officers from the Imperial Army and the Bolsheviks. How could the
party guarantee their reliability?

On the other hand, the Bolsheviks clearly needed these officers. The
simple fact was that the Bolsheviks did not have anywhere near enough
trained military experts to staff the new army. The only source of trained,
competent officers were those who had served in the Tsarist Army. Some
of these individuals had gone over to the Bolsheviks of their own free will
and could be considered at least partially reliable. But they would not suffice—especially with the Civil War looming on the horizon. This meant
that the Kremlin would have to find additional, less reliable military specialists.

Faced with the influx of large numbers of officers from the former Imperial Army, the Bolsheviks did exactly what Kolkowicz suggested: they in-

troduced a number of direct, intrusive political controls. The purpose of these controls was to ensure the loyalty of these "outsiders." In addition, the controls were also set up so that the Bolsheviks could be certain that over time those who remained in the military, as well as those who were subsequently inducted into it, would begin to adopt and internalize the new value system. After all, it would be much more efficient to have officers and NCOs who willingly supported the new regime than it would be to keep a constant eye on their every action.

### Reliance on the Old Order

One of the Bolsheviks' prime objectives was to destroy the old army. On November 23, 1917, for example, the leadership issued a decree on the gradual demobilization of the military, only to be followed several weeks later by two additional decrees. One was entitled "On elective command and the organization of discipline in the army," and the other, "On the equalization of rights among soldiers." The first destroyed the old hierarchical command structure, and the second ended the use of all insignia, decorations, and officer organizations in the Red Army. As a consequence, the only officers who could serve in the Red Army had to be elected by their compatriots. The result was anarchy as the authority of officers was undercut, including those who were elected.[1]

The ineptness of these "elected" officers was evident in the overwhelming defeat suffered by the Red Guards and the remnants of the Imperial Army in early 1918 at the hands of the Germans. Meanwhile, to make matters worse, Japanese troops appeared ready to pounce on Siberia, and segments of anti-Red forces seemed poised to attack in a variety of areas. The new Soviet state stood in peril, and it was obvious that in order to survive the army that Lenin had worked so hard to destroy had to be rebuilt. In rebuilding it, however, the Bolsheviks had to mold it into a tool of the party—a tool which would be both Red and expert.

It is one of the ironies of the period that despite their hatred of the past and of the officers who staffed the Imperial Army, the Bolsheviks found themselves increasingly dependent on this very group of individuals. Operating a military (even in 1917) was a complicated undertaking, and the Bolsheviks quickly realized that, given the threats they faced (from the Germans and the approaching Civil War), they had no alternative but to make use of these hated symbols of the old regime, the so-called "military specialists." As Sergey Gusev noted, it was a "natural and inevitable means for creating detachments to repulse the attacks of the White Guards."[2]

One of the first uses the Bolsheviks found for the military specialists was as advisors. This permitted the Kremlin to use their expertise, while at the same time keeping them out of operational matters. For example, the

Bolshevik's principal military advisor in 1918 was Mikhail Bonch-Bruevich, a former general in the Imperial Army. Similarly, "practically all" of the twenty-six members of the Higher Military Council in 1918 were former officers from the Imperial Army—"13 of them had been members of the General Staff."[3]

The leadership also used military specialists as teachers and professors. The problem was simple. The Bolsheviks had thousands of officers who were politically loyal—even fervently committed to the new regime—but the vast majority of them lacked the necessary technical training. It was vital that these officers (who were called Red Commanders, or *Kraskom* in Russian) be trained to assume critical positions. Accordingly, on February 10, 1918, a decree entitled "The Basic Conditions for Accelerated Courses for the Preparation of the Command Staff of the Workers and Peasants Red Army" was issued. These courses aimed at "preparing instructors for the infantry, cavalry, artillery, engineering forces and machine gun units." The courses lasted three or four months, depending on the officer's specialty. To gain entry, candidates had to satisfy minimal educational standards and present proof of political reliability. To provide the necessary expertise at the thirteen training courses set up at this time, the Soviets again were forced to rely on military specialists. As one Soviet writer put it, ". . . for the general military schools for the workers, a tremendous number of instructors were required. It would have been difficult to solve that task without the old military specialists."[4]

The Bolsheviks also used military specialists as instructors for longer-term courses. In fact, they put military specialists in charge of reorganizing the entire educational system. For example, they placed the General Staff Academy (formally the Nikolaevskiy Academy) under the command of A. K. Klimovich, who had been an officer in the Imperial Army. It formally opened on December 8, 1918. The first course contained 183 students and lasted seven months. Other academies focused on the study of artillery, engineering, medicine, and naval affairs. In each case, military specialists made up the bulk of instructors. To quote one source, "Instructors at the Academy were drawn from former professors and teachers at the old Nikolaevskiy Academy of the General Staff and commanders of the Red Army, who had combat experience and as a rule, higher military education."[5] The faculty included a number of officers, such as N. A. Danilov, V. F. Novitskiy, A. A. Svechin, and N. A. Suleyman, all of whom had a profound effect on Soviet military thinking. Of all the areas in which they served, the military specialists most completely dominated the educational arena. One source reports, for example, that more than "90 percent of the instructors and line officers serving at military academies, higher schools, accelerated and short-term courses were military specialists."[6]

When Trotsky took over as Commissar of War on March 4, 1918, it was clear that the Bolsheviks had to completely reorganize the Red Army if it was to meet external or internal challenges. This was true throughout the armed forces. In this regard, Trotsky argued that Soviet Russia had to expand the role played by military specialists. They should serve not only in staff positions as educators and advisors, he argued, but also in operational command positions. Reflecting his pragmatic approach to such problems, Trotsky suggested that ideological concerns be subordinated to the needs of the time. To satisfy the concerns of those who opposed such an action in principle, Trotsky emphasized that the state had no alternative, and pointed out that such individuals would play a limited role:

> Yes, we are utilizing military specialists because the task of Soviet democracy is not to dispose of technical forces which we can make use of for our historical work. . . . Military specialists will supervise technical matters, purely military questions, operational questions, combat issues. . . . At the current point in time, we have no alternative. It is important to remember that besides enthusiasm . . . technical knowledge is also necessary.[7]

Despite Trotsky's attempt to explain the need for military specialists in operational command positions, strong opposition remained. Using them as advisors and educators was one thing, but giving them operational command was more than many Bolsheviks could stomach. After all, in addition to undercutting their authority, Bolshevik propaganda had made the military specialists into one of the most hated symbols of the old regime.

Nikolay Krylenko and Nikolay Podvoysky were outspoken in their opposition to the use of these officers. They argued that the military specialists, "cannot understand any other kind of war other than a war utilizing large masses of regular troops . . . a situation that always demands bureaucratic centralization." They feared that such individuals would have little concern for Marxist ideology, and would be insensitive to the Bolshevik military doctrine of maneuver and offense. Instead, they would cling to the old ways.[8]

The Bolsheviks continued to be concerned about political reliability. These concerns were not without merit. There were instances when "military specialists joined the Red Army with the purpose of undercutting its combat capability from within." The actions of such "traitors caused considerable losses."[9] Despite these objections, however, Trotsky won on this issue. The Fifth All-Russian Congress of Soviets adopted a special resolution which stated that "in order to create a centralized, well educated and supplied army, it is necessary to utilize the experience and knowledge of the many military specialists from the ranks of officers of the former army."[10] The need for these officers was great. Soviet government plans foresaw the creation of 60 divisions, but by the end of 1918 only 1,773 Red Commanders had finished even the short courses. As a result, it was decided that 55,000 military specialists were needed, "just to fill command positions." By the end of the year, Shatagin reports that 8,000 had volunteered and another 5,000 had been drafted.[11] And the number continued to grow. By the end of the Civil War, for example, Soviet sources state that of the 130,000 officers serving in the Red Army, between 70,000 and 75,000 were military specialists.[12] In addition to their role in educational institutions and operational commands, these officers figured prominately on staffs.

Military specialists played a critical role in the war effort—not only as educators and staff officers, but as commanders on the battlefield as well. In fact, such officers dominated senior level operational command positions. For example, of the twenty officers who commanded the Eastern and Southern fronts between 1918 and 1920, seventeen, or 85 percent, were military specialists. Likewise, all of the chiefs of staff of fronts, 82 percent of the army commanders, and 83 percent of the chiefs of staff of armies came from this group.[13]

The Bolsheviks took two special measures to ensure the political reliability of military specialists. First, they forced all who joined to go before a special "Attestation Commission, which evaluated their political reliability."[14] Second, and more important from the long-term perspective, the leadership introduced the political commissar. As originally conceived, the commissar's primary role was to supervise the actions of military specialists. In theory, these individuals were not to become involved in technical/ operational military affairs. They were in the army to ensure that military specialists did not engage in treasonable activity. To make certain that the actions taken by military specialists accorded with party instructions, the Kremlin instituted a system of "dual command" (*dvoevlastie*). Under this system, only those orders signed by both the military specialist and the political commissar were valid (i.e., authority was split between the two officers). The logical implication of such an arrangement was that once a new cadre of politically loyal and technically competent officers had been educated and had assumed their positions within the Red Army, the system of commissars would become unnecessary. The latter system, known as the "unity of command" principle, placed all authority in the hands of one individual—the commander. Indeed, Soviet sources claim that this latter approach was always the goal, a principle which "the Communist party always viewed as the most efficient organizational form of leadership of the Red Army."[15] Whatever the truth—and one has the impression that while this may have been the goal in principle—at this time the freedom of action of the military specialist was severely limited. In addition, the leadership subordinated commissars to higher-level military-political organs, a situation which only widened the split between the two.[16]

The relationship between commanders and political commissars was an uneasy—in some ways artificial—arrangement from the start. While some worked well together, other cases produced conflict or at least antagonism on the part of both men. For their part, military specialists resented limitations placed on them by the commissars. After all, many of them believed they had proven their loyalty on the battlefield, where they had displayed considerable courage and dedication to the new regime. The situation was made worse by the close working relationship forced on the two men. As Fedotoff-White put it, "The commissars roomed with the commanders to whom they were attached. They accompanied them wherever they went, so that each step made by the commanders was immediately known to the commissars."[17] Conflicts between military specialists and commissars also impacted on troop morale and behavior. As von Hagen put it, "From the beginning . . . dual command had introduced ambiguity, tension, and often hostility into officers' relations with commissars, thereby diminishing the authority of both groups in soldiers' eyes."[18] Command in any military is sensitive and it is very difficult to split. Who is in charge? What does a soldier do if he receives two different and mutually contradictory orders? The only long-term solution in the eyes of the military specialists was to remove the commissars. Most of the military specialists believed that the political commissars—who often had only a rudimentary knowledge of military affairs—contributed little to the unit's combat capability.

Meanwhile, commissars resented the military specialists. The commissars were the ones who had given their lives to the revolution—in many cases long before most of the military specialists had joined the Red Army. Besides, many of them had discovered that political work at the unit level was boring and unrewarding. They had seen combat, believed they understood the basics of military affairs, and wanted the opportunity to command troops themselves.

Needless to say, both the commissars and their ideological supporters opposed abandonment of the dual system. They argued that the creation of a system based on the unity of command principle would weaken the role and influence of the "true Communists" and could lead to a reemergence of the old order.

The question of whether military specialists should be given greater freedom came to a head in March 1919. By this point, the positions of the two sides were polarized. As one individual put it, "There are two points of view; to utilize military specialists and military technicians socialized under capitalism or to get rid of specialists, and in military affairs utilize only those individuals who are completely sympathetic to us."[19] Both of these positions were clearly articulated at the Eighth Party Congress, held from March 18-23. On the one hand, it was argued that the issue had been "historically decided"—the fact was that "there are tens of thousands of military specialists" in the armed forces. They had served well, a point Trotsky never tired of pointing out. For example, in an article on the topic published a couple of months earlier he had stated,

> The broad public knows about almost all of the cases of betrayal and treachery by military specialists, but unfortunately, not only the broad public, but even more close party circles know very little about all of those military specialists, who honestly and consciously died for the cause of the Workers and Peasants of Russia.[20]

Even if they had wanted to, the Reds could not have functioned without the specialists for the simple reason that "it would be impossible to substitute our Communist officials for military specialists."[21] In essence, this side argued that the military specialists had proven their value and that as a result the unity of command principle should now be introduced.

The other side, led by Vladimir Smirnov, a party official, maintained that the vast majority of military specialists still sympathized with the Whites. Rather than introducing the unity of command principle, Smirnov pushed for strengthening the role of political commissars and claimed that responsibility for military operations should be placed in the hands not of the commander, but of revolutionary councils. If military specialists played any role at all, it should be limited to that of an advisor. Unity of command for these people would be a recipe for disaster.[22] To quote a Soviet source on the issue, "Some members of the Revolutionary Military Council and in the army considered the principle of unity of command in the leadership of military operations, unacceptable, 'disastrous' for the revolution and insisted on retaining the collective form of command."[23] For these people, class background was more important than technical competence. Lenin himself took on this group, arguing that "when you propose theses which are completely directed against the military specialists, you violate the entire tactical position of the party. This is the basis of the difference of opinion."[24]

Faced with the imminent threat posed by Kolchak's forces then moving on Moscow and the deep splits at the congress over the peasant question, not to mention disputes over military matters, Soviet leaders were in no mood to further antagonize the left wing. As a consequence, the congress made a concession to the "military opposition" by passing a resolution which strengthened the commissars by making them representatives of both the Soviet state and the party. They were also given the right to inflict summary punishment, and the dual command principle was expanded to include problems dealing with administration and supply—i.e., both officers were required to sign any orders dealing with such matters, a clear expansion of the authority of the political commissar. In addition to strengthening the hand of the political commissar and calling for intensified political work, the program adopted by the congress also called for further efforts to train ordinary soldiers for command positions.[25] Finally, it is important to note that the congress refused to go as far as the military opposition wanted. Just as the party leadership recognized the need to make concessions to its more radical elements, it also was aware of how dependent it was on these officers. As one speaker put it, "Whatever area you take, supply, technical, communications, artillery—for that we need military specialists, because we don't have them."[26] In the end, the resolution emphasized the importance of the role played by specialists and commended them for their loyalty to the Soviet state.

Despite the decision of the Eighth Party Congress, this issue refused to go away. By the end of 1919, Ivar Smilga, the head of the Political Administration and a Trotsky ally, again raised the issue, arguing that those commanders who had proved their loyalty be allowed to function without the presence of political commissars. In units commanded by individuals of proven loyalty, Smilga maintained that the post of commissar should be abolished. Smilga argued that the political organs and the party organization that had been created in 1918 were sufficient to control the commanders.[27]

Publicly, Trotsky tried to occupy the middle ground—as he had on the issue of military doctrine. This was clear in a speech he made on December 12, 1919. On the one hand, he argued that it was possible to dispense with political commissars in some cases: "If military specialists are good workers, there is no reason not to trust them completely in a political sense; it is always possible to organize observations of their actions. And that does not have to be done by a commissar."[28] At the same time, he carefully avoided offending those who favored retaining political commissars. For example, he made it clear that while he favored the principle of unity of command, he was not advocating the abolishment of the commissar. In reality, however, political commissars were becoming dispensable. As Fedotoff-White put it, "As soon as the Red Army had become a regularly organized armed force, commanded by men welded into it by the fire of battle, the commissar had no place in it."[29]

Despite Trotsky's suggestion that military specialists were becoming more reliable, and that serious attention should be devoted to introducing the unity of command principle, primary attention continued to be focused on improving the education of the Red Commanders. The logic was simple; first, there were not enough commanders available to fight the Civil War, even with all of the military specialists. To quote one Soviet source writing in January, "Success in combat demands that in the position of a commander there be real commanders. . . . and the supply of commanders from military specialists has almost run out. . . . In one division on the Southern Front five regimental commanders were wounded or died the other day."[30] Second, with sufficient training for the Red Commanders and the young people entering the service, military specialists would gradually become unnecessary. The Kremlin was clearly making a serious effort in this area as indicated from the following figures. By 1920 the number of such training courses totaled 153. Of this number, sixty-four trained infantry officers, eighteen were for artillery officers, three were devoted to training officers to deal with machine guns, seventeen were for cavalry officers, eight for engineers, and the remaining forty-five were for a variety of specialties. In all, this "net" of military schools "served 81,000 individuals."[31]

By the end of the Civil War, the 130,000 officers of the Red Army were split into three groups: revolutionary commanders from the industrial sector, NCOs and warrant officers from the old military, and the military specialists. Given the opposition they had faced on the question of utilizing military specialists, the leadership's preference was to minimize dependency on the military specialists in favor of concentration on the Red Commanders. Reality, however, was to turn out to be more complex than many of them thought. Training takes time—even if it is accelerated—and in the meantime, the expertise of the military specialists would continue to be indispensable.

### Focus on the Red Commanders: The Transition Period

Personnel reductions during the early 1920s provided the military leadership with an opportunity to focus on quality rather than quantity, i.e., from trying to upgrade the qualifications of masses of officers to focus its attention on fewer, but better quality officers. For example, instead of 130,000 officers, Voroshilov reported that by 1921 there were only 48,000. Of the 48,000, by 1921 14,000 were Red Commanders.[32] Logically fewer officers to train meant an easier educational task. However, despite all the efforts that the military leadership had made to educate the new class of Red Commanders during the Civil War, they remained hopelessly out-classed by the military specialists, in terms of numbers, education, and technical competence.[33]

Instead of helping the Red Commanders, the cutbacks hit them hardest. When it came time to discharge officers in order to reach the lower ceilings, the generals opted in favor of the better-trained military specialists. In fact, Red Commanders were often singled out and relieved of their command positions because of their "lack of theoretical knowledge."[34] The situation reached the point where by 1920 only 10.5 percent of all officers were Red Commanders.[35] This issue was raised at the Tenth Party Congress, which was held from March 6-16, 1921.

The congress took a hard line in favor of the Red Commanders, calling for an immediate halt to the practice of releasing Communists from the military because of their lack of technical qualifications. The resolution adopted by the congress called for those having military rank to be reinstated and for greater attention to be paid to a "planned and systematic use of Red Commanders in command positions."[36] Recognizing the enormity of the task ahead, the congress called for "increased attention by soviets, party, and professional institutions and organizations to the all-around improvement of the conditions of military-educational affairs."[37] In a follow-up statement a month later, the Central Committee called on local party organizations to help educational institutions by assisting them in recruiting politically reliable young people, and in improving living standards at such schools. The main result of this effort was the introduction of an educational reform in 1921.

The 1921 reform had a twofold goal. On the one hand it was aimed at educating a new generation of politically reliable young officers who would form the backbone of the army in days to come. On the other hand, the reform tried to upgrade the educational level of the Red Commanders so that they would be in a position to gradually replace the remaining specialists.

The educational reform ended short-term courses, so that primary attention could be focused on longer courses and a wider group of subjects. It expanded the length of these schools to three to four years, depending on the student's specialization. At the same time, Moscow appointed a new commander for the General Staff Academy—the energetic and talented Mikhail Tukhachevsky. It also became "the leading center for military education." In 1921 Moscow established a political academy, followed the next year by an air force academy. As a result of the educational reform, by 1923 there were "55 normal schools, 13 commander's courses, and 10 higher military educational institutions."[38]

As with other aspects of military affairs, the issue of officer qualifications was also caught up in the power struggle between Stalin and Trotsky. For example, the commission that was set up at the end of 1923 to investigate the status of the Red Army sharply criticized the quality of the officer corps. The poor level of education in the Red Army, the report stated, was a result of the poor qualifications of the instructors. It went on to blast the political and military qualifications of all officers. "From a social standpoint up to 45 percent of the officers do not satisfy the demands of the Red Army (former White Officers make up 5.3 percent of officers)." The report also noted that a significant segment of the officer corps lacked technical qualifications, "a third have no combat experience, and up to 12 percent lack a military education."[39]

Opponents of military specialists joined in the attack. Gusev, for example, criticized the make-up of the officer corps, noting, "In all of our main directorates we find that the domination of old military specialists, and generals has significantly increased." Gusev then read a letter from Uborevich criticizing the army's leadership for having the ossified spirit of "the old Tsarist military specialists."[40] While the attacks were mainly directed against Trotsky—who as Commissar for War bore direct responsibility for the situation in the army—they were also aimed at military specialists.

This desire to limit the role played by military specialists was evident in the commission's call for a reduction in the number of such officers. "The commission pointed to the need . . . to keep in the army only those specialists from the former Tsarist army who, as a result of their actions during the Civil War, showed their commitment to Soviet power; it also called for a review of the professors and instructors on the staffs of academies and at other military-educational institutions."[41] As it was, the relationship between the commander and the commissar would only be settled by the Frunze reforms.

### The Unity of Command Principle Is Implemented

If the Frunze reforms introduced during the mid-1920s accomplished anything, it was to get rid of the old dual command system in favor of the unity of command principle. Military specialists could remain in the military, but only in limited numbers and only if they showed they were completely loyal to the new regime. The bulk of the officers would be either Red Commanders or committed young men prepared to master modern military technology. Andrei Bubnov, who was head of the Political Administration of the army, described this policy as aimed at "the regrouping of the personnel of the military organs to permit a more rapid advancement of the young military Communists and of the young 'Red Commander' element trained in Soviet military schools or promoted to command positions from the ranks during the Civil War."[42]

Before anything could be done, however, personnel policy had to be standardized. It was clear that the military lacked a clearly defined personnel policy, not surprising given the need to recruit every able-bodied man to fight in the Civil War. This was true of conscripts, volunteers, and non-commissioned officers as well as officers. As a result, beginning in 1922 steps were taken to inject a sense of rationality into the process. For example, the leadership issued a directive which laid down strict rules for military service for enlisted personnel. It listed periods of service, set up a twice-annual call-up of conscripts, and prohibited those with "hostile" class backgrounds or who actively opposed the new Soviet state from serving in the Red Army.[43]

Despite this effort to standardize personnel policy, by 1924 it was clear that the party had to take additional steps. To begin with, the different lengths of service (infantry, a year and a half; the navy, four and a half years), created considerable dissatisfaction among conscripts. Second, the one-and-a-half-year obligation, together with the twice-a-year call-up, caused economic and training difficulties. Third, it was clear that a year and a half was not enough time to train non-Russian minorities. As a consequence, in 1924 the government issued a new directive which standardized service at two years except for those in the navy and certain specialties (the latter were set at four and three years, respectively). As a consequence, especially with the passing of the law on obligatory military service in September 1925, the Soviet Union had a standardized approach for dealing with conscripts for the first time in its history.[44]

Meanwhile, the military leadership continued to focus on raising the educational qualifications of the officer corps, a prerequisite to the introduction of the unity of command principle. In fact, Soviet figures indicate that the educational background of officers in the Red Army was still unsatisfactory—at least in the eyes of the Kremlin. For example, 56 percent of officers had received their military training in the Imperial Army, 12 percent did not have military education at all, and only 37 percent had gone through Soviet military institutions.[45]

Faced with this situation, the leadership began a full-scale effort to improve both the political and technical qualifications of its officer corps. And this policy appears to have had some success. By September 1, 1924, the percentage of Communist party members in the central military apparatus increased from 12 to 25 percent. At the same time, the percentage of those older than 50 (the vast majority of whom were military specialists) dropped from 21 to 5 percent.[46] In addition, the leadership made progress on the question of Red Commanders. By 1922 the percentage of Red Commanders in the officer corps was only 22.5. By 1923 it reached 29.5 percent and by 1924 it was 31.8 percent.[47] Meanwhile, those who had gone through Soviet military academies increased ten times, while the number of Red Commanders went up three times. These changes were made easier by the reduction of the Red Army from around 5 million to just under 562,000.[48]

While the cutback in forces made improvements in the military's educational system easier, the Kremlin left nothing to chance. Accordingly, the leadership stepped up efforts to raise the educational qualifications of officers. For example, a decree was issued on November 26, 1924, entitled "A Network of Military-Educational Institutions." This decree ordered that the best commanders be sent to military schools as teachers, that minimum educational standards for entering students be increased, and that a program under which cadets would serve with active-duty units during their time at the school be created. In addition, the leadership increased the number of instructors from 21,348 on November 1, 1924, to 24,028 one year later. It also added short-term courses aimed at helping officers improve their qualifications. By the mid-1920s it was clear that the educational reform process was making progress. "In 1924 military educational institutions produced 6,848 commanders, in 1925—9,193 individuals. Besides, during 1925, 258 individuals graduated from military academies." By the end of 1926, officers with a military education had increased to 95.5 percent.[49]

Meanwhile, the purge of military specialists continued. By January 1, 1925, the number of military specialists on the main army staff had been reduced from 2,598 (June 1, 1923) to 397. Speaking about those who were retained, one source emphasized their political reliability, remarking that "the majority of them had shown their devotion to the working class."[50] Similarly, the percent of officers having a working-class background increased from 13.6 percent on June 1, 1923, to 20 percent on January 1, 1925, while those who were party members rose from around 20 percent to 40.9 percent during the same time period. Meanwhile, party membership and appropriate class background were being stressed for those wishing to attend officer's schools. Again to cite figures from the period: the graduating classes of 1925 were made up of 33 percent workers, 52 percent peasants and 15 percent others, while 51.4 percent were Communists, 15.5 percent were members of Komsomol, and only 33.1 percent were non-party.[51]

As a result of the considerable efforts made to get rid of potentially hostile military specialists and to improve the lot of Red Commanders and Young-Communist officers, by the end of 1925 Soviet writers could argue that the Kremlin had succeeded in

> wiping out of the differences between the Red Commanders and the military specialists; between officers having finished Soviet educational institutions—the Red Commanders and the officers of the old army, who as a result of their honest and selfless service in the Red Army, have demonstrated their loyalty to Soviet power.

The emphasis on quality was beginning to pay off.[52]

With the end of the split between the Red Commanders and military specialists, the leadership began to focus attention on implementing the unity of command principle. The problem, however, was how to operationalize it. Should commissars be completely dropped and the commander made the sole decision maker in all military matters? Or should the commissar be retained in a weakened, but still important form? The first steps toward modifying the institution of political commissars were taken in 1922 when a number of commanders who had completed military academies and higher military courses, and who had been members of the Communist party for at least two years, were allowed to combine both functions. In such cases, a political assistant would replace the commissar. In reality, very few officers were allowed this freedom of action, and even in those cases where a political assistant was introduced, he retained the right to sanction personnel changes and played a key role through the political fitness reports he wrote on all line officers, including his commander.[53]

The unity of command principle was addressed at a meeting in mid-June. Frunze argued that all of the conditions for a transfer now existed, as did Bubnov when he observed that "we have in the ranks of the Red Army in sufficient measure selected, firm and in all areas qualified officers." Stalin also supported this position. In the end the commission adopted a resolution stating that it "recognizes that unity of command is the most efficient principle for the development of the Red Army." The commission left the details on implementing such a policy to the leadership of the Red Army.[54]

The Revvoensovet addressed this issue at a meeting in December, when it passed a resolution calling on commissars to restrict their activities to the "morale-political condition" of the unit to which they were attached. At the same time, recognizing that not all officers fully accepted the new regime, the Revvoensovet noted that in some units the unity of command principle would only be partially implemented. This resolution was followed by a directive entitled "On the Involvement of Officers in Political Work," which ordered officers to take part in the political education of the troops under them. The directive also made it clear that their performance in this area would be noted in their fitness reports. Frunze explained the logic behind the new approach in a speech he gave the same month. There were three types of unity of command. The first dealt with those line officers who would be responsible not only for combat and administrative/ logistical affairs, but for political work as well. Given the newness of the system, it would not be possible to assign this "broad" responsibility at that time. The second type dealt with the commander who was responsible for military as well as administrative/logistical affairs. This would be the most common form of command in the Red Army. Political structures would be responsible for political work. A third type would be introduced into administrative organs such as staffs or directorates. A month later Frunze abolished the titles of military specialist and Red Commander and instituted one title for all officers.[55]

For some in the Red Army, these steps did not go far enough. There were, for example, efforts to get rid of political commissars and political education in the military altogether, a point Frunze acknowledged in an article published in 1925 when he wrote that "some commanders underestimate and minimize the importance of political work in the Red Army in general."[56] Not surprisingly, the political commissars fought back, arguing in November 1924 that the unity of command principle should only be adopted if the officers involved were Communists. Non-party officers could only exercise the unity of command principle on an exceptional basis, and when they occupied staff positions. "Unity of command cannot be viewed as a liquidation of the institute of commissars, because it is not possible to liquidate elements of the party leadership and political education in the army. Unity of command must be viewed as the joint function of party leadership, political education, and military training in one person—the single commander."[57]

Unity of command was one of the hottest topics at a plenum of the CPSU held at the end of November and the beginning of December 1924. Recognizing the need to take steps to deal with the issue, the plenum argued in favor of increasing the limited autonomy enjoyed by regular officers. It resolved that unity of command should be introduced in two forms. The first—

called "incomplete" unity of command—was aimed at those commanders not yet ready to take full responsibility for the political leadership of their troops. The commander was to assume complete control over military, administrative, and housekeeping functions. The commissar, meanwhile, was responsible for morale and political affairs. For them to be valid, orders dealing with transfers, inspections, operational and political matters had to be signed by both officers. The second or complete form of unity of command introduced at this time gave the commander total freedom in issuing orders. The political commissar became his political deputy. This approach was implemented with the issuance of Directive 234 in March 1925.[58]

Despite all of the fanfare associated with the introduction of Order 234, progress toward unity of command appeared to be more symbolic than real. Of 44,326 officers in command positions as of October 1, 1925, only 1,184 of them (2.67 percent) were appointed unified commanders. This was especially true at the middle and lower levels. Among middle level commanders, for example, only .83 percent were given that title.[59] The political commissars were still very much in charge. On the other hand, the dam had been broken. A trend toward greater independence on the part of regular officer corps had begun. This was especially evident in a comparison of the new directive with the January 3, 1922, act then in force. According to the 1922 directive, the role of the political commissar was to carry out "political control and the direct observation" of line officers. The new directive, however, spoke of their role as "leading and the immediate supervision of party-political work and ensuring the training and education of personnel of the Red Army and the Red Fleet in a spirit of class unity."[60] It would only be a matter of time before sufficiently trained—and loyal— officers would emerge to permit the full introduction of Frunze's unity of command principle. As far as the commissars were concerned, the writing was on the wall and they did not like it, a situation evident from an article which Frunze wrote in the summer of 1925 in which he remarked that "it is impossible not to mention that in some units our commissars continue to act negatively toward all of these reforms."[61] This led the Kremlin to launch a campaign offering commissars appointments as line officers if they improved their technical qualifications, and in "early 1925 the certification commissions reviewed the service records of the entire political and officer staffs and promoted large numbers of political workers to military commands."[62]

Further movement toward implementation of the unity of command principle (Frunze's second category as outlined above) soon followed. The percentage of line officers enjoying such status grew to the point where by September 1926 100 percent of corps commanders, 54.7 percent of division commanders, 36.5 percent of regimental commanders, 37.7 percent of company commanders, and 75.5 percent of the chiefs of military educational institutions operated under the unity of command principle.[63]

The next, and most important, step occurred in 1927, when Voroshilov, who succeeded Frunze as Commissar for War, issued Order No. 11. Under this order, a commander who did not have a political commissar (i.e., one who functioned under the unity of command principle), could sign any order himself except for those dealing directly with political affairs. In this case, the political officer would function as the commander's deputy. Any disputes between the two officers were to be reported to the next highest political organ. As the commander's deputy for political affairs, the political officer was responsible for political work as well as morale, discipline, and training-housekeeping matters. The most important component of this directive, however, was its notation that the political officer and the commander *together* "bear complete responsibility for political and morale condition of the unit as well as combat readiness." Some units would remain under the old system, but for those commanders who came under the unity of command principle, they were now more firmly in charge of their units than at any time since the end of the Civil War. As a consequence, in the majority of cases, the chaos of the dual command procedure became a thing of the past.[64]

Both Erickson and Fedotoff-White have argued that despite the introduction of the unity of command principle, the autonomy enjoyed by commanders was still seriously restricted. After all, political officers were still in charge of political work and the fact that disputes could be reported to the next higher political organ placed the commander at a disadvantage.[65] In addition, as von Hagen points out, officers in the Red Army lacked one of the key elements of institutional autonomy—the ability to determine the criteria for entrance into the institution and promotion within it.[66] While all of this is true, it is important to keep in mind that even though a political officer was in a position to harass and in some cases hurt a commander, in practice the two men soon learned that they had no alternative but to work together.[67]

By the beginning of 1930 the percentage of regimental commanders enjoying the unity of command authority had risen from 48 percent in 1927 to 73 percent. Similarly, the percentage of company commanders enjoying this authority rose from 36 percent in 1927 to 52 percent in 1930.[68] To aid these commanders in dealing with political affairs, the Military-Political Academy set up courses to provide them with the necessary knowledge. By end of 1931 the process of transition to the unity of command principle was almost complete. The overwhelming majority of units operated under it. The only exceptions were the navy and the air force, where the "party stratum" included fewer party members. With the exception of those cases where an individual commander may have been forced to accept the "half" form of unity of command from time to time, this arrangement remained in place until May 1937, when the dual command system was reintroduced during the purges.[69]

## Conclusion

Of the four areas discussed in this section, this one most closely reflects Kolkowicz's conflict model. There is no question that party officials saw the military specialists—which in the 1920s counted as the real professionals—as a potential threat. Accordingly, party officials set out to limit their autonomy and freedom of action by designing political structures to maintain control over them.

Political commissars were intended to make sure that regular military officers remained loyal and reliable. Indeed, interference in regular military affairs by commissars was deeply resented, and on many occasions led to open conflict between the two men. Military specialists opposed what they perceived to be actions by incompetent, unqualified ideologues, while the commissars argued that the military specialists were not loyal.

In this sense the conflict model makes some sense. At the same time, it is important to note that this chapter also makes clear, as Odom noted, that the values held by the officer corps were slowly changing. The party was carefully weeding out those opposed to the new regime. The leadership permitted those who adapted to the new realities—even if they had been military specialists—to continue to serve in the Red Army. Indeed, if one looks at the Red Army during the late 1920s, it is clear that the strong feeling of antagonism common in the very early 1920s had begun to disappear. The relationship between the regular and political officers was becoming more symbiotic. As a result, by the end of the decade the relevance of the Kolkowicz model had decreased significantly.

Given their concern over control and their fear of Bonapartism, the Bolsheviks would not have relaxed their commissar control method as they did if they had not believed a value change had taken place. In short, they saw no need to continue it—since it led to military inefficiency.

Colton's model would be hard to apply to the 1920s, primarily because it would be difficult to determine institutional lines. Assuming one classified military specialists as the military, and others as coming from the civilian side, military participation actually decreased during the 1920s. In fact, this was a period of institutional formation—the military as a Soviet institution was still being built. Once it was formed and began to function as an institution (by the late 1920s) its ability to determine its own personnel policies increased—although the Stalin years would soon lead to a loss in institutional autonomy in this area as well, an action that had the most serious implications for the Red Army. Were it not for the purges in the late 1930s, Moscow would have had a core of highly trained and well-educated officers to staff the Red Army during World War II. As it was, most of the gains made in improving the quality of the Soviet officer corps during the 1920s would be lost in the purges of the 1930s.

# II

## *The Gorbachev Period*

# V

## GETTING CONTROL OF
## MILITARY DOCTRINE

> Of particular interest are the writings of our
> military theorists active in the 1920s and
> early 1930s. They form a unique part of our
> cultural heritage. Without studying and
> updating these works, we can hardly carry
> on a deep or exhaustive discussion on major
> military political problems.
>
> Andrei Kokoshin

> I'm getting the impression that all those
> with nothing to do today have decided to
> choose the Armed Forces as their target and
> have turned into Ministry of Defense
> advisors.
>
> Gen. Mikhail Moiseyev

### The Problem

When Gorbachev came to power in 1985, he was faced with a situation
where the military had almost total autonomy when it came to military
doctrine. The High Command determined military doctrine with minimal—
if any—interference from the civilian world. In a certain sense, the situation resembled the period of the Civil War, when professional military officers believed that determining doctrine was their prerogative. To succeed,
he would have to overcome military opposition by forcing the High Command to adopt a new, more defensive military doctrine: one which would
be more in tune with his new approach toward the West.

In attempting to rally support for a new, less threatening doctrine,
Gorbachev's allies turned to the writings of Aleksandr Svechin, the military officer who played such a key role during the 1920s. Svechin and his
ideas were cited both as evidence of the importance of an open discussion
of this topic and as proof that a defensive doctrine was a viable alternative
for the USSR at a time of fiscal stringency.

Because military doctrine plays such a central role in Soviet military affairs, the stakes were very high. Changes in doctrine would inevitably lead to modifications in force structure, not to mention battle plans and operational procedures. This was one of the reasons why the military monopolized public commentaries on this topic. Too much was involved to permit outsiders—especially civilians —to get involved in the process.

### The Issue Emerges

When Gorbachev came to power, Moscow's foreign policy was in disarray. Soviet troops were mired in Afghanistan, in spite of the sacrifice of thousands of Russian lives and considerable material outlays. And this was only the most obvious example. As Sakwa put it:

> In Eastern Europe political stagnation and economic crisis threatened a new wave of unrest. Relations with the West were at their worst in thirty years. Detente had been broken on a number of policy issues, including wars in Africa, human rights, the deployment of Soviet SS-20 missiles, the invasion of Afghanistan and the imposition of martial law in Poland. Brezhnev's foreign policy had culminated in the nightmare of encirclement by hostile powers.[1]

Overcoming this sense of encirclement was one of Gorbachev's top priorities. Unless there was movement in this area, he could not hope to improve relations with the West and reduce military spending. Taking on the military establishment would not be easy, but he had no alternative. Political realities dictated, however, that he would have to be cautious—initially at least. Gorbachev fired the opening salvo at the Twenty-Seventh Party Congress in February 1986. During his report to the congress he stated that "the character of modern weapons does not permit any state hope of defending itself by military-technical means alone—even by creating the most powerful defense." Furthermore, he continued, ensuring security was primarily a political task; it could not be maintained by military means. It was not a question of the "amorality" of mutual deterrence; rather it was a fact that "security cannot be built forever on a fear of retaliation." The concept of deterrence led to a speeding-up of the arms race, which sooner or later would get out of control. Security, to be effective, had to be mutual. Then, in a section devoted to military doctrine, Gorbachev introduced a new idea; reasonable sufficiency. "Our country favors the destruction of weapons of mass destruction, the limiting of military potential within the limits of reasonable sufficiency."[2]

Gorbachev's introduction of this undefined term left the generals in a quandary. From their perspective, it had both positive and negative connotations. To begin with, Gorbachev's rejection of the concept of victory in a nuclear war was an idea shared by a number of leading Soviet officers. Marshal Ogarkov had argued some years previously that the future lay not in nuclear weapons, but in high-tech, precision-guided weapons. Second, the idea that cuts in the budget loomed on the horizon was nothing new. Indeed, Gorbachev had made this clear to the generals in April at a Central Committee meeting, had reiterated it in a meeting with senior military officers in Minsk in July, and he had suggested in his speech to the Twenty-Seventh Party Congress that the budget would be a key criterion in determining the country's military needs. The idea of "preventing war," a concept included in the party platform, did not upset the generals since it did not appear aimed at the military. But what would the term "reasonable sufficiency" mean in practice? As the generals saw it, the political half of military doctrine was being changed, with unforeseen and potentially very serious implications.

Many of the country's senior officers were already suspicious of the direction in which the country's national security policy was going. For example, Gorbachev had proclaimed a unilateral test moratorium in August 1985 and extended it several times, he had adopted a more flexible approach to verification, and some of his decisions at the summit at Reykjavik were difficult for some in the military to accept. Budget cuts were one thing, but this new policy could impact on all aspects of Soviet military policy.[3]

The key question facing the generals was just how far was the civilian leadership prepared to go in dictating and changing the military-technical nature of Soviet military doctrine? Soviet generals and admirals had always argued that Soviet military doctrine was defensive. But this new, undefined concept was sufficiently ambiguous to justify a doctrine so defensive that it would call for a complete overhaul of not only doctrine, but the force structure and operational procedures that were so closely tied to it as well. For example, did defensive mean only having enough forces to repel an attack? If so, this would mean a major change in how the Kremlin planned to fight a war. What about a counteroffensive capability? Would the generals be forced to give up the plans and forces required to implement existing doctrine—which was primarily offensive in nature? What about parity? Furthermore, the introduction of this term by civilians reinforced the general's fear that these outsiders would try to undermine military autonomy in this critical area.

The only clue Gorbachev provided concerning the meaning of reasonable sufficiency was his suggestion that security was mutual—a point that was also included in the party program adopted at the congress. The logical conclusion of such a statement—and one the generals drew—was that reductions in Soviet weapons would be dependent on similar actions by the West., i.e., the continued existence of parity. Such an approach ruled out the unilateralism that was already present in the country's policy toward nuclear test moratoriums.

Given their skepticism toward a policy that placed a premium on diplomacy, their confusion over the new term's meaning, their unpreparedness to deal with this radical new concept, and most importantly their fear that the new concept of reasonable sufficiency was a Trojan Horse for a major, radical restructuring of the armed forces to be guided by outsiders, the generals' immediate response was to ignore it. Until they understood it better, they did not want to give it legitimacy; something that their use of the term would have implied.

Writing in May, Marshal Sergey Akhromeyev, chief of the General Staff, supported Gorbachev's call for a new approach to security, arguing that defending the country's security was primarily a "political task," which "must be resolved by political means . . . and not by means of arms or doctrines of 'containment' or 'deterrence.'"[4] Then in a speech in December, Akhromeyev argued in favor of "approximate military parity," and noted that the Soviet armed forces "are maintained at the necessary level of combat readiness with the sole purpose of holding back a potential aggressor from waging war and defending the peaceful labor of the Soviet people." In discussing the results of the Geneva Summit he emphasized the importance of a strong military while the USSR waited to see if the U.S. would approach the problem of arms limitations "from a more realistic standpoint." In essence, Akhromeyev favored improving East-West relations even if that led to changes in military doctrine. But, he believed that military parity must be maintained at all costs.[5]

While publicly avoiding the term "reasonable sufficiency," the Soviet military was beginning to grapple with the new term and its implications. An editorial in the General Staff journal *Voennaya mysl'*, emphasized the importance of preventing war and of approaching military matters in a new way:

> A threat to the end of world civilization has arisen. . . . In these circumstances, the conclusion of our Party that in the contemporary nuclear-space age one must not think in old categories, that a new approach to the problem of security was necessary, is an important matter of principle.

The article went on to discuss the importance of preventing war and the uselessness of nuclear war.[6]

Gorbachev returned to reasonable sufficiency in February of the following year. During a speech to the Moscow Peace Conference, he again argued that the level of defense should be limited by "reasonable sufficiency," and he insisted that any attempt to push it to higher levels was pure "madness." He labeled deterrence a policy of "political threats," and he suggested that such a policy increased the danger of military conflict.

Arms races of all types—including conventional ones—must be avoided.[7] Two weeks later, Gorbachev insisted that the USSR would "not take a single step in excess of the demands and requirements of sensible, sufficient defense." Unfortunately, Gorbachev again did not define the concept.[8]

Given the continued ambiguity of reasonable sufficiency, it was easy for the generals to emphasize their own view of the term. Akhromeyev, who was probably closer to Gorbachev than any other military officer, reiterated the army's stand in an article in May. In this piece he observed that "the 27th CPSU Congress particularly stressed the *defensive thrust of Soviet military doctrine*," and reiterated that war of any kind would lead to "unpredictable disasters and suffering." He also repeated the military leadership's favorite line; namely, that the military threat from the West, "requires that the Soviet Armed Forces be maintained at a level that ensures our homeland and its allies are reliably defended." If there were any doubts in the reader's mind as to what Akhromeyev meant, he answered them when he remarked that "our principle is to maintain the Armed Forces and our military potential in a state of rough military equilibrium and at a level sufficient to ensure reliable defense of the Soviet Union."[9]

One of the most important developments in the evolution of Soviet military thinking occurred in May 1987 when the Warsaw Pact Consultative Committee issued a document entitled "On the Military Doctrine of the Warsaw Pact Member States." To begin with, the document codified the Gorbachev line in favor of "preventing" war. As it stated, "The military doctrine of the Warsaw Pact, just as of each of its members, is subordinated to the task of preventing war, nuclear and conventional." Second, for the first time it suggested that reasonable sufficiency referred to an inability to initiate offensive operations. This meant that conventional weapons should be reduced "down to the level at which neither side, in ensuring its defence, will have the means for a sudden attack on the other side or for starting offensive operations in general." By making defense the key to Soviet military doctrine, and stressing the importance of preventing a war, Gorbachev forced the generals to take these terms seriously. At a minimum, the political-social aspect of military doctrine had now been formally changed.[10]

The military leadership was confused. Indeed, this move toward reasonable sufficiency "caught the Soviet military and national security establishment largely unprepared."[11] The confusion and unpreparedness were evident in Defense Minister Dmitri Yazov's initial reaction to the pact document. Acknowledging the overriding importance of war prevention in Soviet military doctrine, the impossibility of solving the world's problems by war, and emphasizing the defensive nature of that doctrine, Yazov supported Gorbachev's new concept. In doing so, however, he carefully qualified his support by introducing a new phrase, "defensive sufficiency":

In general terms it means having precisely the magnitude of armed forces necessary to defend oneself against an attack from outside. Specifically, it means that the composition of the armed forces and the quantity and quality of the means of armed struggle are rigorously measured against the level of the threat of war and the nature and intensity of imperialist military preparations and are defined by the requirements of ensuring the security of the Warsaw Pact countries and rebuffing aggression.

There were two interesting elements in Yazov's statement. First was his use of the term "defensive sufficiency," which served two purposes: it emphasized the view that military-technical matters were a topic best left to professional military officers, and it underlined their continuing belief in the critical importance of parity. Without parity, Yazov and his colleagues believed, the military would not be able to "give a crushing rebuff to the aggressor." Or as Yazov put it with regard to conventional weapons, "sufficiency amounts to a quantity and quality of armed forces and armaments capable of reliably ensuring the collective defense of the socialist community." The key question was who would decide the appropriate level of parity. For Yazov the answer was simple—the military leadership.[12]

## Offering an Alternative Approach

In an effort to mobilize support for doctrinal change and to open a dialogue on the nature and content of the new defensive doctrine, Soviet writers who were close to both Gorbachev and the military establishment published articles that drew heavily on the country's past experience. Their message was that in spite of the many differences between the past and the present in military affairs, the former offered a number of useful ideas on how to deal with the newly imposed defensive strategy.[13]

The first such article was written jointly by Andrei Kokoshin and Valentin Larionov. It dealt with the World War II battle for Kursk. Noting that the defensive military doctrine adopted by the Warsaw Pact would require "a definite change in the way of thinking of professional military officers," the article went on to argue that the battle, "showed just how advantageous a reliable defense can be, even when one enjoys superiority." In fact, the authors maintained, the idea that some political and military leaders hold—that it is possible to conduct military operations only on the territory of the opponent—"is practically excluded." Citing Svechin and others on the importance of strategic defense, the authors admitted that to be effective a defensive strategy must be carefully prepared—as was the case with the Battle of Kursk.

Turning to 1987 and the new doctrine, the authors noted that despite significant differences between the past and the present, the Battle of Kursk showed that a carefully prepared defense could be effective. In the final analysis, Kokoshin and Larionov maintained that "the Battle for Kursk is convincing evidence of the possibilities for skillfully opposing the offense when the defender possesses variegated and sufficient forces and the means for anti-tank defense, good organization and a conscious decision has been made to refrain from attacking ahead of time."[14]

An article published in *Pravda* in September 1987 made it clear that Kokoshin and Larionov's ideas carried considerable political weight. Gorbachev called for the restructuring of Soviet forces so that they would be able "to repel possible aggression, but not sufficient to conduct offensive operations."[15] A number of civilian writers and academics echoed Gorbachev's position.[16] Clearly matters were not moving in a favorable direction from the point of view of the country's top military leaders.

Despite civilian pressure for change, Yazov remained stubborn in his refusal to back down on the issue of parity. For example, he stated in a book he authored at this time that "defense is the major form of military operations. . . . Defense, however, alone cannot defeat an aggressor. Therefore, after repulsing the attack, troops and fleets must be capable of waging a decisive offensive. The transition to it takes the form of a counteroffensive. . . ."[17] General Makhmut Gareyev, considered by many to have been the USSR's leading military theorist at that time, published a pamphlet in which he took an equally hard line on the question of parity. He talked of the importance of maintaining "military parity at its lowest possible level" as an important goal and noted that "military parity . . . is of crucial significance for restraining aggression and carrying out of missions in a war by the armed forces." Gareyev believed that without parity the Soviet military could not defend the country.[18]

Insofar as the historical analogy of the 1920s, or Svechin, was concerned, Yazov ignored them. Compared with the issues raised in the next two chapters this response was unique. In the latter instances, the generals dealt with those issues directly, arguing that while those solutions might have been appropriate during the 1920s, they were not compatible with the military realities of the 1990s. Yazov may have recognized the relevancy of Svechin's arguments concerning doctrine and for that reason believed that the best approach was to ignore them.

Kokoshin and Larionov published another article in mid-1988, which attempted to differentiate between four types of defensive strategies. The first concerned a situation in which the country attacked immediately counterattacks. The counterattack soon becomes a strategic offensive operation, with the goal being "a victory . . . ending with the final defeat and destruction of the enemy." The authors labeled this type of thinking "traditional military thinking," the very thing they wanted to change.

The second variant, which most closely resembled the Battle of Kursk, suggested that both sides would refrain from going on the offense, instead limiting themselves to defensive actions. As with Kursk, to be effective a well-developed series of defensive positions had to be prepared. Furthermore, the side attacked had to retain considerable reserves so that it would be able "to transist decisively to the counteroffensive carrying it to the complete defeat of the enemy on his territory."

Kokoshin and Larionov's third variant limited both sides to the ability to defeat an opponent on the attacked country's territory without engaging in counteroffensive operations beyond the country's borders. "The essence of this type of defense consists in the fact that military operations will not be carried to the territory of the country that started the war." Finally, the fourth variant assumed that on the basis of an agreement or "mutual example," each of the countries would engage only in purely defensive operations without the "material possibility of carrying out offensive or counteroffensive operations."

The authors recognized the difficulties involved in transisting to a nonoffensive strategy, especially in variants three and four. How did one define what was an offensive or a defensive weapon? The same was true of force structure. Even more difficult, how to relate qualitative and quantitative factors? Rather than providing answers to these difficult questions, the authors suggested that consideration be given to steps which would strengthen the defensive aspect of military doctrine. For example, they proposed limiting the number of large military exercises and maneuvers, and designing technical criteria for comparing qualitative and quantitative factors (i.e., mobility, speed, multipurpose usage of a given system, all-weather use, etc). Kokoshin and Larionov both knew and understood the military establishment. They knew that the generals would not accept variant three or four, but they hoped that these articles, and their political connections, could help force the generals to move to variant two.[19]

Lest there be any doubt in the minds of Soviet readers concerning the relevance of the 1920s for understanding the nature of defensive doctrine, Kokoshin published an article a few months later that focused directly on Svechin and his relevance for the discussion on doctrine. Arguing that "hardly any of our military theorists of the time—not even Tukhachevsky—could match Svechin in his capacity for so multidimensional an analysis of strategic problems," Kokoshin maintained that one of Svechin's most important contributions was his idea that works on military subjects should encourage "independent thinking." Kokoshin believed that Svechin was unique in his understanding of the interrelationship of politics and military strategy.[20]

Turning to the question of doctrine, Kokoshin emphasized Svechin's contribution to Soviet military understanding of the role of defense in modern warfare. For example, Svechin had argued that the goals and the means available must be in unison. Kokoshin clearly had the military leadership in mind when he quoted Svechin as stating, "real activity consists primarily in taking sober stock of the conditions for struggle; one should see everything as it really is and not make illusory plans."[21] The country was not economically capable of supporting an offensive strategy, and Gorbachev had ordered the military to develop a defensive one. Or as he put it in the latter instance, "Since the summer of 1987, a number of important innovations have occurred in Soviet military doctrine. . . . One of the major changes is its military technical part . . . that the principal mode of action by the Armed Forces of the USSR in resisting aggression will be defensive and counter-offensive and not offensive."[22]

Looking at World War II, Kokoshin maintained that the failure to give careful consideration to Svechin's ideas had cost the USSR dearly in the beginning, and that contemporary Soviet literature on the war failed to note that many of the victorious operations carried out by Soviet troops during the war were possible only because of "successful strategic offensive operations in the second half of the 1943-1945 period."[23]

Placed against the backdrop of the four variants of defensive strategy suggested by Kokoshin and Larionov in their previous article, Svechin would be found somewhere between the second and third categories. A man who saw defense "as a means of providing conditions for an effective counterattack," would certainly not advise moving to a situation where a counterattack was impossible. Insofar as the third variant was concerned, given his belief that military matters should always be subordinate to politics, Svechin would leave the decision of crossing the country's boundaries in pursuit of an enemy in the hands of politicians. His primary concern was that the Red Army be capable of conducting such operations.[24]

Recognizing the threat to its autonomy, the generals continued to insist on the importance of parity and defensive sufficiency. In a major speech in February, Yazov expressed support for "sufficiency," although he carefully avoided attaching the term "reasonable" (or the adjective "defensive"), while at the same time he quoted Gorbachev's comment that the country would do everything necessary "to preserve our defense might at a level which precludes the military superiority of imperialism over socialism."[25]

From the military leadership's perspective, a key question was the army's ability to conduct offensive operations. Surely, Gorbachev was not suggesting that the Soviet Army should be neutered to the point where even counteroffensive capabilities should be eliminated? Just stopping an opponent made no sense if he could not be repelled and his war-making ability destroyed.

It was at this point that fissures began to appear in the military leadership's position. When he was interviewed for the journal *Novoe Vremya* in February 1988, General Vladimir Lobov (at that time first deputy chief of the General Staff) repeated the standard line to the effect that "Soviet military doctrine has a defensive character, with defense regarded as the principal form of military operations." When it came to the question of parity, he observed that "the Soviet Union is building up its Armed Forces on the principles of adequate defense."[26] Within a few months, however, Lobov's position had become more flexible.

Writing in *Voennaya mysl'*, for example, he criticized the Soviet military's tendency to overemphasize the role of surprise in modern warfare.[27] Then in another article he blasted Stalin's World War II strategy because of its overemphasis on the offensive. The result, he maintained, was a "deformation" of Soviet military strategy.[28] He followed up this article with an interview in October in which he mentioned both reasonable sufficiency and defensive sufficiency, but unlike some of his military colleagues he came down more on the side of the former than the latter. He noted, for example, that the weapons held by both sides must be considered in determining what level of military forces was necessary, but quickly added that the West was beginning to "think in a new way." Furthermore, he admitted, "one cannot solve everything by armed means—cannot keep arming oneself all the time, but should undertake measures towards disarming as well." Turning to the concept of defensive sufficiency itself, Lobov added a new twist to the military's position. Acknowledging that "the character of the military threat is considered primary," he argued that Soviet arms control proposals should "be based on minimum defensive potential, not the maximum." Then turning to the question of offensive operations, Lobov came out somewhere between Kokoshin and Larionov's second and third variants. "Material conditions in the sphere of arms must be created that would deprive any state of the possibility of conducting sudden offensive actions. . . . In essence, this is reasonable sufficiency in its specific and feasible manifestation. We are ready for this today."[29]

## The Battle Continues

Despite Lobov's more forthcoming position on doctrine, the generals continued to fight Gorbachev's attempt to undermine their power to determine military doctrine.[30] In September, for example, Andrei Kokoshin published an article in which he took the generals to task for their attitude toward strategic stability. While admitting that parity was important, Kokoshin insisted that *"parity is not a synonym for strategic stability."* Even if it were maintained, it would be possible to create an unstable situation by increasing the level of "military forces." The way out of this situation was for military and civilian experts to work together and come up with a better understanding of strategic stability and the accompanying force structures.[31]

Faced with attacks from a variety of fronts, the generals dug in their heels. General Staff Chief Mikhail Moiseyev, for example, charged that Soviet analysts were underplaying the importance of the military threat.

> The existence of a military threat from imperialism is thus a fundamental
> issue. And success in implementing the party's instructions on defense
> questions will depend largely on the nature of public opinion on this is-
> sue. Yet in their published items some authors try to cast doubt on the
> reality of the military threat and on the correctness of the defense mea-
> sures which are being taken.

There were good reasons for the generals' hardening position. Two
months prior to Moiseyev's speech, Gorbachev had announced a unilateral reduction of some 500,000 troops and 10,000 tanks in his speech to the
United Nations. In addition, as Moiseyev noted, the military leadership
was launching a major restructuring of Soviet forces, one which he claimed
involved "the very backbone of the Armed Forces." For example, motorized rifle and tank divisions were to be restructured so that offensive operations would become more difficult, and 30-35 percent of their tanks,
artillery systems, and assault river-crossing equipment would be reduced.
Concurrently, defensive weapons would be increased by a factor of 1.5-2,
and arms production in the USSR would be reduced by 19.9 percent.[32]

Yazov tried to make the best of these unilateral steps when he stated
that their purpose was to remove the "potential for a surprise attack, which
for a long time was used to intimidate the public in the West European
countries." In the course of restructuring, a number of motorized rifle divisions would be transformed into machine-gun and artillery formations,
"which, as is known, are earmarked only for defense." In addition, the
military leadership was withdrawing clearly offensive structures, such as
combined arms formations from Europe.[33] In reality, however, Gorbachev
was increasingly restricting the military's flexibility when it came to doctrine.

There is a certain irony in the High Command's position. On the one
hand, the generals did not show any interest in Svechin or his defensive
strategy. However, it was clear by mid-1989 that Svechin's strategy was
becoming a blueprint for the revision of Soviet doctrine. The unilateral actions announced by Gorbachev could be justified as an effort to implement
a strategy similar to that outlined by the famed Russian theorist. Even
though they were accepting many of Svechin's ideas in practice, there were
two reasons why neither Moiseyev nor Yazov invoked his name. To begin
with, civilians such as Kokoshin had already usurped Svechin (and this
would legitimize their involvement in the policy process). Second,
Gorbachev's action had caught the generals by surprise and they had not
been able to work out a new concept, although the generals claimed they
were preparing a document on the subject. Most of what they were doing
was being undertaken on the run.

It was at this point that Lobov again came to the fore. Lobov was unusual for a senior Soviet military officer. The possessor of three doctorates

(one in history and two in military science) and the author of several important articles and books, Lobov was very much at home in discussing the 1920s and their relevance for the present. In February 1989 he published an article in *Voenno-istoricheskiy zhurnal* in which he noted that an understanding of the 1920s "is extremely important today." Lobov outlined the views of a number of Soviet theorists, including Svechin. He was singled out because of his contribution to understanding the role of defense. Lobov's primary message to his military audience was that just as there was an open and free discussion in the 1920s, the military leadership should not be afraid of one today. Indeed, many of these issues, such as Svechin's concept of strategic defense, were undeveloped and warranted further analysis and discussion. As he put it,

> Together with the interesting scientific views of the military theoreticians of that time, a matter of special importance for the present day is the level of democracy, scientific controversy, pluralism of opinions, which characterized the conditions of that time, which, without a doubt, made possible progress in military-strategic thought and which was a manifestation of real democracy and the development of Soviet military science.

The situation deteriorated in the 1930s, according to Lobov, as Stalin imposed his own doctrine on the General Staff. The result was the catastrophic defeat suffered by Soviet forces in the early part of World War II.[34]

Lobov suggested to his colleagues that a discussion of the 1920s was relevant for an understanding of the current problems facing the Soviet armed forces and that the best way to develop a new and more effective defensive strategy was through open debate. He carefully avoided taking sides on the content of a defensive doctrine (e.g., the role of the counteroffensive) as well as on the meaning of parity. Nevertheless, the generals were upset at his attempt to serve as a bridge between the civilian and military worlds. Such efforts not only would result in greater civilian influence over military affairs, but they could force the generals into taking steps they wanted to avoid. As a consequence, on February 25, the military leadership announced that Lobov was being reassigned to become Chief of Staff of the Warsaw Pact. Moving from one of the most senior and important positions on the General Staff to the number two position in an alliance that was losing its relevance was a clear demotion.

### The High Command Compromises

By the middle of 1989 the generals recognized that they had no choice but to compromise. In April Yazov published an article in *Red Star*, in which he approvingly quoted Gorbachev's U.N. speech to the effect that the task of the Soviet armed forces was "to maintain the country's defense capability at the level of reasonable and reliable sufficiency. . . ."[35] Yazov hedged his use of the term "reliable" by tying it to the need for the Soviet armed forces to be able to resist the external threat facing them. Nevertheless, it was clearly a step forward compared to what he had been saying only months earlier. By the end of the year, however, Yazov (and Moiseyev) were again relying on "defensive sufficiency." In a major article published in *Kommunist* in December, for example, Yazov used the latter term exclusively in his new "model of security" for the USSR.[36]

The issue of a counteroffensive remained confused and unsettled. General Geliy Batenin told a British audience that the heart of reasonable sufficiency was the "conviction that your armed forces are such that you can repel aggression without moving on to the opponent's territory."[37] Another and even more important statement on this issue came from Marshal Akhromeyev. In answer to a question from a Western correspondent concerning the army's attitude toward a counterattack, Akhromeyev, like Yazov, admitted that in the past, "Our ability to repel aggression was . . . more offensive than defensive. . . . In the early 1980s, we realized that this posture was causing anxiety in Western Europe."[38] Turning to the conduct of operations, Akhromeyev went beyond Yazov when he suggested a new wrinkle in Soviet defensive strategy.

> In theory, and in our exercises in the field, we are planning for long defensive operations to repel a possible aggression, if it proves impossible to end this aggression by political means. Then, and only then after around 3 or 4 weeks, we might launch a counterattack.

In evaluating the comments of Batenin and Akhromeyev it is important to keep in mind that both had a loose relationship with the country's senior officers. Batenin was assigned to the Central Committee as a military advisor, while Akhromeyev no longer served on the General Staff. As a consequence, they did not necessarily speak for the military leadership.

Akhromeyev's suggestion of a wait of three to four weeks after an attack before a counterattack was launched made sense from a political point of view, but there was no sign that the country's top military officers were ready to embrace the idea.[39]

Meanwhile, Kokoshin, together with Lobov, reentered the debate with a hard-hitting piece published in February 1990. The article stressed the relevance of the past, and especially Svechin, in an attempt to convince the generals to be more forthcoming on the question of offense. Calling the 1920s one of the country's most creative periods in military affairs and Svechin as the most important military thinker, the authors provided the most in-depth analysis of his writings and ideas published since the 1920s. After once again noting the importance Svechin assigned to an open and frank discussion of military issues, the authors focused on his ideas concerning the relationship between offense and defense. Svechin, according to the authors, saw a dialectical relationship between the two. Acceptance of a defensive strategy by no means meant a renunciation of the offense in the form of a counteroffensive. Indeed, the authors maintained, history has shown that he was right: World War II took the form Svechin had predicted. The country was attacked and forced to engage in defensive operations as it fought the enemy on Soviet territory. The Germans were slowly removed from Soviet territory by the skillful use of defense and counteroffense (e.g., the Battle of Kursk). Thus, in contrast to most of the Soviet histories of World War II—which had influenced generations of Soviet officers—it was the defense and not the offense that played the primary role in winning World War II. The past was a guide to the future.

> Now, when these problems of the theory of strategy, the art of war as a whole, and limiting and reducing armed forces and arms are being widely discussed, it is important to consider them in an historical context and to turn to the forgotten or half-forgotten works of Soviet politologists and military theorists of the 1920s and early 1930s, a prominent place among whom belongs to A. A. Svechin.[40]

Kokoshin and Larionov published another article in which they noted that it was impossible to say anything coherent about the nature of the military doctrine adopted in 1987, "without making a certain excursion into history," and they attacked what they called the "ideologization of military doctrine" in the late 1920s. Despite the warnings of individuals such as Svechin that the offense was "dangerous" and could lead to a "catastrophe," it became the basis of Soviet military doctrine. As they put it, "Although the declarative political portion of Soviet military doctrine of that time stressed a defensive orientation, as opposed to what was the case at the beginning of the 1920s, military-strategic planning was oriented primarily to offensive actions." Reliance on offense, according to the authors, "served as one of the most important, if not the main factor in the extremely severe defeats and huge losses incurred by the Red Army in the initial period of the war."

Turning to the present, Kokoshin and Larionov criticized the generals attitude toward doctrine, arguing that

> It is evident . . . that political declarations on the defensive nature of Soviet military doctrine are not reinforced by corresponding provisions in its military technical portion. And the reassessments of military policy being conducted today in this sphere signify nothing other than a surmounting of our offense-oriented genetic background. Today those who assert that the military-technical sphere of our military doctrine remained

defensive as well—and in this sense there was no need to focus on reviewing its provisions—will hardly be able to find evidence to support their view.

To make Soviet military doctrine truly defensive (a "nonoffensive defense"), the authors called on the generals to "acknowledge that the antithesis of offense is not defense but retreat." Defense is simply an intermediate condition between these different combat operations. Defense is designed to bar the way of an attacker and avoid retreat. In order to make the situation more stable, the USSR should reduce "to the minimum level necessary for executing only defensive functions (passive and active)." For a mind trained in the Soviet tradition, such a suggestion was heresy. How could one hope to evict an aggressor without engaging in a counteroffensive operation?[41]

If there was any doubt about Lobov's relationship to the senior military's position on doctrine, it was removed by an article he published at the same time as the Kokoshin-Larionov piece, also in *Kommunist*. Lobov led off with a sharp blast at those who objected to the involvement of civilians in the doctrinal debate. "I categorically disagree with that point of view that having a view about military reform is the exclusive prerogative of the military," he wrote. In addition, Lobov attacked the pace of military reform, maintaining that it "lags behind the processes underway in the country," and called for "greater radicalism and action than has occurred in the last three years."[42]

The military leadership published its last major statement on the nature of Soviet military doctrine late in 1990, in the form of a draft document. This carefully worded document attempted to walk a tightrope between the High Command's desire to retain as much flexibility as possible on issues such as parity and counteroffense on the one hand, and its effort to satisfy the politician's calls for greater movement toward the fourth variant proposed by Kokoshin and Larionov on the other. To begin with, the document avoided coming down on the side of either "reasonable" or "defensive" sufficiency. It simply used the term "sufficiency." In explaining the meaning of this term, the document divided the concept into two parts, nuclear and conventional. In defining the former, the document stated that

> The sufficiency of nuclear forces and assets is determined by the quantitative-qualitative parameters of the nuclear potential necessary for delivering a retaliatory strike, the consequences of which would wipe out any of the aggressor's advantages; such sufficiency is considered an intermediate stage on the path to the total elimination of nuclear weapons.

This language enabled the generals to retain the idea of deterrence (delivery of a retaliatory strike) and the importance of parity with the other side. At the same time, the document acknowledged the significance of arms control and admitted that quantity was not the most important measure of military power.[43]

Insofar as conventional weapons were concerned, the document stated that

> Sufficiency in the sphere of conventional arms and armed forces envisages the minimum quantity of them necessary for ensuring reliable defense, but insufficient for conducting large-scale offensive operations.

Turning to the resulting force structure, the document stated that primary emphasis was being placed on "personnel and equipment earmarked for repelling possible aggression." What the document did not mention was the nature of the offense. What type of offensive operations would be permitted?[44]

In drafting this document, the High Command was attempting to make the best of a bad situation by giving some coherence to the many changes it was being forced to accept. Meanwhile, the unification of Germany became a fait accompli and the withdrawal of Soviet troops from the former GDR, Poland, Czechoslovakia, and Hungary was only a matter of time. In essence, the military's world was turned upside-down and increasingly chaotic. As a consequence, the generals paid less and less attention to military doctrine per se and devoted more time to managerial issues, i.e., how to keep the armed forces together at a time when new demands and changes were being forced on it every day?[45]

Early in 1991 Lobov published an article in which he attempted to show that defense could play an important role in defeating an enemy. As he put it:

> Sufficiency in conventional weapons and forces provides for the minimal quantity which is needed to ensure a reliable defense, but not sufficient to wage large-scale offensive operations. The defense might be tentatively assessed by its ability: to destroy a specific number of armored vehicles, to inflict the appropriate damage to the opponent's air force, to disrupt his communication lines, especially those at sea, to ensure the reliable and steady functioning of command and control of one's own armed forces and to undercut the ability of the enemy to engage in offensive operations.[46]

By the time the attempted coup occurred in August, military autonomy in this area was at its lowest level since the Khrushchev period. Civilians like Kokoshin and Larionov or dissident military officers such as Lobov appeared to be calling the shots when it came to military doctrine. The military leadership was playing the role of a beleaguered manager attempting to keep the military together and operating in a coherent fashion, and of an observer sitting on the sidelines while others determined the basic outlines of the country's military-technical policy. Gorbachev had succeeded in re-penetrating the military in this critical area.

## Conclusion

Gorbachev's interference with the military's autonomy in the area of doctrine contrasted with the situation in the 1920s. Then, the Bolsheviks were concerned about the reliability of those determining doctrine as well as its ideological content. Under Gorbachev, by contrast, there was no question about the compatibility of the values held by the civilian and military leadership. The question, rather, was one of introducing a new and more pragmatic doctrine, one that more closely corresponded to the needs of the time. Similarly, the approach taken by Gorbachev differed from that used by Frunze and his colleagues in the 1920s. Where the Bolsheviks had enforced a single, highly politicized "Weltanschauung" on the military, Gorbachev sought—successfully—to open a dialogue with the country's military leaders. To move doctrine so that it would support the policies favored by his regime, Gorbachev had to undermine the high degree of autonomy enjoyed by the military in this area. At the same time, he made no effort to cut off debate or to restrict the military's ability to make its views known. By the time of the coup attempt in 1991, Gorbachev had largely won the battle. When it came to military doctrine, the military's voice was important, but it was not the only authoritative one in the Soviet regime. Viewed against the background of Soviet civil-military relations under Brezhnev, this was quite an accomplishment.

None of the three models discussed in the introduction to this book fully explained the nature of civil-military relations as reflected in the battle over doctrine. To begin with, the military possessed far more autonomy in this area when Gorbachev came to power than Kolkowicz's model predicted. Indeed, what is interesting in looking back over the period prior to Gorbachev is the degree to which the political leadership accepted military autonomy in this area. Given the battle that ensued during the 1920s over military doctrine, one would have expected a constant battle between the generals and politicians as the former fought hard to keep the latter from dictating doctrinal policy. Furthermore, as the case of Lobov shows, the military was nowhere near as united as Kolkowicz believed it would be in a situation of this type.

Once Gorbachev decided to force a change in military doctrine, the situation became much more conflictual than Odom's model predicted. As a textual analysis of the second half of the 1980s indicates, the generals resisted every effort by Gorbachev and his colleagues to get them to agree to a more defensive strategy. They were far from the "executants" that Odom assumed they would be. As far as Yazov and Moiseyev were concerned, doctrine was the prerogative of the military. Regardless of how knowledgeable some of them might be in military affairs, civilians had no business getting their noses into military matters.

Of the three paradigms, Colton's was the most useful. While it would have been necessary to fine-tune his matrix to account for the subtle changes that were occurring, it would have been possible to chart decreases in military autonomy in this area throughout the Gorbachev period. Military participation—to use Colton's phrase—gradually diminished during the six-year struggle between Gorbachev and the military leadership.

# VI

# RESTRUCTURING THE ARMED FORCES
## HOW PROFESSIONAL A MILITARY?

> I feel it will be impossible to work out a
> modern concept of democratizing the army,
> if we do not hark back to the experience of
> the military theoretical debates in 1917-1925.
>
> Lieutenant Colonel Aleksandr Savinkin

> In contemporary conditions a professional
> army, because of the limited size of the
> reserves trained under such a system of
> manning, is incapable of waging protracted
> military operations, especially in defending
> territories extending over a considerable
> area.
>
> Marshal Dmitri Yazov

## The Situation

When Gorbachev came to power, the situation with regard to force structure mirrored that of doctrine in one important aspect. The military enjoyed almost total autonomy. It was up to the generals—without sniping
from civilians—to decide when, how, and under what conditions changes
in the existing system should be adopted. After all, the generals were the
experts in the application of violence. They understood these issues far
better than civilians. Before the military's personnel system could be
changed, Gorbachev would have to break the military's autonomy in this
area as well.

The debate over a militia was central to the question of what type of
manning system the Soviet Army should possess. It was becoming clear
that the army of the future would be smaller, that fewer funds would be
available to support it, and that many procedures would undergo major
changes. Turning to the manning system, the question was what kind of
system to adopt. Should the currently existing conscript system be continued? Should the armed forces move toward a more professional, if not
fully professional, armed forces? What about the "mixed system" that ex-

isted during the 1920s, one that combined a professional armed forces with a militia as a reserve system?

In contrast to the discussion of doctrine, those who invoked the past in discussing a manning system had in mind the specific model that existed from the mid-1920s to the mid-1930s. These individuals believed that in spite of the many changes in warfare over the last sixty-odd years, the manning system in use at that time was directly transferable to the current situation.

Another difference between this situation and the changes discussed in the last chapter was that events forced action in this area. Doctrine was in flux, Moscow was reducing Soviet forces and the Kremlin was introducing major changes in the number and types of weapons, not to mention the new operational plans being introduced with more to follow. As a result, the country had to come up with a new manning system. Furthermore, while civilians were also involved, the primary push for the 1920s model came from military officers. While the generals attempted to strike back at them, many were members of the Supreme Soviet, which gave them a degree of immunity. It is also significant that over time large numbers of regular military officers began to side with the reformers on this issue.

The military leadership's public response to the reformers' attempt to use the example of the 1920s was to argue, first, that the earlier period was not applicable to the current situation and, second, that the existing system had proven its value in World War II, and was now protecting the country. Why change something that was functioning so well?

To a certain degree, the tactics adopted by the reformers influenced the leadership's very negative, rhetorical reaction to the military reformers and their policy suggestions. Unlike the situation with doctrine, they were confrontational. They demanded that the generals adopt the "mixed system" of the 1920s and when the Kremlin's top military officers objected, their views were dismissed out of hand. In fact, a number of these objections had merit—at least from a military standpoint. As a result, the generals dug in their heels, opposing any change in the country's manning system.

The push for a modification in force structure similar to that which existed in the 1920s was not an original idea on the part of the Gorbachev administration. Such proposals had been heard earlier, most specifically during Khrushchev's time in power.

### Khrushchev and the Militia Idea

Khrushchev was the first postwar Soviet political leader to suggest the revival of the "mixed system." As in the 1920s and the 1990s, his call for a reform of the personnel structure was tied to his plans to cut the armed forces in order to save money. Like the reformers of the 1990s, Khrushchev argued that the militia system aided by improved military technology could do the same job as the larger regular armed forces for much less.[1]

In 1955 and 1956 Khrushchev announced that Soviet forces would be reduced by some 1.8 million men. In fact, by 1960 Khrushchev had succeeded in reducing the size of the Soviet armed forces by 2,140,000 troops to a low of 3,623,000. In 1960 he announced that he planned to further reduce Soviet forces by 1,200,00 to a total of 2,423,000.[2]

Khrushchev's logic was simple. Because of the development of nuclear weapons and the existence of parity between the superpowers, he believed large standing armies were obsolete. This opened the door to large-scale cutbacks in conventional force structure. Anticipating the military's argument that ground forces would always be necessary, if for no other reason than to occupy territory, and that large forces would be needed in the event of a war, Khrushchev proposed that the USSR adopt a system similar to that which existed during the 1920s. In an interview with the editors of *Time* magazine in 1958 he stated,

> In the final analysis we favor the liquidation of the army and the transition to a militia system. . . . It was necessary for our country to create its mighty army to defend the Soviet state from enemies. But I want to emphasize that we do not favor the existence of a standing army. It was a result of specific circumstances.[3]

A month later, Khrushchev reiterated his support of a militia system when he stated on March 20 that "in the period immediately after the end of the October revolution we did not have the intention of creating a standing army, but instead proposed moving to a militia system."[4]

Khrushchev came back to the militia concept again in January 1960 in his speech to the fourth session of the Supreme Soviet. He argued that large standing armies, surface navies, and bomber aircraft were becoming obsolete. Nuclear weapons were the basis of Soviet military strength. As a result, "in modern times a nation's defense capability depends on firepower, not the number of men under arms." This made it possible to reduce the size of the country's conventional forces in favor of a manning system such as existed in the 1920s. "It is possible that we will repeat that which was done by Vladimir Il'ich Lenin in the first years of Soviet power, although under different conditions and under a somewhat different plan." Arguing that a militia system would provide the necessary cadre and that the populace could master modern weapons, he continued,

> Looking to the future, I can imagine that we will have military units formed along the territorial principle. Their personnel will master military matters without a break in production, and when necessary, the appropriate means of transportation—airplanes and other military technology—will

make it necessary to bring them together on our territory in the appropriate areas. I'm speaking about this so that in taking a decision on the current reduction in our forces, you will have in mind those questions which
may come in up the future in the absence of an arms control agreement.[5]

With Khrushchev's ouster in 1964, the question of moving toward a militia
system receded into the background, although it continued to be mentioned
by academics as a possible alternative to the existing manning system.[6]

### The Militia Concept Reemerges

By the late 1980s a number of individuals, including some military officers, believed that the old manning system had to be modified. As one
officer put it in a roundtable discussion of the issue, "Certainly, the army
which we now have, which for practical purposes preserves the postwar
structure, is no longer necessary. New conditions demand a basic restructuring of the entire army structure. A modern army should be built on an
entirely different basis." In discussing what type of army should replace
the existing one, one officer suggested that it be based on the militia principle, while another was "convinced that we need a professional army." A
third suggestion was made by a lieutenant colonel and political officer
Aleksandr Savinkin, who maintained that a small professional military by
itself would be isolated from the population at large and would create tensions between the military and civilian worlds. The alternative, he argued,
was to return to a system similar to that which had existed in the 1920s.
"Under modern circumstances there is every possibility to establish such a
system." Sounding like the proponents of the "mixed" system some fifty
years earlier, Savinkin observed that

> Under such a system in the face of a necessity it is possible to create a well
> trained military force in a short period of time. And during peace time it is
> possible to exist with a small core of officers controlling a large net of
> territorial-militia formations.

According to Savinkin, such an approach would be more democratic
and help build ties between the populace and the military.[7]

Savinkin followed up on his roundtable suggestions in a major article
two months later in which he outlined his proposal in greater detail.
Savinkin argued that a militia system made sense for a number of reasons.
First, it would lighten the economic burden on the country, and provide
added manpower for the civilian economy. Second, it would counter foreign perceptions of a Soviet military threat. Third, it would improve the
military's prestige, which had dropped to the point where young men were

showing a "dwindling interest in the service." In terms of structure, Savinkin's military would be composed of "a relatively small, technically equipped, professionally trained and mainly voluntarily staffed military organization supported by a broad network of local militia formations." As in the 1920s, members of the militia would serve "short terms of reserve service." The fact was, Savinkin maintained, a small professional military by itself could not "safeguard the country, given its vast territory." This could only be done by a combined professional-militia structure.[8]

Public reaction to the Savinkin proposal was mixed. Toward the end of January, *Moscow News* published three letters to the editor on this topic. The first, which opposed the idea, argued that the force structure proposed by Savinkin would not be sufficient to deal with the external threat faced by the USSR, and that soldiers trained under a militia system would be unable to master modern weapons systems. The other two letters supported Savinkin.[9]

First signs of the military leadership's reaction to this attack on its autonomy came in a series of essays published in January 1989 in *Kommunist vooruzhennykh sil*, a journal under the control of the Main Political Directorate of the Armed Forces. Of the seven essays, five expressed opposition to the idea, one provided limited support, and one argued that the Savinkin article was full of factual errors. The major theme of the essays opposed to a mixed system was that to offset the military threat from the West, the USSR had to retain a standing army. The most articulate opponent of a militia system, Major General Tabunov, argued that while the militia approach as suggested in the 1920s had a number of advantages (i.e., it was cheaper, more closely tied to the people, and less threatening to other countries), it was not as combat capable as a regular military. Furthermore, in an effort to turn the historical tables on Savinkin, he argued that just as Frunze had recognized that a regular army was inevitable because of the complexity of weapons systems in the 1920s, "It is even more correct under contemporary conditions, when combat equipment has been improved immeasurably, and its maintenance and utilization require high professional knowledge, abilities and skills."[10]

The general's attempt to downplay the Savinkin proposal was unsuccessful. The plan had aroused considerable public interest, and the pressure to find an alternative approach for staffing the military was increasing. In an effort to end discussion of the issue, the generals went public. After noting that the military was being reduced by some 500,000 men, General Moiseyev, the chief of the General Staff, belittled reformers such as Savinkin. As Moiseyev put it, "the General Staff is now receiving dozens of proposals on how the Armed Forces should be built. There are some competent views, but there are also many which are detached from life." Lest there be any doubt whom he had in mind, Moiseyev openly blasted the Savinkin concept, arguing that "these views ignore the fact that a militia system is absolutely unrealistic given today's most complex means of struggle."[11] The message was clear. We, in the General Staff, are prepared to listen to outside views, but we are the ones who have the expertise and we will decide how to deal with this situation.

The most sophisticated defense of the High Command's position was provided by Vladimir Serebryannikov, a lieutenant general and a professor at the Lenin Political Academy in Moscow. Serebryannikov argued that rather than showing the value of such structures, the experience of the 1920s "proved . . . that territorial-militia formations, even though they cost the state considerably less than standing formations, are noticeably inferior in terms of combat readiness, teamwork, coordination and combat and technical training." Furthermore, Serebryannikov asked rhetorically, "If the militia army outlived its usefulness so long ago, how can it be relied on now, when weapons and combat equipment have moved so far ahead, when substantial changes have occurred in the forms and methods for conducting combat actions?" Continuing, Serebryannikov maintained that movement toward a militia system would have an adverse impact the country's security. It would destroy "military-strategic parity." It would weaken the USSR because militia formations could not master contemporary weapons systems.

Serebryannikov also ridiculed the idea that the USSR should rely on a small professional army. Such a step also would weaken the country's military security. NATO was not making any effort to reduce its forces—consequently, the USSR had to continue to support a large standing army. "Reductions of military contingents . . . are realistic only on a reciprocal basis." Furthermore, he argued, the Soviet military (or at least its officer corps) was already professional. A professional military (i.e., one that includes enlisted personnel) would cost too much. "Where are these additional funds to come from if our state budget is already quite sizeable even without this?" Finally, Serebryannikov remarked, the most serious damage would be moral and political. "This will mean doing away with a citizen's equal responsibility for the motherland's defense and their equal practical participation in this work. . . ."[12]

Defense Minister Yazov soon joined the fray. Writing in March, he reiterated the reasons why movement toward a professional military was not possible. To begin with, it was too expensive. "The point is that a hired army is at least several times more expensive for society than an army manned on the basis of universal compulsory military service." Second, he maintained that a professional military would not produce the necessary reserves. "Because of the limited nature of the reserves that are trained under such a manning system, a hired army is incapable of conducting protracted military operations." Third, Yazov claimed that a professional military would not be as reliable as one relying on conscription. "History testifies to the unreliability of depending solely on incentives of this kind, based on the extent of payment for service, when the high moral content of military service is replaced by material advantage and becomes devalued."

Turning to the question of a militia, Yazov argued that training part-time soldiers would be very costly,

> Under such a system there is a need for a ramified network of special training centers possessing appropriate material and technical facilities and highly skilled specialists. It is perfectly obvious that the creation of such a network will require extremely substantial additional expenditures of material and other resources.

Yazov claimed that it would be more difficult to mobilize militia formations because they were often located in the wrong place.

> Militia units are stationed not where the situation requires, but where they are manned and camps are held, and as a result they cannot gain control of a theater of operations and in fact are incapable of resolving the task of repulsing possible aggression and reliably ensuring the country's security.[13]

Yazov's April 13 article was the most authoritative statement on the question of a professional-militia force up to that time. In it Yazov added a few new disadvantages to such a system. To begin with, he argued that a professional military was more likely to be isolated from the populace. As he noted, "Moreover, if the social base of a professional army is narrowed, it loses touch with the life of the people, and becomes a kind of caste with its own specific interests, sociopolitical guidelines, and moral values." In raising the specter of a separate caste, Yazov was playing on the long-standing Soviet fear of Bonapartism—the development of a military independent of party control. A second disadvantage was that a militia system would take away from the productive process, or as he put it, "the mass diversion of urban and rural working people for military training at their place of residence is bound to affect the economic indicators of labor collectives' work, especially in conditions of self-financing. . . ."[14]

The leadership's initial position was full of inconsistencies and it was not well thought out. Indeed, the generals appear to have been taken off guard both by the Savinkin proposal and the degree of public support for it. Their confusion was evident in the way they avoided dealing with Savinkin's basic point—that the most effective way of dealing with the problem was by a *combined* professional-militia approach.

Seen from the perspective of the 1989-1990 period, there were a number of reasons for the attitude adopted by the generals. First, they deeply resented this outside interference in their affairs, Second, they were in the midst of absorbing major cuts in their force structure. Gorbachev had announced his unilateral cut of 500,000 men at the UN in December 1988, and there were rumors that these would be followed by additional force reductions. To make matters worse, for the first time in Soviet military history civilian analysts had begun to comment aggressively on the need for major reductions in Soviet military force structure and weapons systems. For example, Larionov and Kokoshin published an article in March openly advocating a "mixed" professional-militia approach.

> The young nation's life having been dislocated by the Civil War, the government adopted the most economical mixed pattern of the military establishment (a combination of a standing army and territorial units). . . . This . . . laid the guidelines for a long time to come in improving the battle-worthiness of the Soviet Armed Forces at the lowest possible cost. . . . Today's efforts to achieve a breakthrough in the country's development are, to some extent, reminiscent of the situation in those days. Relying on a small-size regular core, the mixed establishment could train reserves without actually separating the conscripts from their jobs and homes.[15]

To make matters worse, General Lobov, at that time still a deputy chief of the General Staff, published an article on the relevance of the 1920s and 1930s in February 1989. In this piece he provided support to the militia-professional approach. For example, in discussing former chief of the General Staff Shaposhnikov's ideas, he observed that the latter "expressed support for the militia character of the army, believing that in our times we must consider the militia army a permanent factor in a future struggle, not an exception or an indication of a state's weakness." Given the extent of interest in a manning system similar to that of the 1920s, acceptance of the Savinkin proposal as a basis for discussion ran the risk of legitimizing this approach with all the disastrous consequences that that might have had for the generals' control of the reform process.[16]

In addition to its concern about outside interference and uncertainty over the future, the generals also had to deal with a disruption in their complex planning process. Traditionally, the generals devoted considerable time and effort to studying both how best to modify force structure and when such changes were necessary, as well as how to integrate them into military doctrine and weapons systems. The Savinkin approach was dangerous. It was a partial solution—a change from a force structure that had stood the test of time to a new and (from their perspective) amateurish approach. It said nothing of how such changes should be integrated with existing Soviet military doctrine or weapons systems. Suggestions or even hints of an interest in such proposals could place the generals on the slippery slope toward bureaucratic compromise. In short, the generals ran the risk of losing what control they had over the process of reform and inter-bureaucratic change.

Finally, and not surprisingly, the military leadership had reason to fear that such proposals could lead to a reduction in their own privileges. A smaller professional military would mean fewer positions for generals and, as a consequence, lessened chances for promotion. This came at time when the armed forces were already under attack because of their large number of flag officers. To cite only one example from the period,

> ... if you look at the expenditure classes you will learn why soldiers are so poorly supported, and what it costs to keep regiments of colonels without regiments and at least battalions of generals without armies. Who would explain why a lieutenant general must command the society of military hunters? Why do generals command the Central House of the Soviet Army, the military song and dance ensemble, military trade, and the military museum? How much do you reckon it costs to keep one general?[17]

The generals saw no alternative but to keep their wagons in a circle.

## Focus on a Professional Military

By the middle of 1989 the military leadership's decision-making power in this area was eroding. The debate over a militia gave way to a discussion of how professional the Soviet military should become. It was clear that changes would be made. The issue was not only how major they would be, but who would make them. The militia question did not totally disappear— it continued to be mentioned by military intellectuals—but it was increasingly associated with the role to be played by national armies (which many Soviet writers at this time saw as synonymous with a militia).[18]

Moiseyev and Yazov continued to fend off attempts to create a more professional military. For example, in a May 1989 article Moiseyev reiterated his concern about the lack of a reserve system. Moiseyev observed that "the number of volunteers now stands at approximately 35 percent." From a purely military standpoint, he argued, the professionalism and military competency of individuals serving for long periods of time (i.e., 20 to 25 years) or even short periods of service (i.e., 3 to 6 years) were higher than was the case with conscripts. But what if the USSR was forced to mobilize its reserves? If that were to happen the country would be in trouble because "there is a significant reduction in the possibility of building up militarily trained reserves."[19]

The debate continued throughout the remainder of 1989. In October, for example, *Morskoy sbornik*, the navy's main journal, published an article by A. Rogachev, identified as an instructor at Moscow State University, who argued in favor of moving toward an all-volunteer armed forces. Rogachev's basic thesis was that war had not been averted by the presence of large armies on both sides, but the existence of mutual guaranteed destruction in the event of a nuclear war. As a result, the Soviet armed forces should become much smaller and fully professional. Not surprisingly, the commentary on Rogachev's article, written by a Colonel Men'shakov, disagreed. A professional military might be possible in the future, he agreed, but the threat presented by the West together with financial, social and other military considerations made such an alternative impossible for the present.[20]

A number of officers shared the military leadership's position on this issue. By November, for example, General Makarevskiy wrote in *Novoe vremya* that given the massive reductions that would result from the Conventional Arms Discussions then under way in Vienna and the need for better trained enlisted personnel, "the transfer of the Soviet Armed Forces to a professional basis, with the careful selection of personnel, is an objective necessity in the near future." This meant that enlisted personnel would gradually move toward a contract system. Under this latter procedure, enlisted personnel signed a contract obligating them to serve for four, six, or even eight years. What was most interesting about this article was not only the author's support for a professional military, but his willingness to ignore many of the arguments utilized by Yazov and Moiseyev in defending his position.

Looking at the question of expense, for example, Makarevskiy argued that it could be taken from the 19 percent decrease in military production that was expected in coming years. As far as the argument that a professional military was immoral—since it involved payment for military service—Makarevskiy asked the rhetorical question, "What about the nucleus of the armed forces—their officers, warrant officers and re-enlisted men? Everything *Krasnaya zvezda* spoke about was applied primarily to these very servicemen whose total number . . . is about 1 million men." Furthermore, when it came to the question of modern technology, Makarevskiy argued that it was clear that conscripts could not master modern weapons systems in their two or three years of service. Finally, on the question of reserves, he maintained that at half their current size, they would remain "sufficient for defensive purposes."[21]

In spite of the splits in the upper ranks of the Soviet armed forces, the leadership refused to budge; no professional military. In January 1990 Moiseyev was again asked about the possibility of moving toward a professional army. In response, he dug up many of the same arguments that he, Yazov, and others had already utilized. Moiseyev did indicate that the leadership was becoming increasingly sensitive to the need to pay closer attention to servicemen's social needs. In this regard, he noted that the generals were working actively to improve the situation.

> As of 1 January 1990 it is contemplated that officers' pay will be increased by an average of R90 per month; that servicemen without military lodgings will get cash compensation—R30-90 per month—for rented accom-

modations; upon discharge from active duty, compulsory service soldiers will be paid R100 instead of R10-40; the officer corps will also be paid an emolument for a proficiency rating of up to R25 per month, and pay in an amount of 30 percent of salary will be tacked on for flight personnel of the Air Force and for special conditions of service.

What is important about this quote is that it points out that the generals were beginning to recognize that they had no alternative but to take steps to improve living conditions for officers and enlisted men. This was the first step toward a professional military—i.e., improving the quality of life of military personnel so they would serve willingly.

Another topic that came up in the Moiseyev interview was the question of alternative service, or as the Soviets tended to define it, "service without weapons," which was introduced for "persons refusing from religious or other beliefs to serve with weapons." While recognizing that such service existed in other countries (e.g., the FRG and GDR), Moiseyev came out against such a program. He called it "a desire for the legalized opportunity to avoid general military service and to evade active duty in any way." Based on figures available to the General Staff, he claimed that "there is no need for the introduction of alternative service here." The number of people who have refused to take the military oath is "negligible."[22]

Recognizing the firmness of the leadership's opposition to movement toward a professional military, opponents of the existing system decided to advance their own reform program. Their approach was given added weight because a number of them were military officers and deputies from the Supreme Soviet. In effect this meant that not only could the military hierarchy not silence them (since they were Peoples' Deputies), but that as legislators their views had to be taken seriously.

The leader, the most outspoken proponent of military reform and painful thorn in the side of the generals on this question (i.e., movement toward a professional military), was Major Vladimir Lopatin. Lopatin, a political officer assigned to the Soviet Navy, was part of a group of seventeen Peoples' Deputies/military officers, who argued in favor of major reform of the Soviet military. Their plan was reportedly given to the Ministry of Defense on December 7, 1989. Lopatin provided some details on it in an interview he gave in February 1990. According to Lopatin, the plan called for a phased transition to a regular professional army. The issue of reserves would be handled by the creation of militias on a territorial basis. In response to a question concerning the costs of such an army, Lopatin maintained that a professional military actually would be cheaper than the current structure.

Who said that maintaining professionals . . . will be more expensive for the state? Who has worked out how much money will be needed? And we are talking about a phased, I stress, a phased transition. No one, incidentally, has calculated the losses from, for instance, the damage and accidents to highly complex military equipment elegantly phrased in documents as "occurring through the fault of personnel." Being in the Army, I can see that officers are increasingly carrying out duties of mechanics and technicians, that is, they are doing things that soldiers and sergeants should in theory be doing. Are they looking for work for themselves? No, they are afraid of letting anyone near the equipment.

Furthermore, Lopatin continued, a substantial reduction in personnel would lead to additional budgetary savings. Not only would such a move result in fewer soldiers and sailors, it would make it possible to close down a number of military facilities, including schools, and should lead to the use of civilian experts for training military personnel. The transition should begin, Lopatin maintained, with the more technical services such as the "strategic nuclear missile and assault forces, the Navy, the Air Force and then the Ground Forces and Air Defense Forces."[23]

Lopatin was attacked by a number of his military colleagues for these proposals. On April 13, for example, *Krasnaya zvezda* published an article by an economist, Colonel Nikitin. Nikitin accused Lopatin of professional incompetence and irresponsibility. In particular, he blasted Lopatin's suggestion that a professional military would help the country's economy. Reductions in defense output would lead to a rapid drop in productivity in the defense sector and significant increases in the prices of individual defense products.[24] The Nikitin article, however, represented only the tip of the iceberg. In fact, the leadership had already begun a campaign to undercut these officers. Colonel A. V. Tsalko, another leading military reformist, claimed that such officers were relegated to the very back of the hall and had their microphones removed at the All-Army Officer's Assembly held in December 1989. He further argued that the Ministry of Defense had threatened to dismiss all of the officers who had put forth the alternative reform plan.[25] The leadership soon decided that even more severe steps were needed to bring officers such as Lopatin back into line. Indeed, during the remainder of 1990 the MOD went after Lopatin with a vengeance. And they had some success. On April 26 he was expelled from the Communist party in his home district on trumped-up charges and remained in that status in spite of the fact that the CPSU Party Control Commission (which was directly subordinate to the Central Committee) suspended the action by the local party organization. In addition, he was also threatened with discharge into the reserves.[26]

Despite this harassment, Lopatin continued to attack the generals for their handling of the military reform process. In May he argued that the senior military leadership was out of touch with the rest of the officer corps.

"The military leadership does not reflect the army's real interests and does not enjoy the support of the middle-ranking officers, who are the army's principal force."[27] Then in September, he charged that no one in the USSR—including the Ministry of Defense—knew the real size of the country's military budget. "This allows the military-industrial complex to continue to hold uncontrolled sway in attempting to extract profit from any situation." Second, he continued, the army had a major problem with the quality of its recruits. "In 1989, 45 percent of draftees were people with an undermined psyche, 15 percent had been previously convicted, and 37 percent spoke Russian poorly." Third, he maintained that conscripts made many more mistakes than professionals. "In comparison with professionals, they make 25 percent more technical and organizational mistakes, and up to 40 percent under extreme conditions." Fourth, Lopatin claimed that "based on sociological studies of 1990, 87 percent of officers favored having a professional volunteer army." Lopatin also called for major cuts in the size of the military and for its depoliticization.[28]

By the middle of 1990 it was clear that the officer corps was deeply split on this issue. This was true of both military academics and operational officers. For example, Marshal of Aviation Yermakov, the Commander of the Air Force, stated in an interview published on February 23 that "professionalization is a natural process, whether we want it or not. It is especially urgent for those services in the Armed Forces that are equipped with complicated and expensive equipment."[29] Furthermore, as if to remove any doubts about where he stood on the issue, Yermakov noted, "it would be much easier and simpler for me to work with subordinates who are professionals."[30] Colonel General Yu. Yashin, a deputy defense minister, made a similar statement, observing that the only way of improving the quality of the Soviet armed forces was by "increasing the percentage of professional, highly trained servicemen and providing the possibility of voluntary service."[31] Even General Tret'yak, long considered one of the most conservative of the USSR's senior military officers, admitted that a professional military would improve the situation within the armed forces.[32]

Support for a transition to a professional military was even stronger among more junior officers. A political officer, for example, remarked that he favored "a gradual transition, over a three to five year period, to the principle of professional volunteer manning for our state's Armed Forces."[33] Likewise, a captain first rank argued that the Soviet Union had to move to a professional military.[34] A similar position was adopted by a junior lieutenant, who claimed that insofar as costs were concerned, "In the end it is much better to have an expensive army, but at a higher level of combat readiness, than it is to have a cheaper, but less capable one."[35]

This is not to suggest that all military officers unanimously supported the immediate introduction of a professional military. For example, Colonel Ochirov, also a People's Deputy, raised the question of where the military would find volunteers. "Who will enlist? . . . At present we have thousands of vacancies for warrant officers. People do not enlist."[36]

General Ivashov also opposed the Lopatin plan, arguing that "in such a complicated matter as reform, one must obviously adhere to a principle which has stood the practical test of time; do not break established structures and mechanisms without having created a reliable replacement."[37]

Of all the expressions of support for a professional military, none was a greater surprise than that voiced by General Serebryannikov, who only a year earlier had been the leadership's strongest and most articulate defender. In an article published in May 1990, he criticized the military leadership for comparing professional militaries to mercenary armies and for suggesting that conscription was more important than a voluntary military. In addition, he argued that defense policy should be in the hands of state (rather than party) institutions, and ridiculed the Ministry of Defense's plan for military reform. His most complete and most outspoken defense of his position came in an interview in which he argued that professionalism was the only sensible approach to the country's problems. To begin with, he maintained that soldiers in Western professional militaries were much better trained than in the USSR. In the West, for example, only 10-12 percent of soldiers at any given time were untrained. In the USSR, the constant turnover of troops meant that at least half of them were untrained. The only concession he made to the leadership was to admit that the transition to a professional military should be gradual.[38]

Despite agitation both within the military and from civilian critics, the leadership maintained political support for its position. This was evident at the Twenty-Eighth Congress of the CPSU. The resolution adopted by the congress stated that the party was in favor of a staffing system "which combines general servicemen's duty with voluntary enlistment to military service by contract, social justice and equality of all servicemen and men liable for call-up in the eyes of the law."[39] In effect, this meant the continuation of conscription.

### Debating a Reform Plan

Having secured political backing for their opposition to a professional military, the military leadership published its version of a military reform plan in *Voennaya mysl'* in November 1990.[40] In essence, the Ministry of Defense plan stated that the immediate transition to a professional military was not possible at a time when the economy faced serious problems. At the same time, the military leadership made a number of gestures toward the eventual introduction of a professional military. First, in a speech outlining the basic parameters of this reform plan, Yazov noted that the military would introduce a system "by contract" in the navy (other services would be included at a later date). Under this system, the conscript would have the option of serving for two or three years beyond his initial term. If he selected the latter option, he would receive special training and a salary of 150 rubles a month "and higher." Yazov also mentioned that the possibility of cutting the length of conscripted service was currently under study and warned his colleagues that the armed forces faced additional cuts. In addition, he announced that civil defense troops would no longer come under the Ministry of Defense, that the construction troops would be streamlined, that the number of military-educational institutions would be cut by 30-35 percent, that the number of officers at civilian universities would be cut by 30-40 percent, and that the system of command and control would be streamlined. As a result of the latter process, he stated that staffs would be reduced by 15-20 percent and the number of flag officers would be cut by "no less than 30 percent."[41]

Moiseyev provided additional details in a November 18 article. According to Moiseyev, the military planned to introduce the reform plan in three stages. The first stage (up to 1994) involved the implementation of all arms control agreements signed by Moscow as well as a modification in operational and mobilization plans and the adoption of new legislation governing the military. The second stage (1994-95) would complete cuts in the Soviet armed forces, reorganize the army's central apparatus, modify the internal structure of military districts and reorganize military-educational institutions. Finally, during the third stage (1996-2000), a 50-percent reduction in strategic offensive arms would be carried out, and the existing military structure would be modified. In the end, the military would have about 3.2 million men under arms. Turning to the question of professionalism, Moiseyev reiterated the standard line: the current arrangement was the most appropriate for the present, a contract system would be introduced shortly, and alternative service (three-year obligation) would be available to those who objected to military service on religious or moral grounds. In short, the generals had no intention of giving in on the question of a professional military. They had already made concessions on issues such as a contract system and alternative service—and that was all. On December 13 the Supreme Soviet's Committee for Defense and State Security Questions adopted the MOD's proposal as the basis for the future reform of the armed forces. From a practical point of view, this meant that conscription would remain a fact of life, at least until the year 2000.[42]

Critics continued to attack the military leadership in the media. Lopatin, for example, repeatedly blasted Yazov and Moiseyev, arguing that the Ministry of Defense was stone-walling the radical reform plan that he and his colleagues had suggested. Furthermore, zeroing in on the idea of conscription, Lopatin maintained that the current arrangement was not working. The situation was getting worse. "Any further delay is likely to aggravate the crisis in society and the Army and poses the threat of the Army's disintegration." Using figures from surveys taken by the Main Political Directorate of the Soviet Army and Navy, he pointed out that overall interest in serving in the military was sharply decreasing. In 1975, for example, 78 percent of enlisted personnel had expressed "great interest in service." By 1986 the figure had dropped to 63 percent and by 1990 it was down to 12 percent. "And yet the Ministry of Defense assumes that it will be possible to retain all-Union universal military service for at least the next 15 years!" The only way to deal with this situation, Lopatin maintained, was to look to the past:

> Paramount attention ought to be given to the experience of preparing and implementing the 1924-1925 reform. At that time, taking advantage of the stabilization of the international situation, the Army was reduced by a factor of 10 (from 5.5 million to 562,000 men) between December 1920 and the summer of 1924. It is, of course, obvious that quantitative reductions must be compensated for by qualitative transformations.

How was the question handled at that time? "The way out, Frunze said, is to combine a cadre army with a militia system." Such an approach not only provided reserves, it did minimal harm to the economy. Indeed, Lopatin insisted, the past had important lessons for the present.

> This half-forgotten experience of ours is a warning against attempts to maintain the existing system of manpower acquisition by the Army while it undergoes sizeable reductions (which led to the virtual disintegration of the Workers' and Peasants' Red Army in the twenties). . . .

The main objection to a professional military, according to Lopatin, was its high cost. In fact, High Command figures for what it would cost to establish a fully professional military, which ranged from 3.3 to 8 times more than the current arrangement, proved that their figures were spurious. Indeed, in Lopatin's mind a professional military would be a panacea for most of the problems (e.g., discipline, illiteracy) currently facing the armed forces.

> The world's practice has proved: Professionalization of the armed forces, subject to a sizeable reduction of their numerical strength, has a favorable effect on the economic and political situation in the country, boosts the prestige and attraction of military service, and makes it possible to reduce expenditures on the army.[43]

By the end of 1990 the lines were clearly drawn. On the one side were officers like Yazov and Moiseyev, who were determined to hold the line on the question of a professional army. The other side was represented by Lopatin, who continued to hammer away at the need to create a professional military as soon as possible. The majority of other officers found themselves in the middle, although most appear to have supported the Lopatin proposal at least insofar as professionalism was concerned.

The period from January 1991 until the coup attempt in August was characterized, on the one hand, by a slight softening of the positions of the military leadership toward the idea of a professional military and, on the other, by increased support on the part of both civilian and military officials for an end to conscription and the adoption of some form of professional-militia type arrangement.

General Batenin fired another salvo in a lengthy—and balanced—article published in *Novoe vremya* in March. In this piece he argued that the Soviet military currently found itself in a "deep socio-psychological, moral and political crisis," as a result of the clash between a conservative military structure and the demands of perestroyka and new thinking. This situation was aggravated by the Afghanistan experience (which he compared to Vietnam) and the misuse of the army for internal purposes. The American way out of a similar crisis was to make the army professional. Such a military had distinct advantages. First, at a time when military equipment was becoming increasingly complex, they would recruit only the best and the brightest. Second, the military would have its pick of the best qualified—intellectually, physically, and emotionally. Third, a professional military would raise the prestige of the armed forces in the eyes of the Soviet populace. Fourth, it would decrease the number of untrained conscripts serving in the army, and thus result in a more efficient and better-run organization. To make such a system work, the military would have to create a reserve system.[44] This article was followed on March 4 by a call for the immediate creation of a professional army by the radical People's Deputy, Galina Starovoitova, and in April by an article in *Kommunist*, at that time the most important party journal in the country, which criticized the generals for putting off critical military reforms such as the transfer to a professional military. The latter piece, in particular, represented a serious challenge. And then, as if to put salt in the wound, a major article was published in the General Staff's own journal *Voennaya mysl'*, which stated that the mixed system adopted in the reforms introduced in 1924-25 should serve as a model for the present.[45]

The strongest and hardest-hitting critique of the generals' position was written by Vladislav Yanelis in January 1991. Yanelis sharply criticized the Defense Ministry reform plan, arguing that it "presents little that is new and protects more the existing army structures rather than the interests of the country and society." Indeed, he continued, the plan was a stalling tactic, an approach that was devastating the army.

> Who is ready to give the military minister four or five years to get moving? The army, just like society, is being torn apart by conflicts. . . . The leadership of the Ministry of Defense is stubborn in not recognizing that the combat capability is decreasing day by day. Why is this so? Our pilots are not allowed to fly their aircraft in order to economize on fuel. The soldiers are begrudged an extra ten bullets for training. Gunners of infantry combat vehicles are doled out such a minimum amount of ammunition that some, when demobilized, still have not learned how to hit a target. And rocket gunners can go through their entire enlistment without having gone through a single combat training session.

In short, Yanelis asked, "What is a four million man army doing anyway, other than wearing a military uniform?" The sad fact was, he argued, that the military had too many senior officers, too much property, and nothing to do. Turning to the MOD's reform proposal, Yanelis sarcastically asked what the defense minister intended to do to cut back on this over-inflated bureaucracy. He "is planning to decrease the commanding staffs by only 15-20 percent, leaving the army with a total of 3-3.2 million men." But who was going to pay for such a large army at a time when a market economy was being introduced? In conclusion, Yanelis commented that while the Lopatin plan was a bit pretentious, "it is significantly more realistic" than what Yazov and his colleagues were proposing.[46]

By the end of March the leadership began to feel the heat. Yazov, for example, in an interview on Soviet television, was more circumspect in dealing with the professional issue than in the past. When asked what he thought about the idea, he limited himself to suggesting that the army should include both volunteers and draftees, while emphasizing that the military would become increasingly professional as greater numbers of enlisted personnel opted to sign long-term contracts.[47] For his part, Moiseyev also avoided openly opposing movement toward a professional military in his last interview on the topic prior to the coup. In response to a question concerning the country's personnel system, Moiseyev mentioned the newly adopted contract system, calling it, "the first step toward enhancing the professionalizaton of the Armed Forces." This would make it possible, he argued, to reduce the proportion of conscripts in the military. Indeed, he continued, the proportion of professionals in the military was on the rise.

> Whereas at the start of the reform officers, warrant officers and extended-service personnel accounted for a little over 30 percent of the Army and Navy, ultimately we want to reach a point where the number of those recruited by the draft becomes considerably smaller. As it stands now we

have already managed to increase the proportion of professionals in the
Armed Forces to 43 percent.

When asked specifically why then the MOD did not "propose switching to
an Army composed entirely of professionals," Moiseyev hedged, arguing
that current conditions such as the potential threat presented by the West,
and the consequent need for a reserve, made such a step impossible at present.
At the same time, he went out of his way to note that the term of service for
conscripts would be cut and argued that pre-military training would be up-
graded, thereby enabling young men to assume more quickly their positions
in the country's armed forces.[48] Other members of the military leadership,
who dealt in detail with the Lopatin plan, were also careful to avoid dismiss-
ing the idea of a professional military over the long run. One, for example,
qualified his opposition to the idea by commenting that "the Ministry of
Defense does not reject the possibility of even deeper professionalization by
accepting USSR citizens who volunteer for service.[49]

Thus, by the time of the coup in August pressure was mounting for movement toward a professional military. The High Command continued to resist—although it attempted to avoid a confrontation in public—while some
of its most senior officers defected to the other side. For example, General
Achalov, a deputy minister of defense, wrote an article in which he qualified
his continued support for conscription by noting the clear advantages of a
professional military. "Many of the problems encountered by an officer, from
a platoon commander to the minister of defense of the USSR, will disappear
in a professional army of their own accord."[50] In short, by this time it was
clear that the most serious obstacle to the introduction of a professional military (even if it did not follow the Lopatin plan in every detail) was bureaucratic, not substantive. How much the new system would mirror that which
existed in the 1920s was anyone's guess. One military academic argued only
months prior to the coup that there was a significant difference between the
two time periods. During the 1920s there was a concern with thrift and "an
atmosphere of general love and respect for the army." Both of these factors
were now lacking, he claimed. While he was correct in noting these differences, most of the USSR's senior military leaders felt that a professional military would help overcome both of these problems.[51]

The bottom line was that almost all of the country's senior political and
military figures believed both in the importance of a professional military
as well as the need to create a reserve system to back it up. Whether such a
backup system would be called a militia or a national guard mattered little.
It would still signify the adoption of a "mixed system," one combining a
cadre of regular, professional officers with civilian part-time warriors. The
key to adoption of such a system was to overcome the entrenched opposition of those at the top, something the coup and its aftermath would accomplish.

## Conclusion

When Gorbachev came to office, the military's authority over force structure was almost complete. In essence, the generals enjoyed calling the shots in this area. Gorbachev's policies, however, required greater flexibility when it came to the country's manning system. To ensure that this occurred, a way had to be found to "penetrate" the High Command's autonomy on this issue.

While it is probably stretching things to suggest that the actions taken by Savinkin or Lopatin were orchestrated by Gorbachev and his advisors, it is clear that the climate he had created on the question of doctrine made such forays into this area easier. In any case, while the generals had not been completely defeated on this issue by the time of coup (they had not agreed to a completely professional military), they had clearly made concessions in this direction. In order to get control of force structure questions, Gorbachev succeeded in diluting the authority enjoyed by the generals to the point where the country's senior military officers were on the defensive. The generals were making concessions one after another.

When it came to this question, the situation prior to Gorbachev's rise to power differed from both the Kolkowicz and Odom models. Insofar as the first was concerned, civilians acquiesced in the military's autonomy over force structure issues. Indeed, it is not an exaggeration to suggest that civilians often understood little about such matters, and had even less to say about them. This was not the picture painted by the Kolkowicz model. At the same time, it is clear that the generals believed that while general policy guidance from party officials was acceptable, it was their bureaucratic right to determine force structure.

The Gorbachev era was different. Conflict came to the fore. Having enjoyed a major degree of autonomy, the generals objected to Gorbachev's efforts to gain control over force structure. The generals clearly did not see themselves as "executants," to use Odom's phrase. They spent the next seven years fighting Gorbachev's efforts to modify the country's manning system. In this sense, during this period the Kolkowicz model made some sense. At the same time, it is important to note that contrary to one of Kolkowicz's primary assumptions, the military was hardly a cohesive organization. Military officers led the charge for the militia concept, and toward the end they were joined by a number of senior officers. As far as the country's most senior officers were concerned, the bureaucratic line between the military and civilian worlds was clear. As this study illustrates, this was not the case with other military officers.

Insofar as Colton is concerned, use of his paradigm would have shown that military participation (i.e., autonomy) in this key area was rapidly decreasing. Civilians were involved in areas from which they had previously been excluded, and they were influencing the decision-making process.

# VII

## THE REVIVAL OF NATIONAL MILITARY FORCES

It is true that national formations existed in our armed forces from 1918 to 1938 and from 1941 until the mid-50s. . . . A return to them would not only be a backward step, but would be detrimental to the cause of the country's defensive capabilities.

Marshal Dmitri Yazov

Things would not be so bad if all the military formations were under unified command, but we can see that combat operations are being conducted by sundry groups without plans or goals, and motivated by just one thing: ethnic hatred.

General V. Samsonov

### The Problem

By the time Gorbachev came to power, national or territorial formations were a vestige of the past. Moscow had disbanded them in the 1950s and there was little talk of resurrecting them. When the subject did arise, the generals argued that they were irrelevant.

For the country's senior military officers, this issue went to the core of its concerns. If necessary, they could live with a professional army backed up by a militia system even though they found such an arrangement distasteful. But they believed that territorial armies would destroy the military's combat readiness, threaten its cohesion, and if they became national armies not subject to Moscow's total control, they would lead to the collapse of the Soviet Army.[1]

Gorbachev and most civilians agreed with the generals—the emergence of national armies could result in the collapse of the Soviet Union. Nevertheless, pressure for the creation of such military forces increased as the period progressed. The rise of national armies was not planned, but it was an inevitable result both of disintegrative forces in the former USSR as well as Gorbachev's attempt to gain control over the military.

## Ethnic Problems Emerge

While the issue of territorial or national armies did not become a serious problem until 1989, ethnic questions, and especially ethnic nationalism, played an important role throughout the 1980s. In the beginning of the Gorbachev period, the military's primary concern was ethnic relations at the unit level, i.e., how to ensure that the various nationalities worked together in harmony. Later, however, as the Soviet armed forces became increasingly dependent on non-Slavs for conscripts, nationality problems increased. A lack of Russian language skills, and a tendency to form ethnic based cliques intensified ethnic consciousness and led to an increase in ethnic conflict.

Intensified agitation for independence resulted in a further increase in nationalistic feelings, and a call for the creation of territorial forces or at least restrictions on where local conscripts served their time in the military (e.g., Latvians to serve only in Latvia). As the breakup of the Soviet Union became more of a possibility, the question of fully independent national armies became more urgent.

For their part, the generals worked hard to deal with ethnic tensions during the 1980s. Indeed, the generals went so far as to create their own version of an affirmative action policy in an effort to better integrate the various ethnic groups. Later, as it became increasingly clear that territorial formations would be established, the generals' attention shifted to ensuring the total subordination of such units to Moscow. However, by the end of 1990 the generals realized that national units—independent of Moscow's control—would be created. Accordingly, the generals again switched tactics, this time working to tie these forces to the Kremlin through devices such as a joint strategy, common weapons systems and forms of supply, a common training program, etc. In the end, the generals lost the battle to stop the formation of both territorial formations and national armies. In the process their worst fears were realized—the Soviet Army as a militarily effective institution ceased to exist.

## A Multi-Ethnic Army

By the late 1980s the need to rely on non-Russians had resulted in a more ethnically diverse military. This point was made by a military sociologist, who revealed in 1988 that "eight years ago there were 5-7 nationalities serving in companies and batteries, whereas now the number of nationalities has risen to 9-18. In the early 1980s the army numbered 20-30 nationalities, and today 25-37." According to this source, this was the result of an increase in the percentage of Central Asians and individuals from the

Transcaucasus in the military. The effect on the army was dramatic. As this source put it, this meant that "whereas 28 percent of conscripts in 1980 were from these regions, 37 percent of them are in 1988."[2]

The increase in non-Slavs led to a number of serious problems. As one source noted, non-Slavs were more "inclined to join together than are the Slavic peoples," thereby forming cliques. Second, they also had different temperaments, habits, opinions, and ideas than Slavs. The result was the formation of small groups—based on ethnic origin—within the various units. This in turn led to an intensification of nationalistic sentiments. "It is precisely in such informal associations that trends toward national exclusiveness and sentiments of national arrogance manifest themselves."[3]

The fact that many of these people knew little or no Russian made the problem worse. As one Soviet officer put it, "A poor knowledge (or ignorance) of Russian on the part of soldiers from the national republics is becoming one of the principal reasons for the formation of closed national groups in the troop collective."[4] As another source put it,

> Of late we are increasingly frequently coming up against cases like the following: Private Sh. Tashtemirov is a graduate of the Fergana Agricultural Technical School, but his Russian is very poor, and the Russian vocabulary of Privates G. Gorgadze from Georgia and B. Turunov from Uzbekistan, who have received 10 years of schooling is limited to a dozen words.[5]

Indeed, in some cases, the language problem reached disastrous proportions. According to the same source, in certain units 40-70 percent of the soldiers from Central Asia and the Transcaucasus did not speak Russian. Faced with such a situation, their sudden exposure to a different lifestyle, as well as racist attitudes on the part of many Slavic officers and soldiers, they took refuge in their ethnic groups.

By 1989 the situation within the armed forces had reached the point where Soviet officers openly expressed concern about the explosiveness of the situation. To quote one such officer:

> Servicemen who were multinational in make-up arrived in the messhall and took their seats. One soldier stood up and shouted: "Hey, Chernyy (Black)! Bring some bread." (He was addressing his comrade named Chernyy.) Fellow soldiers from the Transcaucasus sitting two tables away thought it was addressed to them. A conflict could have broken out in a matter of seconds. It was well that an officer was in the messhall.[6]

One of the worst manifestations of ethnic tensions was the tendency for hazing (the so-called *dedovshchina*) to take on an ethnic orientation. What this meant was that instead of hazing being directed at all incoming recruits (who under this rubric were expected to be subservient to the "deds," or more senior conscripts), the majority ethnic group began to direct its wrath against other ethnic groups in the unit.

The generals were only too aware of the many problems they faced in this area, and for some time they had been making a serious effort to deal with them. For example, in 1984 an affirmative action program was created, according to which "representatives of the indigenous nationalities of a number of union republics" were offered the opportunity to attend officer schools under a "special admissions policy." The idea was that the presence of officers of non-Russian background would help ameliorate, if not eliminate ethnic tensions. Being sensitive to the unique characteristics of their own national groups, the generals believed that such officers would serve as a role model for soldiers of a similar or related ethnic background.[7]

Those admitted to officer schools under this program did not take regular admission tests. Instead, a Republic Admission Committee reviewed their educational records. In some cases, individuals were admitted "in spite of their inadequate knowledge of the Russian language." In other cases, the committee admitted young men who did not have the necessary background in mathematics or physics. Unfortunately, the failure rate in this program was high. As one officer put it, "It is common knowledge that in 1986 300 Kirghiz boys were forced to part with their dream of becoming officers because of a poor knowledge of Russian."[8]

As in the United States, affirmative action programs were controversial and drew considerable criticism. *Red Star*, for example, published a letter from teachers at a school in Kirghizia attended by young men who were given special training to enable them to attend a regular officer's school. The authors complained that even though all students (i.e., Russians and non-Russians alike) took the same courses, non-Russians did not have to take an examination to enter an officers' school, while Russian students (about 15 percent of the class) had to pass these difficult tests. As a consequence, the authors contended, "after graduation some of them do not have an 'equal opportunity' to enter a military school and become an officer. This is hardly justified."[9]

The military also took other steps to ameliorate ethnic conflict within the armed forces. To begin with, they established Russian language "study circles." Under the supervision of a political officer, the military set up a tutorial system involving Russian soldiers with higher education. The aim was to work with ethnic minorities on a one-to-one basis during non-duty hours, thereby helping the soldier gradually to bring his Russian up to a level where he would be able both to perform his job and to communicate with his Slavic colleagues.[10]

In addition, the military created ethnic sensitivity training courses at the unit level for both officers and cadets. These programs had a twofold purpose: first, to convince Slavic soldiers and officers that non-Slavs come from a highly civilized culture. The second purpose was to show non-Slavs that the military valued their specific cultural backgrounds. To ensure maximum efficiency in the implementation of such programs, the regime made party organs responsible for monitoring the program. Those who took a "formalistic" approach to such problems were sharply criticized. As one officer put it, "There is still quite a bit of 'a toast to your health and holiday,' interpretation of those who have national problems and there are many simplifications." As an example, the author cited the following case:

> The political section in which Colonel V. Cherepukhin serves formed an inter-ethnic relations group and included three of its workers and several major unit staff officers on its staff. They did not even try to concern themselves with including representatives from among those nationalities who serve in its units and subunits. I ask you, who does this group represent: what benefit can be expected from such a formal approach to the very delicate matter of establishing inter-ethnic relations?[11]

In spite of the generals' best efforts, the situation did not improve. By March 1989 one source stated that ethnic conflicts were the most serious problem confronting the military. Another officer noted that "cases of national egoism, arrogance, and cliquishness, according to national origin continue to occur," and added that "a number of flagrant incidents due to so-called dedovshchina have a nationalist overtone."[12]

Yazov himself recognized the severity of the situation. While he maintained that, when investigated, many reports of dedovshchina turn out to be untrue, he nevertheless admitted that it was a serious problem in the Soviet Armed Forces.[13] For example, in an address to the Nineteenth Party Conference of the Group of Soviet Forces in Germany, he warned that problems associated with ethnic relations "need the closest attention these days. The events in Armenia and Azerbaijan and in the republics of the Soviet Baltic region confirm the danger of underestimating internationalist education." The officer on the spot must resolve such problems. To quote Yazov, "The leadership of multinational collectives commanders must rigorously observe the fundamental demands of Lenin's nationalities policy and show special concern for strengthening friendship and fraternity between servicemen of different nationalities."[14] Aleksey Lizichev, then head of the Main Political Directorate, went further, warning officers that they would pay the price if they permitted activities such as hazing to continue.

> We and only we—commanders and political workers—are responsible for hazing, responsible before the people and before our conscience. . . . When commanders and political workers do not take decisive measures to curtail such ugly and shameful phenomena and use neither the educational possibilities nor the full force of the authority granted to them for

this purpose, we make them strictly accountable. We expel them from the party and the Komsomol.[15]

The military leadership also ordered medical personnel to report any "bruises, injuries and wounds they find on servicemen that are clearly not accidental."[16] However, these warnings and calls to action by two of the country's most senior officers did not have much impact. As one source put it,

> 55 to 70 percent of officers do not take the multi-ethnic composition of military units into account during educational work; up to 80 percent have not been taught to control interrelations among subordinates of different nationalities; approximately the same number do not know how to conduct preventive work for the prevention of conflicts based on nationality.

The same source also reported that the special admissions policy outlined above was not being fully utilized, and that certain ethnic groups (e.g., those from the Transcaucasus) continued to place themselves in "privileged" positions. "They refused to clean up their living quarters, wash floors, etc. (They said, 'men do not do women's work')."[17]

Despite these efforts by the leadership to deal with ethnic developments, the situation worsened for two reasons. On the one hand, the movement toward national independence in a number of the republics—most particularly in the Baltics and the Transcaucasus—intensified nationalistic feelings. On the other hand, bitter ethnic conflicts broke out around the country. In April 1989 a violent clash between soldiers and demonstrators occurred in Tbilisi. In May both Lithuania and Estonia announced that they were planning to declare their independence. Then in June, Uzbeks attacked Meskhetian Turks in the Fergana Valley, and the next month Latvia declared its independence. In the meantime, tensions between Armenians and Azeris over Nagorno-Karabakh intensified.

In essence, an interdependent relationship between ethnic nationalism and ethnic conflicts existed in the armed forces. The worse ethnic conflicts within the military became, and the more the military became involved in putting down such conflicts, the stronger became the calls for national militaries. Similarly, as calls for independence grew, so did the hazing of recruits from those republics. Slavic soldiers resented those they believed were turning their backs on the USSR.

Efforts by political authorities to deal with these issues only made the situation worse. As early as June 1988 the Nineteenth Party Conference emphasized the need for a new approach to dealing with ethnic problems. The Conference Resolution condemned past practices, arguing that they represented a departure from the Leninist principles on nationalities, and that they violated Soviet law. As a result, the resolution stated, "The negative phenomena built up over decades were ignored for a long time, driven under the surface, and not duly assessed by the party." The conference also called for greater independence (*samostoyatelnost*) for the republics, while at the same time it argued for a struggle against "hometown nationalism and chauvinism." The political leadership was attempting to take two incompatible steps at once: trying to maintain central control, while at the same time granting greater autonomy to the republics. The actions taken in pursuit of the latter eventually led to the breakup of the former. In the process, ethnic tensions in the military worsened and the drive for independent militaries intensified.[18]

## The Call for National Armies

Savinkin was the first Soviet officer to call for territorial armies. Savinkin tied his proposal for a mixed system to suggestions that Moscow should create territorial formations, similar to those which had existed some fifty years earlier. This "mixed system" would be made up of a professional military and a militia. As in the 1920s, the latter would be split along national and regional lines. For example, Savinkin argued that in an area such as Uzbekistan, the militia should be national, i.e., made up primarily of Uzbeks. In metropolitan areas such as Moscow and Leningrad units would be made up of local inhabitants regardless of their national origin.[19]

The push for national autonomy provided an impetus for Savinkin's call for territorial armies. For example, Sajudis, the Lithuanian Independence Movement, included a call for territorial formations in its program. The idea in 1988 was to widen areas of national/ethnic autonomy within the republic, not to create totally independent ethnic armies.

One of the early arguments by Baltic nationalists was that rather than ship recruits all over the Soviet Union, it would be cheaper to permit them to serve in their home district (e.g., Latvians in Latvia, Estonians in Estonia). This would alleviate many of the health problems that arose from forcing recruits from the Baltics to serve in areas such as the mountains of Tadjikistan. Insofar as hazing was concerned, the official line—i.e., that service in the Soviet Army helped to build national unity by integrating the various nationalities—was not working. As one writer put it, the victims of "non-regulation behavior" (i.e., dedovshchina) were usually the non-Slavs. By creating territorial formations, such excesses would be avoided and the result would be a stronger sense "of patriotic feelings, and the creation of a real school of internationalism."[20]

The idea of territorial armies was given a semiofficial endorsement when Al'fred Chepanis, a Latvian candidate for the Supreme Soviet, called for the creation of such formations within the Soviet Army. As evidence of their practicality, he cited the Latvian Rifles that existed during the

Civil War Period.[21] Support for the creation of such units was not limited only to the Baltics. *Moskovskie novosti*, for example, published an article in February 1989 by a captain from the Far Eastern Military District who argued that "national problems cannot be resolved by setting off one nationality against another"—individual ethnic differences had to be recognized.[22]

The military leadership stubbornly opposed any movement toward greater national autonomy. It argued that control of military units came within its sphere of autonomy. Speaking at a election meeting in February 1989, for example, Moiseyev dismissed the idea of territorial armies or, as he put it, "distributing the Army among national barracks," while Serebryannikov, the officer who figured prominently in the debate over a professional military, cited World War II hero Marshal Zhukov to the effect that soldiers trained under a territorial system "did not know how to fight against aviation, they were not familiar with tanks and therefore, as you may recall, our Army was in the grip of fear of tanks."[23] Moiseyev returned to the topic two weeks later, when he criticized suggestions that "each union republic could have its own national military formations, and even its own army."[24] With the exception of Serebryannikov's reference to Zhukov, no reason was given for the High Command's opposition to such formations. Indeed, in a speech in March Yazov sidestepped the issue, arguing that "what is needed is the systematic study of the feelings of personnel and concrete work with people . . . that is based on knowledge of the peculiarities of national character, customs and traditions."[25] It was as if the problem was primarily one of hazing, and that it would go away if only enough time and effort were devoted to overcoming dedovshchina. The problem, however, went deeper than hazing.

Insofar as the 1920s were concerned, several military academics rejected the idea of bringing back these national formations, arguing that "they were rejected" in the 1930s both because of the worsening international climate and the increasing complexity of the weapons systems then in use. Another officer, General Tabunov, came out in favor of extra-territoriality (i.e., the idea that individuals should be available for service anywhere in the USSR), maintaining that "an extra-territorial principle of manning that makes possible the successful formation of military units in the necessary amount through young men called up from various regions of the country is more suited to the USSR." This position was supported by another officer who argued that without extra-territorial service it would be impossible to man units in areas east of the Urals, "where just 20 percent of the population of the USSR lives."[26] Meanwhile, another source noted that the financial costs entailed in setting up such units would have to be borne by the republics, many of which could not afford to pay for them. The next month, an editorial criticized those who wanted to repeat the experience of the 1920s, arguing that

> During the 70 years of its existence, our Army has gone through . . . na-
> tional military formations within the framework of a single army. Having
> experienced all of this, frequently through the trial and error method, it
> began to be structured on the existing system of military organization
> which was developed by the party. This system withstood trial by war.
> And this is the main argument in defense of the existing principles of our
> military structure.[27]

To make its point, the generals enlisted the assistance of individuals with
the appropriate ethnic background in areas like the Baltics, where the call
for territorial formations was strongest. In one case, for example, a Colonel
Kulpinskas wrote an article in the Latvian newspaper, *Sovetskaya Latviya*,
in which he argued against the idea of independent armies or even limitations on service outside of the various republics. "Imagine . . . that the
territorial principle . . . actually exists. . . . Then all of a sudden a military
conflict breaks out. . . . What happens then? Will each republic begin to
protect its own borders, waiting until the adversary reaches them? This is
quite absurd."[28] Major General Duda, the military commissar for Latvia,
citing letters reportedly received from citizens in Latvia, also upheld the
High Command's position. He argued that more than 30 percent of those
drafted in Latvia were already serving in the Baltic region. In addition,
while dedovshchina must be eliminated from the military, he noted that
the "Army is currently waging a fierce struggle against it using both educational and administrative measures. And this struggle is producing definite results."[29]

Throughout the remainder of 1989 the military leadership continued to
attack national armies. Yazov, for example, argued in May that "the Army
cannot be composed along ethnic lines," suggesting that this would lead
ultimately to the breakup of the military, a situation in which each village
had its own army.[30] Then in June, General Varennikov, the commander in
chief of ground forces, entered the fray, arguing that the idea made no sense
from a military point of view. He maintained that such units would intensify ethnic differences between the various republics and undercut military efficiency because there would be an immediate drop in the number
of military personnel who spoke and understood Russian. "Let us say it
openly: this idea appeals only to those who want to destroy our fraternal
union."[31]

By October Yazov admitted publicly that ethnic problems were a major
problem in the armed forces. For example, he acknowledged that draft
evasion was spreading beyond the Baltics and Georgia to other regions.[32]
On September 29 the Supreme Soviet of Lithuania adopted a resolution
calling on the Kremlin to limit the military service of Lithuanian-born youths
solely to the three Baltic nations, and in November Georgia followed suit
with a request that Georgians serve only in Georgia.

Yazov returned to the issue in November when he blasted "manifestations of anti-army feelings," by which he meant "a well-orchestrated and
coordinated campaign to discredit the Armed Forces." Such actions included
not only urging young men to avoid military service, but a refusal to provide the necessary housing, social, cultural, and consumer facilities to military families—not to mention incidents of harassment of officers and their
wives and children. This whole approach, he argued, was aimed at the
destruction of the armed forces.

Returning to the question of extra-territorial service, Yazov cited the Strategic Rocket Forces: "How can you organize these forces and the performance of compulsory active military service in them according to the national territorial principle, which is, in part, what the Lithuanian legislators' resolution seeks?" In fact, he continued, "Formations and units of
particular branches of the Armed Forces are deployed where defense tasks
and the specific military-political situation require it." Turning to the 1920s,
Yazov argued:

> It is true that national formations existed in our Armed Forces in 1918-38
> and from 1941 until the mid-1950s. They played a part in enlisting the
> peoples of our country to the common cause of the defense of the socialist
> Fatherland.
>
> With the appearance of radically new types of weapons this way of
> organizing the Armed Forces became obsolete. A return to it would not
> only be a backward step, but would be detrimental to the cause of the
> country's defense capability, since with this kind of manning system it is
> impossible to ensure the necessary level of combat readiness of the Army
> and Navy, the manning of formations and units with servicemen of the
> relevant combat specialties, and the training and accumulation of suffi-
> cient mobilization resources.

Furthermore, Yazov continued, "the number of servicemen who were
representatives of the indigenous population in these formations was only
30-40 percent."[33]

Moiseyev attempted to convince republic leaders that movement toward
national armies was not only *not* in their political-military interest, but it
was also a recipe for military disaster. He reiterated Yazov's argument that
such units were no longer militarily relevant because of the complexity of
modern military weapons and equipment. Turning to the role of national
factors in the Soviet armed forces, Moiseyev argued that three demands
were now being made. First, the number of recruits serving outside of each
republic should be reduced. Second, that servicemen be permitted to serve
in national units so they would be able to maintain their ethnic traditions
and culture, and third, that conscripts not be forced to serve in climatic
conditions which differ significantly from their home republic. According

to Moiseyev, the adoption of any of these demands would undermine Soviet security.

In response, Moiseyev maintained that "there is not one republic that can independently create and maintain a modern army; they do not possess the economics and potential for that." Second, he claimed that the purpose of the armed forces was not to make it easy for conscripts to do military service, but to enhance the country's defense. How, he asked, can one get servicemen to serve in more difficult parts of the country under these proposals? What about Kamchatka? Who would want to serve there? "Therefore, from the military point of view, the proposal . . . is absurd." Furthermore, how does the military decide which republic should have how many men under arms? "In Uzbekistan, there are approximately 10 times more people than in Estonia. However, the interests of defense do not demand having 10 times more troops in Uzbekistan than in Estonia. . . ."

Moiseyev also listed other negative factors associated with territorial formations. They could not provide the type of training needed on modern, complex weapons systems—and this was true even of infantry units. "For motorized rifle divisions alone, it is necessary to train servicemen to the tune of several hundred military registered specialists." Turning to the country's past experience with such units, Moiseyev noted that such formations required national officer cadres, something that was lacking. The republics were not in a position to create officer schools. Sensitive to the linguistic nationalism then sweeping the country, Moiseyev argued that territorial forces also created serious problems for command and control. Military forces must operate in one language: "One cannot allow the headquarters of the Baltic military district, or another region—the Transcaucasus—to issue their orders and directives in several languages. What command and control can one speak of in this case?" Likewise, what about manuals, regulations and textbooks, something that was a major problem in the 1920s? Or translators? Finally, he argued that history had proven that the extra-territorial principle was best for the USSR.[34]

By the end of 1989 it was becoming obvious both that regional nationalism was becoming very serious, and that the generals' nerves were frayed. Moiseyev admitted in his December speech that ethnic-related hazing continued to be a serious problem, that many young men were refusing to serve in the military, and that a number of Soviet military officers had been killed by civilians during 1989. It was also clear from a transcript of a meeting between Yazov and other high-ranking military officers with Lithuanian deputies that the generals were bitter. Yazov accused the Lithuanians of ignoring Soviet laws, of insulting and harassing Soviet military personnel and their families stationed in Lithuania, and claimed that Sajudis's support for national armies had little to do with either dedovshchina (as some of the Lithuanian deputies claimed) or national aspirations. "It is struggling for power and needs an army to support its government," he argued. Furthermore, Yazov and Lizichev, who took part in the meeting, claimed that the military had already made considerable concessions to the Lithuanians in that 27 percent of those inducted into the Soviet Army from Lithuania were serving in that republic, and Yazov argued that he personally would look into any cases of hazing or other complaints submitted to him by Lithuanian deputies.[35]

### The Push for Territorial/National Armies Intensifies

The idea of territorial armies not only did not go away, pressure for them intensified throughout 1990 as nationalistic feelings rose even higher. During January tensions between Armenia and Azerbaijan over Nagorno-Karabakh worsened, Soviet troops intervened forcibly in Baku to restore order, and the Tallinn City Council refused to enforce military draft regulations. January also saw mass demonstrations in Moldova for reunification with Romania. The following month Armenians were attacked in Dushanbe, leaving almost forty dead. All of these actions intensified local dislike—even hatred—of the Soviet Army, which was often called upon to maintain order in these bitter and often irrational ethnic conflicts. Then on March 11, Lithuania declared its independence, thereby forcing the generals to come to grips with the possibility both that the Soviet Union would break up and that independent military forces could become a reality.

For their part, Lopatin and his allies made national armies an integral part of their military reform plan. Their plan called for "all people living in a specific territory to serve in national formations, irrespective of their nationality." These formations would be subordinated "in administrative terms to the central and local leadership, but in operational-strategic terms only to the center."[36] These forces could be used by local authorities to control internal disorder or to help with national disasters. In order to train the reserve system, Lopatin suggested utilizing DOSAAF (the organization that is charged with providing military training for young men prior to their entry into the military).

As was the case with his advocacy of a professional military, Lopatin tied the territorial concept to the experience of the 1920s. Noting that the need for such units was dictated not only by economic conditions, "but also by historical preconditions," Lopatin stressed their importance in resolving ethnic problems when he stated that

> Various national-territorial units have existed as part of the Armed Forces of Russia since the time a central Russian state was formed. In the period from 1917 through 1938 organization of such force elements significantly contributed to a positive resolution of the ethnic question

by eliminating the actual inequality of peoples of the USSR in the military sphere.

Furthermore, he continued, by 1935, 74 percent of all divisions were territorial, and during World War II up to eighty units in action were "made up of all nationalities living on the territory of a republic or district."[37]

Lopatin was not calling for independent military forces. Rather, he was suggesting the re-creation of units similar to those which existed in the 1920s with one—important—exception. Control would still be in the hands of central authorities in wartime, but during peacetime, republic authorities would command these forces, a situation somewhat analogous to the relationship between the various state national guards and the federal government in the United States.

From the point of view of the military leadership, the situation continued to worsen. Yazov revealed that the use of Soviet forces in Tbilisi had a serious demoralizing effect within the army. As he noted,

> I do not want to say that everything turned out as I would have wished. At first one psychological factor I would call the 'Tbilisi syndrome' hampered things and paralyzed initiative. The vacillation with it hampered the military from acting in a clear-cut manner according to regulations, according to orders, and ultimately, according to their duty. This is a new phenomena.

Furthermore, while admitting that hazing continued to be a major problem, he argued that in every instance when it was reported, "a careful investigation is initiated and specific and urgent practical steps are taken." Turning to charges that soldiers had been brutalized and killed as a result of ethnic hazing, Yazov reiterated his position that the majority of charges were untrue.

> In January this year, the writer V. Yasukaytite made sharp and serious accusations against the Ministry of Defense. I am forced to say that they were all highly strung and emotional in form, totally without foundation, and simply false in terms of their content. In particular, the writer stated that in December of last year six soldiers of Lithuanian nationality died. This is not so; no Lithuanian soldier died. The statements about the existence of some kind of norms for losses on exercises and maneuvers, and that AIDS is allegedly widespread in the Army, are absolutely groundless.

If nothing else, Yazov's statement revealed a strong sense of frustration, a feeling that no matter what he or the armed forces did to deal with ethnic problems, the situation was getting out of control—and he was right.[38]

From the generals' standpoint, the creation of territorial/national units would not only lead to operational problems, they also added fuel to ethnic fires. Furthermore, not only could such units use any weapons they obtained against their neighbors, they could also use them against Soviet forces attempting to keep peace in these regions. Moiseyev gave vent to his frustration on this question in February when he commented,

> I can say with certainty that today it would be not merely impermissible, but criminal to entrust weapons to such military formations. The events in Transcaucasia are an illustration of this. Enough blood has been shed there already. Both military men and civilians are dying.[39]

In an effort to shore up support for the generals within the officer corps, and to provide senior officers with the requisite ammunition to defend the military's position, General Varennikov, gave an intellectual defense of the military's position on this issue. Varennikov reviewed the history of national forces from 1918 to 1938, as well as their role during World War II. Like Yazov and Moiseyev, he lauded their performance, noting that they played a critical role during both periods. Turning to the present, however, Varennikov argued that current demands for national formations were not realistic.

> As a result of the contemporary level of the development of military affairs, the character of the conduct of military operations, the priority assigned to qualitative parameters in the development of all branches and units of the Army and Navy mean that the acceptance of these demands will lead to a lowering of the country's defensive ability, the quality of training, exercises, and the combat and mobilization capability of the army and navy.

Varennikov's message was simple; national formations were important in the past, but the past was not a prologue to the future.[40]

While a number of senior military officers differed with Yazov and Moiseyev on the question of a professional military, there was little disagreement on the question of national forces. All opposed it. Marshal Yefimov, for example, commented that "from a purely military standpoint, they cannot represent a real force capable of resolving defensive tasks independently. I think this is obvious even to an amateur."[41] Similarly, General Sukhorukov remarked, "The principle of the formation of the Armed Forces is extra-territorial; the principle of their formation is based on the principle of general liability for military service. . . . Obviously, it must not undergo any changes, because that is even impossible in practice."[42] General Krivosheyev was equally outspoken, stating that "a deeper study of the territorial principle makes it possible to see a whole series of shortcomings in it."[43] Other officers echoed this concern. Lieutenant Colonel Durnev, a political officer, observed that "if you are talking about the principle of manning the Army on the basis of the territorial principle, I am against it. I do not think the Army can be Uzbek, or Armenian, or any other nationality. The army must be all-Union."[44]

These efforts to stem the tide of nationalism were of no avail. By March all of the Baltic states refused to assist military commissariats with the spring draft. Similarly, there were calls for the withdrawal of Soviet forces from the Baltic region. Indeed, one Lithuanian deputy went so far as to claim that "the Soviet Army for us is a foreign army."[45] Meanwhile, in Moldova young men were urged to refuse service in the Soviet Army, while in Georgia the Social Democratic party called for the creation of a national defense ministry and compulsory military service for young men only in the Georgian armed forces. Likewise, Yazov stated that calls were being heard in Armenia and Azerbaijan for conscripts from those republics to serve "only on their own territory and calling for the creation of national armies." To make matters worse, Yazov claimed that desertions and draft dodging were increasing.[46]

Meanwhile, interest in national military formations began to draw public attention. In contrast to the militia issue, lines between civilians and the military were very clearly drawn on this topic. Civilians—even those who did not appear to have had an ethnic axe to grind—favored the idea of introducing such units, while military officers (with the exception of reformers such as Lopatin) continued to argue against them. For example, in April Lipitskiy suggested that the reforms of the mid-1920s, including the creation of national forces, offered a good model for the 1990s.[47] On the other hand, a group of military officers rejected it, claiming that it would both weaken the country's military defense and lead to a further deterioration in ethnic relations.[48]

By the latter part of 1990 the proposed Union Treaty took the issue of national armies out of the military leadership's hands. Gorbachev decided that the solution to the ethnic problem would be a new Union Treaty—a voluntary association of the republics—and he created a working group made up of representatives of all the various republics to draft it.

In the meantime, the push toward republic sovereignty continued. By the middle of 1990 the process was well under way. The declaration by Ukraine in July, in particular, had serious potential consequences for the generals since it called for the complete withdrawal of Soviet troops, the creation of its own armed forces, and the establishment of Ukraine as a nuclear-weapons-free zone. The following month Armenia, Turkmenistan, and Tadzhikistan followed suit with declarations of sovereignty.[49]

The draft Union Treaty was published on August 19. Unfortunately, the treaty tried to satisfy two masters at once. On the one hand, the Kremlin's main purpose—which was supported by the military—was to retain as much central control over the country as possible. On the other hand, a number of the republics—especially Moldova, Ukraine, and the Baltic states—wanted the maximum degree of sovereignty. In the end, central authorities drafted the treaty and presented it to the republics for approval. A true federation, however, would only come about if the various states gave up some of their rights to the center. By the end of the year the level of frustration in several republics had reached the boiling point. Moldova, for example, decided in November that "the process of multilateral negotiation had proved pointless and Moldovian sovereignty could only be upheld by bilateral relations with other sovereign republics." Thus, for the military leadership the future looked bleak indeed.[50]

### Attempting to Salvage an Army

Faced with the increasing disintegration of the country, the generals began to focus almost exclusively on holding the armed forces together. To be fair, however, by this point it was not clear that they could have done much to change the situation. The train of Union disintegration had already left the station.

Speaking in September and November, both Yazov and Moiseyev avoided direct mention of territorial or national armies. Yazov blasted those whom he accused of attempting to split and destroy the military for their own "selfish" purposes.[51] Moiseyev, meanwhile, acted as though the problem did not exist. Indeed, reading his November interview the reader gets the impression that the Soviet Army of the future would differ little from that of the past—insofar as the national/ethnic question was concerned. He acknowledged the need to reduce personnel, expenditures, and reorganize the country's force structure, but he said nothing about the need to create national armies.[52]

There was a good reason for Moiseyev's failure to mention the subject. There was a lot of support for the Lopatin proposals among Supreme Soviet Deputies; i.e., a plan for the creation of all-Union strategic professional formations and republic (territorial) troops. However, the generals had succeeded in keeping such language out of the draft Union Treaty, and as a consequence both Yazov and Moiseyev probably opposed raising the issue anew at this critical juncture. In particular, the draft treaty called for a unified army, although each republic was to have a representative on the Defense Council. In addition, while the republics were to have a greater say on issues such as military policy, the stationing of troops, the handling of conscripts, the budget, and manning levels, operational control of the military was to remain centralized and the principle of extra-territoriality was to be retained. From the military's standpoint the draft treaty was not perfect, but it was better than the alternative suggested by Lopatin and his colleagues.[53]

In the meantime, the ethnic situation within the country deteriorated to the point where the military was forced to take specific steps. In September Moiseyev told the *Washington Post* that Moscow had quietly withdrawn nuclear warheads from those areas of the country in which ethnic unrest was a problem. "In those areas where the situation doesn't fully correspond to the concept of national security, the warheads have been put in a more secure place."[54] Then in November, Gorbachev issued executive orders prohibiting republics from controlling nuclear weapons on their territory and sanctioning the use of weapons against nationalists who attacked or harassed Soviet troops.[55]

Calls were again heard for the creation of national armies at the Fourth Congress of the USSR People's Deputies, held in December. As one might expect, both Yazov and Moiseyev repeated their standard positions. Yazov, for example, when asked about a speech by a G. Kh. Popov proposing the creation of territorial forces, responded that "talk about how the Army should be distributed among the republics or organized along two horizontal lines . . . are . . . frivolous." Furthermore, he continued, creating such forces would intensify "interethnic differences."[56] Moiseyev, when asked a similar question, responded that such ideas were "without real foundation." From a military standpoint, "this is a naive approach."[57]

The effort to maximize republic sovereignty, while at the same time retaining unified armed forces, was destined to fail. Indeed, by the end of 1990 tensions between the generals and republic officials had reached the point where senior officers were claiming that local officials were not only discouraging young men to report for the draft and harassing military personnel, but they were interfering in operational matters as well. On December 3, Yazov threatened the use of force if local authorities cut off services to military garrisons. "We will take the electric power stations and the water supply under our protection if the need arises."[58]

The period from January 1, 1991, until the attempted coup in August was one of continued deterioration from the point of view of the generals. In January General Dmitri Volkogonov, who had been forcibly retired by the High Command for his "liberal" views and an individual who became one of Yeltsin's closest military advisors, published an article in which he argued that "it would be possible . . . to have a national guard within the framework of the republic in order to feel the reality of sovereignty." He suggested that such formations be used in the event of national disasters. At the same time, he maintained—as had Lopatin—that strategic forces must remain in the hands of the central government. Volkogonov's comment suggested that at least one of the country's generals believed that territorial forces were inevitable.[59]

Matters came to a head on January 7, 1991, when paratroops were sent to Lithuania and Latvia to seize draft evaders. On January 13, Soviet forces attacked unarmed civilians attempting to prevent a takeover of the local radio and TV stations. At least fifteen people were killed and many others injured. Similar actions followed a few days later in Latvia. Claims by the political and military leadership that the people and the army were one began to ring hollow.[60]

As the push for national armies intensified, republic analysts began to look to their past—just as Soviet reformers such as Savinkin or Lopatin had done previously—for clues on how to structure their new, emerging armed forces. Discussing the need to form an Azerbaijani Army, for example, one analyst pointed to the Army of Azerbaijan of 1922.

> The republic had its own fleet, air units, and armored vehicles. Military cadres were trained on a regular basis. Military education began during adolescence. An army formed from Red Military Academy students was active.
>
> After the USSR was established, military forces from the Transcaucasian republics which had been included in the composition of the All-Union army were added to a separate Caucasian army. Despite major difficulties, the Azerbaijan division was quickly turned into a well prepared military unit. I have to add that other Soviet republics of the Transcaucasus also had their own national army units.

The author proposed the immediate establishment of divisions similar to those which existed in the 1920s. They would be made up primarily of Azeris, but other nationalities would be free to join.[61]

Despite his opposition to national armies, Yazov made a slight concession in this direction by approving the creation of Cossack units as part of the Soviet Armed Forces in May. Cossacks would take a different oath (omitting reference to the CPSU), but in terms of command and control they would be subordinated to the Soviet Army.[62]

In spite of its more forthcoming stance on Cossack units, the generals' position continued to come under public criticism. An especially hard-hitting article appeared in April. It blasted the generals for putting off military reform and accused it of acting like an ostrich. In the words of the author, Sergey Rogov, the military reform plan proposed by the generals the previous year, "ignores the process of the radical transformation of the national-state arrangement of the USSR which has already begun." Furthermore, he continued, "The disregard for national problems during the implementation of military reform can only impart new impetus to the centrifugal trends in the country." Calling continuation of the current situation "intolerable," Rogov demanded public debate on a reform plan that would involve both national and republic authorities.[63]

## Conclusion

When Gorbachev came to power the military was a highly bureaucratized organization, and questions such as how military forces were staffed came under the purview of the armed forces. Military autonomy in this area was almost complete.

From 1989 on, however, events over which the generals had no control took hold and gradually destroyed their ability to control events insofar as national armies were concerned. Indeed, it was not so much Gorbachev's attempt to undercut military autonomy that undermined military autonomy in this area as it was events in the former Soviet Union. By the time the coup occurred in 1991, military autonomy had been effectively destroyed— even more so than was the case with doctrine and a professional army. The armed forces were on the point of disintegration. The situation had gone far beyond what Gorbachev intended when he set out to repenetrate the armed forces.

Seen from the perspective of the three models, the experience with national armies suggests that the military had far more autonomy when Gorbachev came to power in 1985 than any of the models would have predicted—although the Colton model would have certainly shown that the military had a monopoly on decision-making authority in this area.

Insofar as the other two models are concerned, neither of them was especially helpful—except for the focus that the Kolkowicz model places on the importance of modern technology in the minds of military officers; i.e., the weapons systems were becoming too complex for national forces. Beyond that, the question of national forces was not an issue for civil-military relations. Both Gorbachev and the generals opposed the idea of independent national forces because both sides realized that their existence would signal the end of the Soviet Union. Even reformers like Lopatin or Rogov— who in this area did not represent Gorbachev—believed that national forces should be recreated—but only under Moscow's strict control.

However, events had their own momentum and before long the generals' autonomy was gone—not because Gorbachev wanted power in this area, but because events dictated this course of action.

All of the country's senior leadership would have agreed with General Makashov, one of the most conservative of Soviet generals, who in response to a question on the topic said, "In the final result they could lead to the destruction of the Armed Forces of the USSR, even to the collapse of the Russian state, which our ancestors created over the centuries."[64] He probably did not realize how correct and prophetic he was.

# VIII

## CADRE AND PARTY

> An important role in the construction of the
> Armed Forces was played by the military
> reform of 1924-25. Many of (its) ideas and
> approaches, especially those connected with
> . . . the style and activity of military cadres . . .
> keep their relevance even today.
>
> Marshal Dmitri Yazov

> Just as 60 years ago, there is the urgent
> problem of converting the Army, Air Forces
> and Navy from quantitative parameters to
> qualitative ones.
>
> Lt. Cols. P. F. Vashchenko and V. A. Runov

### The Problem

By the mid-1980s the relationship between the party control mechanisms
in the military had changed significantly from what it had been in the 1920s.
The party was still present in the military, and party officials could cause
problems for officers who did not go along with the Kremlin's wishes.
Nevertheless, in the majority of cases party structures in the military worked
to support the military. For example, party structures were critical when it
came to containing ethnic tensions within the armed forces. The same was
true of the battle against dedovshchina. Political officers worked overtime
to combat the problem.

While it would be pushing things too far to suggest that the situation
was an example of Odom's unitary model, it was a lot closer to that paradigm than it was to Kolkowicz's approach. The military had co-opted the
party-political apparatus. In practical terms this meant that the military
leadership largely determined what the Main Political Administration did
and how it functioned. Civilian party officials could and did have a say in
such things, but to implement their ideas they had to rely on the Defense
Ministry.

The main impact of the Gorbachev period in this case was that it destroyed the party—that glue that was used to keep the military together.

As a consequence, the generals lost a major vehicle for maintaining organizational cohesion. In short, rather than freeing the military from party rule (although technically this occurred), the end of the Communist party hurt the military's ability to maintain internal order.

When it came to political structures, Yazov and Moiseyev opposed changing their functions, arguing that such institutions were critical for the maintenance of discipline, morale, and cohesion. Indeed, toward the latter part of the Gorbachev era the generals argued that the significance of such organs had increased in light of the many centrifugal forces pulling the armed forces apart. In essence, the generals maintained that just as these structures held the Soviet Army together in the past, they were even more critical now.

## Perestroyka and the Officer Corps

The military leadership had long favored upgrading the quality of the Soviet officer corps. Marshal Ogarkov, for example, blasted Soviet officers as early as 1971 for their failure to adapt to the changing circumstances. "There is . . . I believe a more substantial reason for the shortcomings pointed out. It lies in the fact that individual military leaders do not keep pace with life and the development of scientific thought."[1] For his part, Marshal Akhromeyev, Ogarkov's successor as chief of the General Staff, took a similar position in 1985, declaring that history "offers many examples when the armies of some states prepared for future wars, basing themselves only on the experience of the past without taking into account the evolution of the military field."[2]

Gorbachev too favored increased emphasis on quality in personnel issues. Speaking to a plenum of the Central Committee of the CPSU shortly after taking over as secretary general, he criticized the party-political structures. Turning to personnel, Gorbachev attacked past practices and introduced what became the key elements of personnel policy in the military. In describing the model party worker, Gorbachev listed the following factors: "The main slogans of the present . . . are creative work, the unity of word and action, initiative and responsibility, and placing demands on oneself and his comrades."[3]

Despite similarities between Gorbachev's personnel policy and the positions articulated by Ogarkov and Akhromeyev, the generals' initial response to Gorbachev's speech was ambivalent at best. For the country's military leaders, Gorbachev's call for an acceleration of the economy was welcome. However, it was primarily a problem for the civilian world. When it came to implementing such a policy in the military itself, the generals chose to interpret Gorbachev's speech and the resulting plenum resolution as a call for greater discipline and improved efficiency. Insofar as the question of management was concerned, two areas of special concern—which followed the lines of Gorbachev's April speech—were singled out in the military press.[4]

The first was closeness to people. The ability to work with people was considered a critical aspect of leadership. Those who set high standards for themselves and their troops would have fewer disciplinary problems. To quote an editorial, "It is a question of activating the human factor, of the need to strive so that everyone works conscientiously at his place with full efficiency, deeply conscious of the purpose of the demands placed on him."[5]

The second factor was personal responsibility. In the past, officials of all types, including military officers, had avoided accepting responsibility for their actions. This was no longer acceptable. "The importance of occupational characteristics such as competence, a sense for the new, initiative, boldness and a readiness to take personal responsibility, the ability to follow the task to its final resolution is constantly increasing."[6] Any system of management would only be effective if those who occupied the upper ranks were responsible for their actions.

The military assigned primary responsibility for implementing perestroyka to the political-party apparatus. A May 1985 meeting of party activists called on party organizations to become more responsible for their actions and those of the troops serving under them. A month later, Admiral Aleksey Sorokin, first deputy chief of the Main Political Directorate of the Soviet Army and Navy, complained that the political apparatus was not working as hard as it should. He also called on the party-political apparatus to ensure that each member of the military took perestroyka seriously.[7]

In spite of the attention given to perestroyka, the majority of officers ignored Sorokin. The latter complained about the work of party structures and especially their inability to eliminate "formalism" from party work.[8] Gorbachev responded to the army's foot-dragging at a meeting in Minsk with senior military officers. In that meeting he told the generals, "We need energetic leaders who can command and communicate, people with initiative who are competent in their work."[9] Despite his comments, the attitude of most military officers changed little.

Speaking at the Twenty-Seventh Party Congress, Gorbachev emphasized that progress depended on developing a new Soviet-style meritocracy in which party or family connections would play little or no role. As he put it, "The criteria for all advancements and transfers are the same—the political and professional qualities, abilities, and real achievements of a worker, and his attitude toward the people."[10]

If nothing else, Gorbachev's comments at the Twenty-Seventh Party Congress got the generals' attention. Increasing numbers of articles were published in military newspapers and journals on the topic. *Red Star* began a special section devoted to perestroyka and published a number of letters to the editor on the topic as well. In spite of this increased attention, however, problems remained. Lizichev, the newly appointed head of the Main Political Directorate, complained at a meeting held in November 1986 that

> Even the election-and-report meetings are far from taking a demanding look at perestroyka, from achieving fully collective work in the search for new forms and methods in effectively resolving tasks. In some places, criticism carries a formal, superficial character. At many meetings, criteria characteristic of bygone days, an insufficiently fresh form of analysis, and a lack of sharp conclusions and self-criticism predominate.

By the beginning of 1987 it was clear that the military was not rushing to embrace perestroyka.[11]

Gorbachev was clearly irritated over the military's reaction to perestroyka. Speaking at the January 1987 plenum, he called for "truly revolutionary, comprehensive transformations in society." The key was cadre. "It . . . happens that certain executives find themselves in the wrong position and in no way up to the mark. . . . It seems essential to admit such errors, to rectify them, and without dramatizing them, to assign the person concerned to a job that corresponds to his abilities."[12]

When the West German civilian Mathias Rust landed his Cessna 172 in Red Square at the gates of the Kremlin after having flown through some 700 kilometers of Soviet air space, Gorbachev was presented with a direct challenge. Given that one of the key components of his personnel policy was individual responsibility, a failure on his part to demand a personal accounting for this humiliating event would raise questions throughout the country concerning the viability of perestroyka.

In response to the Rust incident, Gorbachev called an emergency meeting of the Politburo on May 30. The Politburo charged the Air Defense Forces with "impermissible lack of concern and resolve in intercepting the intruding aircraft." It also criticized the Ministry of Defense for serious organizational and managerial shortcomings. Marshal Koldunov, the head of the Air Defense Forces, together with Marshal Sokolov and numerous other generals were retired. The relatively unknown General Yazov was chosen as the new defense minister.[13]

Yazov lost no time in making it clear that he shared Gorbachev's concern about the personnel situation in the Soviet armed forces. In July he delivered a speech in which he blasted senior officers for failing to wipe out "negative tendencies" in the armed forces. "We must look truth in the eye: certain of us have lost our sense of duty and responsibility for the fulfillment of our duties and tasks."[14]

Yazov intensified his campaign for perestroyka in the personnel area in an article in which stated that "generals, admirals and officers have still not completely grasped the essence of restructuring," Yazov wrote. They fail to understand that the new approach must begin with them. Hitting where it hurts, Yazov stated that "the criterion for all promotions and moves remains one . . . that is, the political, moral and professional qualities, the capabilities and actual accomplishments of the worker and his attitude toward others and toward restructuring." In case anyone failed to understand fully what he had in mind, Yazov warned that

> The certification of officer personnel carried out in 1986 showed that certain officers have little knowledge of their official duties, the provisions of the general troop regulations and other documents governing relations in troop collectives and for this reason do not carry them out with sufficient clarity and consistency. Moreover, a certain portion of officer personnel are removed from the men, closing themselves off in highly specialized, technical and administrative problems and are not concerned with establishing a high moral atmosphere, a situation of collectivism, mutual respect and strict prescribed exactingness in the military collective.

Yazov thus made support for an improvement in the personnel area not only the prime criteria for promotion, but for retention as well.[15]

Yazov expected every officer, regardless of his functional specialty enthusiastically to support perestroyka. At the same time, like Gorbachev, he assigned special responsibility for implementing perestroyka to the party and the political apparatus. A policy of perestroyka, he remarked, means above all, "that each leading officer steadfastly implements the policy of the party, relies on the party organization, goes all out to support and develop an active and enterprising approach among Communists and the entire personnel, and to guide them in resolving the tasks at hand." Or as he put it elsewhere,

> Being in the vanguard means always being in the midst of the mass of servicemen, knowing their sentiments, responding to the most burning problems in life of military collectives, and doing everything to resolve them fighting persistently to assert a Leninist style of work, a creative businesslike style to achieve high final results.[16]

Yazov's emphasis on the role of the party in carrying out perestroyka helps explain why the generals would later become so concerned about attempts to abolish the party. The party fulfilled an important function; it not only helped in maintaining discipline, it served as an important transmission belt between the military leadership and the rank and file. When the generals decided to implement a new personnel policy, the party-political apparatus could always be relied on to assist in implementing it. After all, the vast majority of Soviet officers were members of the party, so they were subject to party as well as military discipline.[17]

In his effort to upgrade personnel qualifications, Yazov also emphasized qualitative as opposed to quantitative factors. A resolution adopted at the Twenty-Seventh Party Congress noted that "all defense building must henceforth be geared predominantly to qualitative parameters—with regard both to equipment and military science and to the personnel of the armed forces." Yazov referred to this resolution in August when he noted that "the introduction of qualitative parameters with respect to armed forces personnel presupposes a rise in the standard of the operational combat training of troops and naval forces and the utmost intensification of this training." Once again, Yazov singled out the party-political structures as the key organs charged with making this policy a reality. Inherent in the suggestion that cadre policy should be based on quality rather than quantity was the implication that from a personnel standpoint the Soviet Union could survive with fewer resources. In fact, most officers understood that the overall size of the armed forces would probably be decreased in accordance with the country's emerging defensive doctrine. Few of them, however, expected the quantitative axe to fall as quickly and as harshly as it did, only a few months later.[18]

Yazov continued to be frustrated with the approach taken by Soviet officers to personnel problems. Writing in January, for example, he focused on areas such as combat training (it is too formalistic in many cases), paperwork (it is "totally unabated") and stated that the new ideas "brought forth by restructuring in the activity of command and political cadres and party organs have not yet produced a noticeable improvement in the overall results in troop training and the strengthening of discipline."

The writing was on the wall: Those officers who opposed perestroyka— or were lukewarm in their support—could always be released or retired.[19]

### A Leaner, More Competent Military?

Throughout 1989 the emphasis was on upgrading the quality of the Soviet military. As Moiseyev noted, "The future of the armed forces must be conditioned by qualitative parameters, not quantitative ones." Meanwhile, General Lizichev commented that "the efficiency of Soviet military organizational development must be determined primarily by qualitative parameters with regard both to technology and military science, and to the composition of the Armed Forces."[20]

The generals recognized that in spite of all their warnings, implementing perestroyka in the Soviet military would take a long time. Indeed, to be effective a complete change in the psychological make-up of the officer corps was necessary. Moiseyev addressed the issue in the following fashion:

> Improving command is unthinkable without the eradication of a habit, which took root during the years of stagnation in the style of work of a certain section of command and political cadres. This is the habit of waiting for orders and instructions from above on any matter, of displaying a lack of initiative.

In accordance with this new policy, the military adopted special efficiency reports.[21]

Normally, in the Soviet armed forces, officer efficiency reports were prepared once every four years. During 1989, however, every officer was evaluated. The focus of such reports, according to General Sukhorukov, who was in charge of cadres in the Ministry of Defense, was on "qualitative parameters." In practice this meant that each officer was evaluated on his technical competence, his knowledge of military science, and how he related to enlisted personnel. Those who were ranked low were asked to leave the army.[22]

While figures are not available on how many officers were judged substandard, it is clear that a major turnover in officer personnel was under way. One source reports, for example, that "as many as one half of the generals, admirals and senior officers at the leadership level have been replaced in the past three years."[23] In practice this led to a decrease of approximately two years in the average age of the top fifteen officers—from 65.2 years to 63.2 years.[24]

Meanwhile, the generals began a campaign to improve the quality of military schools. The military closed a number of them in order to concentrate resources on fewer schools. Cadets affected by the closings were given the option of continuing their education at other military or civilian institutions. Those considered substandard were discharged. Concurrent with the closing of military schools, the leadership also began an effort to overcome another of the army's more serious problems. As General Lobov put it:

> The problem of improving the methodological expertise of commanders may thus be said to be the most acute problem that we face at the present time. The source of the problem is to be found in military educational institutions, where future officers undertake only minimal study of even the most elementary methodological procedures. It is in the military educational institutions that the improvement of work with cadres must begin, because it is here that the foundations are laid down for the future of the Army and the Navy.[25]

The military streamlined training procedures, and introduced computers and computer-simulated training devices. In addition, the leadership began to place greater emphasis on an officer's psychological, pedagogical, and leadership skills. The leadership also devoted considerable effort to training military academics on how to teach in a more creative fashion—a problem inherent in the Soviet educational system as a whole.[26]

Meanwhile, Gorbachev was pushing the military to democratize. At first glance, such an idea contradicts the military's command structure, but like glasnost it was a key part of Gorbachev's new approach to political life and as such could not be ignored by the armed forces. It put the generals in a quandary, however. As one participant in a roundtable put it, there was the problem of an autocratic, dictatorial commander. "One can scarcely deny the fact that the existing system of sole leadership has frequently been turned into a form of sole rule, and centralism has been turned into absolutism and a dictatorship of the commander." The alternative to such a situation was one in which the commander listened to the views of his subordinates.

> Generally speaking, I prefer to view democratization in a broader context: as the democratization of interpersonal relations, as a certain style of leadership which makes it possible to maximally increase the activeness of the army community and rely on it. In this context the role of the officer and relations in the officer corps increase substantially. Of great importance is the democratic procedure of conducting officer meetings, personnel meetings and courts of honor. Their status, incidently, could be changed making them more active and less dependent on the commander.

Or, as another participant put it, "In my understanding the degree of army democratization is determined by that social distance which exists between the officer and the soldier."[27]

The leadership tried to deal with this contradiction by introducing officer meetings, an idea taken from the Imperial Army. The purpose of such meetings was to provide officers with an opportunity to express their views, to bring their problems (e.g., housing, lack of promotions) before their colleagues in the hope that the officers' group as a whole could help resolve them. In any case, the leadership hoped that the meetings would provide the individual officer with an opportunity to air his concerns without fear of retribution from a senior officer.[28]

The problem with officer assemblies was that it was impossible to overcome the contradiction between a commander's authority and the open criticism of some of his actions that often occurred. For example, the commander presided at the meeting "on the basis of a recommendation from above." A report on the importance of honor was read, and the assembly adjourned without any discussion of the difficult issues it was set up to deal with.[29]

Despite efforts to improve the quality of the officer corps, it was obvious by the beginning of 1990 that events were overtaking the leadership's ability to deal with personnel issues. In May 1989, for example, the Supreme Soviet voted to discharge from the military some 175,000 students whose studies had been interrupted by military service. It was also decided not to draft students in the future. To make matters worse, Yazov faced serious opposition in being confirmed by the Supreme Soviet. It was only after Gorbachev himself intervened that he obtained the 256 votes necessary for confirmation. As it was, 77 deputies voted against him and another 66 abstained.[30]

Despite his problems, anyone reading what Yazov had to say on the

topic of personnel in mid-1989 would come away with the impression that
the army was making progress:

> [A] consistent and firm line is being pursued toward observance of the prin-
> ciples of social justice, and toward putting a resolute end to instances of
> protectionism. A regulation of assemblies of officers has been formulated,
> and permanently operating efficiency-report boards are active and are gath-
> ering experience. The central apparatus of the Ministry of Defense has been
> significantly cut back and rejuvenated and renewed by one-half. Direction
> and leadership of the troops has been assumed by new commanders-in-
> chief and commanders in the absolute majority of cases. A comprehensive
> system of measures is being implemented to increase the quality of the train-
> ing and education process in military educational institutions.[31]

Nevertheless, it was clear from some of the comments Yazov made in an
address to a meeting in December that problems remained. In addition to
his standard criticism that "a relatively significant number of officers are
displaying sluggishness and passiveness in respect to perestroyka," he
noted "the desire among young officers to leave the army." Yazov also complained about public criticism of the military; he maintained that "a certain proportion of officers are divorced from their subordinates," and criticized officer assemblies for not being "more equitable" in dealing with
personnel questions.

The situation was similar elsewhere. In spite of efforts to improve the
educational system, critics complained about the low quality of the students entering officers' schools. "And who do we have entering the military schools today? Among the graduate students there are many who
earned 'twos,' irresponsible people. And these are the people to whom we
will entrust the homeland's defense some day!"[32]

From the leadership's point of view, by the end of 1989 the situation was
getting out of control. Resistance to perestroyka continued, the content of
military doctrine remained vague, pressure for a professional military was
mounting, and the question of national armies was firmly on the negotiat-
ing table. To make things worse, the army was being utilized for internal
purposes, a development that was having a negative impact on morale.
This latter situation "hampered things and paralyzed initiative. The vacil-
lation associated with it hampered the military from acting in a clear-cut
manner according to regulations, according to orders, and ultimately, according to their duty."[33]

As they began to focus increasingly on how to maintain order in a disin-
tegrating military, Yazov and Moiseyev began to rely more and more on
the party-political apparatus. Regardless of how they felt about Communist ideology—or the competency of political officers—the fact was that
these structures were the only supra-ethnic, unifying, non-command ele-

ments left in the armed forces. If they collapsed or were withdrawn, the leadership might lose control. And the danger that the role played by these structures would be modified grew as criticism of them increased. In fact, Yazov utilized one of his rare references to the 1920s in an effort to defend their continued role in the armed forces:

> Together with the attacks on the party and the Army there is a massive offensive against Army and Navy political organs coordinated by destructive forces. What can be said to this? There have been wreckers in the past. The first attempts to wreck political organs were repulsed by V. I. Lenin and the Tenth Party Congress.[34]

Raising the qualitative level of the officer corps remained an important goal, but one that would have to be put aside for the time being—until the leadership was able to restore some order and predictability within the armed forces.

### The Attack on the Party and Political Organs

As was the case with a professional army and national formations, the fight to oust political structures from the Soviet armed forces was led by Lopatin and his military colleagues in the Supreme Soviet. In an interview in February 1990 Lopatin stated that

> The CPSU's role must be characterized by a switch from directly supplanting state organs in defense leadership to implementing its own policy through servicemen who are Communists. This requires a resolute reduction in the number and staff of political organs, the introduction of a system of appointment by election, and reorientation of work toward elevating the servicemen's status and protection.[35]

In reading Lopatin's statement, it is important to note that at this time he was *not* calling for the *total* removal of the party from the army. Rather he was pushing for a modification in the role played by both the political organs and the party. As he saw it, the former should take on more of an educational-morale role, while the latter would not be banned from the military, but would probably lose its status as the only party permitted to exist in the armed forces. Lopatin provided a few more details in an interview when he observed that "the inflated size of the political organs . . . interferes with their ability to fulfill their functions." For that reason he said they should be reduced. Furthermore, noting that he himself was a political officer and understood their conditions of work better than most people, Lopatin charged that many mid-level political officers "act as if nothing has changed, because that approach is comfortable to them." This situation must change. But the unanswered question was, how much should they change? How much authority should they give up?[36]

At about the same time Lopatin was giving his interview, a controversy was brewing over the decision of the plenum of the Central Committee, which was held February 5-7, to draft a platform for the Twenty-Eighth Party Congress. In looking at the role to be played by the party in the military, the plenum adopted a thesis which called for a renunciation of the CPSU's monopoly of power, guaranteed by Article 6 of the Soviet Constitution. The plenum also called for the creation of a new Soviet presidency. The change was ratified by the Third Congress of Peoples Deputies in March 1990. The latter also established the Presidency with Gorbachev as its first (and, it turned out, last) incumbent.

This was not good news for the generals. Moiseyev publicly opposed the removal of Article 6 from the constitution. After noting that neither he nor any other military deputies had been permitted to speak at the plenum, Moiseyev observed that "many questions . . . arise in connection with Article 6 of the USSR Constitution, and in particular with the role of political organizers in these circumstances." The ambiguity of the language included in the party platform was an obvious concern to the chief of staff. From his standpoint, the removal of the party from the army was only a matter of time. If the reformers were given the slightest opening, calls for a modification in the party's role could escalate into a push for its elimination.[37]

A political officer interviewed at the end of February provided an interesting alternative commentary on the role of the party in the military. In response to a question concerning his views on the Article 6 controversy, he replied that he "thought the article must be reviewed." This individual said he believed that the party must provide "a guiding and directing role not declaratory, but on the basis of some sort of legislative acts and its work in society, also including in the Armed Forces." He warned that the party and the political organs must remain in the military. "With all the critical attitude toward the party apparatus and toward the party leadership today, this apparatus is the only real structure of civilian authority and it is a consolidating organization." Then in a statement that could have just as easily been made by Moiseyev or Yazov, he added, "Any violent removal of this organization, in my view, will either result in chaos or in a military dictatorship. The transfer of power from the Party to the Councils is a matter of not only one day or even one year."[38]

The discussion about political organs and the party took place at a time when state organs were increasingly being separated from party structures. As a result, reformers argued that the emerging multiparty system demanded that the army be directed only by state legal institutions such as the Supreme Soviet, the Defense Council, and other governmental structures rather than the party. As one person explained the problem, "It is not very clear to me personally what role the political organs will play in a multiparty system, which we will inevitably have in the future." He suggested "establishing an institution of military psychologists to replace the present political corps. Their functions could probably include the development in personnel of such basic qualities as a sense of duty, honor and dignity."[39]

Lopatin picked up on this latter theme. "I would call the political organs of the future a 'human service.' I mean that they should be made up mainly of psychologists, sociologists, legal experts, psycho-physicists and teachers, most likely civilians." Turning to the function fulfilled by political officers at that time, Lopatin criticized them for engaging in what amounts to sloganeering.

> The answer we hear is that they indoctrinate the personnel (so that they do not drink, do not go AWOL, and so forth). For one thing, however, this is just talk. I repeat, their functions are more those of depersonalization and slogan-pumping, so that they have neither the strength nor the time for the actual indoctrinational—pedagogical—work. Nor do they always have the abilities.

Since he was a political officer himself, the generals found it difficult to criticize his observations.[40]

The leadership fought back by focusing on the need to improve the quality of the work performed by political structures. The commander of the Moscow Military District remarked that the role of the political organs needed to be "enhanced," while at the same time he admitted that there were shortcomings in their operation. We must be sure that "they are constantly and closely concerned with men's lives and can contribute to their civic and military training," he added.[41] Indeed, by this point both sides agreed that the role and function of the political organs had to be changed or "renewed," to use the commonly accepted term. To quote General Vladimirov, "It seems to me that the party organization and the party-political apparatus should be subjected to substantial renewal in the course of military reform." Among the specific changes he favored he listed having party leaders be elected to their posts (rather than being appointed by party officials in the military). In addition, Vladimirov reiterated the call for political officers to be trained in the social sciences. Another officer went so far as to suggest the need to create a Directorate of Education and Culture in the Ministry of Defense to take over the functions of the Main Political Directorate. Its tasks, according to this individual, (also a political officer) would be:

> . . . to educate servicemen in a spirit of Soviet patriotism and internationalism and propagandize civil law; make personnel aware of modern knowl-

edge and achievements of science in the sphere of psychology, political science, sociology and other social sciences, and the values of Soviet and world culture; protect servicemen's social and political rights; make contacts by Army and Navy units and formations with public organizations and the mass media; and work constantly and purposefully to elevate the prestige of service in the USSR Armed Forces.

The key factor missing from this and other proposals insofar as the generals were concerned was that they omitted discipline and inter-ethnic conflicts, both of which were topics political officers dealt with. Who would keep the military together if Gorbachev disbanded the party/political organs?[42]

One of the standard public arguments used by senior military officers in countering calls for a cutback, if not outright disbandment of the political structures, was to maintain that since it was impossible to depoliticize the armed forces these structures were critical. Colonel Ochirov, an influential conservative military officer, argued that "we cannot depoliticize the Armed Forces. Any military always finds itself under the direct political influence of the power that is established in the state."[43] One way out, suggested by two senior naval officers, was to have all officers participate in political work. As they put it, "The word 'political-worker' must be excluded from the military lexicon." Furthermore, they argued, political officers should be selected from regular officers who were then sent to political-military schools for short courses before engaging in political work.[44]

By May the battle lines between the reformers, led by Lopatin and those who supported him, and the military leadership were even more clearly drawn. In an interview published at the end of the month, Lopatin went beyond his earlier calls for renewal or modifications of the political organs to call for their complete removal. "It seems to me that it is necessary to eliminate party structures in the Army. The Armed Forces must serve the people, and not parties." And then he made a suggestion that was to have important long-term implications: "Various political organizations are cropping up everywhere now. Servicemen join them. If follows that the Army risks transforming itself into an arena of political passions. This is intolerable." The obvious implication was that military personnel should not belong to any political party. And if all parties were banned from the military, there would be no need for the Communist party or Communist-dominated political structures.[45]

By June, only a month prior to the Twenty-Eighth Party Congress, the generals' position had changed considerably from the previous year. Now individuals such as Yazov were more than ready to have the political organs take on educational/morale functions.

In the long term, clearly, the political organs must separate their educational and party functions and set up corresponding organizational struc-

> tures. . . . The work of the former is, I think, the political, military, moral, and legal education of military servicemen and organization of the work of social-psychological and juridical services, the mass media, and cultural enlightenment institutions.

Yazov was careful not to argue with the withdrawal of all party structures from the military. With regard to the latter, he said he favored the creation of "an All-Army Party Committee with the powers of a CPSU Central Committee" to organize political activities. He did not say how such a party structure would relate to other non-Communist party organizations that might want to organize in the armed forces, or what should be done with political officers, all of whom were party members.[46]

One of the most interesting discussions of depoliticization occurred at a roundtable just prior to the Twenty-Eighth Party Congress. One speaker equated depoliticization with "depatriotization," and argued that it was nothing but an attempt to "detach the army from politics." In fact, he maintained, "The protection of state interests is a matter of politics, and the Army at all times has been, is, and will be within the framework of politics." Another speaker argued that the idea of depoliticizing the military was aimed at replacing one party's influence on the military with that of another. In a certain sense, this discussion illustrated the dilemma in which many senior Soviet military officers found themselves. They had been imbued with the idea that the Communist party played the "leading role" in society for so many years that they now found it hard to conceive of a situation in which an apolitical military could exist. The idea that military officers could serve the state and the nation without being active in a party never occurred to them. Meanwhile, while officers such as Yazov and Moiseyev probably believed the rhetorical points made by the individuals cited above, their concern on the eve of the Twenty-Eighth Party Congress was more mundane; how to retain the party structures as a way of maintaining cohesion and discipline within the armed forces.[47]

### Preserving the Party Apparatus

The Twenty-Eighth Party Congress turned out to be a mixed blessing for the military leadership. On the one hand, Gorbachev did not discuss depoliticizing the armed forces. However, he did single out the military for special mention. "No one should have any doubt that the Army will continue to enjoy the support of the party. Special concern should be shown toward those who have devoted themselves to the services of the homeland in the armed forces."[48] Furthermore, the final resolution upheld the generals' position. "The congress is against the depoliticization of the Armed

Forces." On the other hand, it called for a restructuring of the political-party structures.

> The activity of the military-political bodies of the Army and Navy is structured in accordance with policy in the area of the country's defense and with the USSR Constitution, and it is aimed at the political, military, moral and legal education of servicemen in a spirit of loyalty to socialist ideas, of the unity of the Army and the people, patriotism, friendship among the Soviet peoples, internationalism, vigilance and constant readiness to defend the motherland.[49]

By making the work of these organs dependent on the constitution rather than party structures, the congress in effect approved the depoliticization of the party-political apparatus. The practical effect was that in a case when state and party orders clashed, the former would triumph. From the military leadership's standpoint, this meant that the generals would gain complete control over the political apparatus, a clear advantage. At the same time, the party's monopoly was now broken—at least in theory. Major changes were under way.[50]

Recognizing the threat to their continued existence, representatives of the party-political apparatus argued that they continued to perform an important function. To begin with, almost as soon as the Twenty-Eighth Party Congress concluded a new chief of the Main Political Directorate, Colonel General N. I. Shlyaga, was appointed. In his first interview he outlined his plans for restructuring the political organs. First, the military would establish new structures, which were subordinate to the military chain of command (thus removing the old system by which political organs came under the next higher political structure). Second, the leadership would revise training programs for political officers, to better acquaint students with subjects such as psychology and sociology. Third, the primary task for the political organs would be the "social protection of servicemen and their family members." Party organizations would thus become independent of the political organs (in the past the senior political officer often served as the party secretary). Finally, Shlyaga said election to party posts would be truly elective.

Turning to the issue of a multiparty system, Shlyaga denied that this meant the end of political-ideological institutions. "Their presence in our Army, as in other armies, including NATO armies, is conditioned by the need to conduct political educational work with personnel and to shape their high morale. And as long as this task exists, the institutions designed to resolve it will exist in the Army." Shlyaga left open the question of how a multiparty system would work in the armed forces, noting that the country did not yet have a law on political parties. It was clear, however, that he strongly opposed their presence in the armed forces. "The realization of the multiparty principle in the Army will hardly benefit its combat ability, organization, or discipline. A multiparty system means political rivalry. In the Army, whether we like it or not, it means disorder and ideological instability." Shlyaga could decry the possibility of a multiparty system in the armed forces all he wanted; it was becoming more of a reality every day—even if such parties were not formally recognized by the military leadership.[51]

For the next several months conservatives continued to argue against what they saw as an effort to break the power of the party-political apparatus. Akhromeyev attacked the idea of excluding the activity of the CPSU from the armed forces as an effort intended to "seriously weaken the moral-political potential and ultimately the might of the Soviet Armed Forces."[52] A month later Yazov argued that "there is no Army outside politics." Yazov said that political-educational structures would continue to instill a sense of devotion to the USSR in the hearts and minds of Soviet servicemen. Furthermore, acknowledging the existence of a multiparty system in the USSR, he maintained that political-ideological structures must, nevertheless, continue to exist in the military.

> That is why the elimination of the Army and Navy party organization which some people are trying to impose on us today means in fact simply eliminating the CPSU's influence. After all it is the CPSU which is today the only real political force in our Armed Forces. As of today, in the Army and Navy the party stratum is over 25 percent—that is, every fourth serviceman is a Communist. And the conversation of the CPSU's role and place in the Army and Navy as the vanguard, ruling party depends directly on the activeness, militancy, principledness, and effectiveness of the daily work of every party organization and every Communist.[53]

The outline for the party-political apparatus suggested by Shlyaga closely resembled the decree signed by Gorbachev on September 3, 1990. According to this decree, political organs were subordinate to governmental structures (in this case, the General Staff). Second, their primary function was the social protection of Soviet military personnel. Third, the connection between the political organs and the party organization was severed. The draft reform plan, submitted by the military leadership, was based on these three principles.

Instead of satisfying reformers, the new decree, together with the MOD's draft reform plan, only served to whet their appetites. On October 24, a *Novosti* writer argued that the decree was only "the first step toward reducing the Army's ideologization." In addition, he maintained that it was necessary to get rid of the old MPD and replace it with a Main Political Directorate of the Ministry of National Defense. He also called for reorganizing the Lenin Political-Military Academy and the reduction in the number of political officer schools, and noted that the presidential decree said nothing about the role of the CPSU party organization in the military.[54]

Meanwhile, the Lopatin plan called for the full-scale removal of any structures "reflecting the interests of particular political parties and organizations." The latter's concern was that unless such a step was taken the armed forces could turn into a debating society, which in the long run would destabilize the military and undermine the country's security.[55]

By the beginning of 1991 there were two clearly distinct approaches to dealing with the party-political apparatus. On the one hand were the reformers who wanted the role played by the political organs to be radically modified and the Communist party excluded from the armed forces. On the other side was the military leadership. The latter had succeeded in getting Gorbachev to sign a decree that went further than they might have preferred—by superficially removing the party's influence from the political organs. At the same time, even these reformed political organs would continue to be staffed by Communists, since all political officers were party members. Furthermore, the role to be played by the Communist party was sufficiently obfuscated to permit its continued functioning within the military. The generals hoped that, combined with the ban on other parties in the military, this arrangement would help bring some order and discipline to the Soviet Army. The new year, however, would turn out to be very unkind to the military leadership.

## Getting Rid of the Party in the Army

On January 11, Gorbachev signed a decree outlining the structure and organization as well as the tasks and activities of the political organs. This document made these structures directly subordinate to the Ministry of Defense. In noting their primary tasks, the document focused on areas such as discipline, education, morale, social justice, and work with civilian organizations. The document's failure to mention the Communist party, combined with the subordination of the political organs to the Ministry of Defense, removed any legal justification for a role by the party in these structures.[56] Shlyaga dealt with this issue in response to a question concerning the relationship between party organizations and the political organs. He stated that "relations between them will be built on a basis of business-like cooperation; however, the direct leadership of party work will fall to the relevant army party committee."[57] Or as he put it in another interview, "The placement of leading cadres ceases to be the prerogative of the CPSU Central Committee. Officials of military-political organs will be appointed by the USSR President, the USSR Defense Minister. . . ." Furthermore, he added, there would be a 37 percent reduction in the number of political officers.[58]

In the meantime, the role of the party organizations within the armed forces was redefined. As one officer put it,

> The reform of party structures will be carried out from top to bottom. Report-and-election and organizing meetings and party conferences will be held in January through May of 1991. These meetings and conferences will form new party bodies—party bureaus and committees and control commissions. The all-army party conference will be held in late March in Moscow and will elect the all-army party committee and control commission.[59]

The All-Party Conference held at the end of March reaffirmed the leading role of the party in military affairs. However, several days later both the military leadership and party officials received a major setback when the USSR Committee on Constitutional Compliance ruled that regulations requiring military authorities to obey directives issued by party organizations were unconstitutional. The committee charged that regulations governing the use of army units within the USSR had not been brought into conformity with changes in Article 6 of the constitution. The bottom line was that army commanders were subordinate only to the orders of governmental bodies.

The committee's specific focus was on two articles in the Soviet Army's regulations—articles 48 and 20. Article 48 stipulated that commanders must carry out orders issued by both the Soviet government and the Communist party. Article 20 obligated commanders to obey the orders of local party bodies. This ruling had important implications for the party-political apparatus, because the party remained a potent force within the armed forces. Cooperation between the political organs and the party organization now took place on an informal basis, and there was some question as to how successful the court would be in enforcing its decisions. The bottom line, however, was that the trend was now clearly away from the party's monopoly of power in the armed forces. Indeed, a statute was issued on July 20 banning political activity of any kind in RFSR state organizations. This meant that henceforth party organizations in the military, if located on Russian soil, would be illegal.[60]

For his part, Shlyaga concentrated on trying to breathe new life into the political organs and the party organization in accordance with the principles outlined in Gorbachev's January decree. He made speeches and wrote articles impressing on political officers the need for a less ideological approach to political affairs, while at the same time stressing the importance of patriotism and concern for the welfare of soldiers and sailors. Indeed, reading Shlyaga's speeches and articles, one comes away with the impression that his purpose was twofold. First, he was urging his fellow political officers to either shape up or be eliminated, while in his dealings with the civilian world, he was repeating the leadership's oft-noted theme; namely that without these structures, the army faced chaos.[61]

Shlyaga, Yazov, and Moiseyev's efforts notwithstanding, events soon took on a life of their own. The attempted coup in August, in which many representatives of the political organs played a supporting role, sounded the death knell for both these structures and the Communist party. From that point on, discussion centered primarily on how and in what way they should be disbanded. The process begun in 1917 had come full circle.

## Conclusion

Based on Kolkowicz's model, one would have expected a constant struggle between the military leadership and party representatives on this issue. While this might have been the case in the 1920s, it was certainly not characteristic of the Gorbachev period. To begin with, by this time the party-political organs had been co-opted by the military leadership. Political officers were military officers. Indeed, many of them had spent a number of years as regular officers before deciding to switch over to political work.

Second, while these structures may have fulfilled a control function on occasion, by this time their primary task was to support the military leadership in carrying out its functions. Thus their concern with discipline, social problems, combat efficiency, etc. In fact, it is clear from the Gorbachev period that during such a major period of change the generals themselves recognized that the political structures were critical. Without them, Yazov and Moiseyev correctly understood that the armed forces faced very serious problems in maintaining order and discipline.

Of all the areas discussed in this book, this is the one to which Odom's paradigm seems the most applicable and Kolkowicz's the least relevant. The line between the political apparatus and the military was blurred to the point that both consisted of military officers. After all, they were all party members. This finding on the role played by the political apparatus during the Gorbachev era also supports Colton's research. As he noted, with the exception of the 1920s, the two—political and regular military officers—worked together in most cases.

# III

## Toward a Russian Army

# *IX*

# THE POST-COUP PERIOD
# AND THE COMMONWEALTH
# OF INDEPENDENT STATES

> Everything to which I devoted my whole
> life to building is collapsing.
>
> Marshal Sergey Akhromeyev
> (in his suicide note)

## The Problem

In August 1991 a group of "conservatives" led a coup against the Gorbachev regime. Although ultimately unsuccessful, it destroyed the old Soviet system, including the army. As a consequence, Moscow's soldiers and politicians faced the tasks of designing a new type of civil-military relationship, as well as devising a new structure for the old army. With the increased pressure for sovereignty on the part of some of the fifteen republics, the Soviet Army could not retain its old configuration.

Initially, primary attention was focused on finding a confederative approach that would recognize the sovereignty of each state and retain some form of unified military structure. In the long run, this approach failed. In the meantime, the process was marked by considerable confusion over both the nature of a future armed forces and the correct relationship between military and civilian authorities.

## The Coup

It is one of the ironies of politics that it was the Soviet Army that saved the reform process, and it was the Soviet Army that in the end was destroyed by the events of August 1991. Once the majority of the military had decided *not* to support the coup, the take-over attempt was doomed. On the other hand, the fact that some segments of the military did support the coup raised fears in the minds of many, especially in the non-Russian republics, that if they did not create their own militaries there was a danger that the remnants of the Russian-dominated Soviet armed forces inevitably would become involved in politics, thereby threatening the stability of these newly independent regimes.

Opposition on the part of the military to the coup was widespread. Not only did the majority of senior officers not support Defense Minister Yazov and the Committee for the State of Emergency, most units also sided with the reformers.[1] In fact, one of the most notable aspects of the coup attempt was the "very limited support that the coup leadership . . . enjoyed among military units."[2] In retrospect, it is clear that without such support the coup never had a serious chance of success. As Gorbachev himself put it, "One of the major reasons for the coup failure is that those who usurped power failed to turn the Army against the people."[3] While favoring institutional autonomy, the military was opposed to becoming involved in politics.

Despite the support Yeltsin received from some of the country's key military leaders, it was clear that those who had backed the coup had to be purged. Clearly their values and those of the Gorbachev government were diametrically opposed. This led to an immediate personnel shake up. According to then Defense Minister Evgeniy Shaposhnikov, "seven deputy defense ministers, ten military district and fleet commanders, and eight commanders of central directorates were relieved of their posts for actions connected with the imposition of the state of emergency."[4] At the same time, Gorbachev issued a decree banning political activity by all parties and movements within the armed forces. Members of the military would henceforth be forced to engage in political activities outside of military bases and on their own time. As a result, while the loyalty of the officer corps increased, the sense of confusion on the part of the average officer concerning his role and the future of the armed forces also intensified.[5]

At the same time that the military was undergoing this shake-up, the various non-Russian republics—from Ukraine and the Transcaucasus to the Baltics—took steps to ensure that the Russian-dominated Soviet Army would not become a political threat. In the Baltics, for example, with their history of Soviet military and internal security involvement in putting down demonstrations in favor of national independence, there was a concern that such forces would act to keep these states Russian, either with Moscow's agreement or in some cases by acting on their own—perhaps in defense of ethnic Russians. As a consequence, pressures for the creation of nationally autonomous militaries or at least militias rose.

## The Commonwealth of Independent States

The combination of the shake-up of the top ranks of the military and the increasing pressure for national independence on the part of some of the fifteen republics raised serious questions about the future of what had been called the Soviet armed forces. Would there to be a Soviet military in the future? If not, what would replace it? What would be the relationship between the Russian military, which inevitably would be the largest formation and those which would be very small and militarily insignificant? How could one be sure that the military would remain subordinate to political officials in Moscow? The resolution of such questions would have a major impact on the nature of military doctrine as well as on the country's force structure. Almost all observers agreed Russia would continue to have a defensive doctrine—but again the old question, what would it mean in practice? Turning to personnel issues there remained the question of how professional should the military be? Who would pay for it? How large would it be? Should it have a reserve system? If so, what shape would it take?

Faced with these difficult questions, the generals adopted a relatively simple strategy: salvage as much as possible by building a new military, which to the maximum degree possible would resemble the old armed forces. One of General Shaposhnikov's first actions as the newly appointed minister of defense was to state publicly that he accepted the sovereignty of the various republics. As he put it, "I have a positive attitude toward the independence efforts of the Baltic republics, of Ukraine, and of Byelorussia. . . . If the parliaments of the republics decide they want to secede from the Union, they must be allowed to do so."[6] At the same time, efforts were under way to set up a military force that would maximize central control. Lobov, who had been appointed chief of the General Staff on August 23, argued that while each republic should be given greater autonomy, the center—meaning Moscow—had to coordinate the actions of all of the military forces. In essence this meant that the various republics would have responsibility for "cadre policy—preparing future soldiers and the necessary reserve, carrying out the draft, taking care of rear services for the troops on their territory, and taking an interest in the training and educational process in the units." Meanwhile, the General Staff—which would be under the supervision of a board made up of representatives from all of the republics—would have operational control over the various military units. As Lobov, who was Chief of the General Staff, stated, "The General Staff and the commanders on the republics' territories should, in my view, take charge of troop management, the planning and organization of operations and the combat training of troops, and the provision of modern combat hardware and armaments."[7]

In an effort to implement a plan along the lines suggested by Lobov, a meeting of the various republican defense ministers was held in Moscow on September 10. According to press reports, there was general agreement on the need for collective defense—with the Russians supporting a centralized system along the lines suggested by Lobov. The Russians created a state commission—under the USSR president—to formulate a proposal for a new defense arrangement among all of the republics.[8]

Despite the efforts of individuals such as Shaposhnikov and Lobov, it soon became clear that efforts to create unified armed forces were running into trouble. In an interview shortly after the second meeting of defense ministers, Shaposhnikov tried to put the best possible face on the situation by arguing that "the absolute majority of republican representatives who participated in our meeting yesterday are in favor of a single armed forces." However, when asked specifically about republics such as Ukraine, which did not attend the meeting, he admitted that problems existed.

> Well, to some degree Ukraine puts the issue like this—to some degree—and from a different point of view—with more independence—Moldova, Georgia, and in particular Azerbaijan put the issue like this: Give us weapons. Well, I think that as there have been no political decisions yet, I think that there is no point in talking about this topic yet.[9]

In fact, there were two concepts for the creation of a new military. To quote Colonel Ochirov, who participated in the October meetings,

> The first is for a unified Army and Navy. This idea is supported by Russia, Belorus, Kazakhstan, and Central Asia. The second is a military-political alliance, which could include the Transcaucasian republics, Moldova, and maybe, the Baltic republics with their armed forces for the purpose of common defense.[10]

For its part, Ukraine decided to proceed on its own. On October 7, the Presidium of Ukraine's Cabinet of Ministers approved a package of draft laws which envisaged the creation of a nuclear-free Ukraine with an army not to exceed 450,000 troops.[11] The next day, Major General K. P. Morozov was appointed defense minister. In one of his first interviews, Morozov noted that Ukraine had already agreed that "strategic forces" stationed in Ukraine were "means of collective defense not owned by Ukraine," but he also made it clear that there would be Ukrainian armed forces under Kiev's control.[12]

Throughout the remainder of 1991 and the first part of 1992, the process of national disintegration continued. Meanwhile, the Kremlin did its best to stem the tide of nationalism and separatism. In an interview in September, for example, Lobov suggested that rather than territorial or national guard units, Union troops should be stationed in the various republics and, in deference to local feelings, they should "wear national distinguishing insignia: emblems, symbols, and so on of the territory or republic on which they are deployed."[13] In an addition, he came up with a number of plans, all of which would have retained a considerable amount of central control over Union forces. He even published an article in which he utilized history to argue for the necessity of unified forces.[14]

But the pressure for national armies was unstoppable. According to press reports, Lobov's continued insistence on a unified army was one of the factors that led to his dismissal as chief of the General Staff in December.[15]

On December 8, the leaders of Russia, Ukraine, and Byelorus formally declared the end of the old Soviet Union and the creation of a Commonwealth of Independent States (CIS) to replace it. The treaty signed on December 21 formally establishing CIS limited itself to "keeping the military-strategic forces under a joint command and for keeping a single control over nuclear weapons." Toward that end, Shaposhnikov was appointed commander of the CIS forces, "pending a solution to the question of reforming the armed forces." The document also called for proposals to deal with military reform to be submitted for the consideration of the heads of state by December 30, 1991, and made clear that with the exception of Russia, the other states intended to gradually eliminate any nuclear weapons on their soil.[16]

Recognizing the inevitability of the push toward national formations, Russian president Yeltsin announced plans on December 29 to create a 30,000-40,000 member Russian national guard on the basis of Czarist traditions.[17] The Kremlin was careful not to establish its own Russian Army—as had happened in Ukraine. Taking such a step would have raised questions about the permanency of the CIS. If all of the former republics—including Russia—had their own independent militaries, why bother with a supranational command such as the CIS—especially once all of the nuclear weapons had been destroyed or removed to Russia? There was still hope that somehow a "joint" (*obyedinennyy*) armed forces could be maintained.[18]

The meeting of heads of the former republics in Minsk at the end of December was a further blow to the generals. In effect, the various states agreed at Minsk that they could decide on their own whether or not to remain a part of a collective defense system or "to set up their own armed forces."[19] As far as nuclear weapons were concerned, the meeting decided that nuclear forces would remain under CIS command. Turning to conventional forces, however, the situation was confused. To quote General Lobov, "As for conventional forces, the only thing that is now clear is that nothing is clear."[20] Ukrainian president Kravchuk probably said it best in discussing the agreement when he stated, "Shaposhnikov must head the unified strategic forces, whereas the Commonwealth states that do not intend to have their own armed forces can transfer their military apparatus to his command. But this will never happen with Ukraine."[21] In fact, as long as Kravchuk and others insisted on independent conventional forces, the chances that the CIS would become a coordinating device, even a loose one for non-nuclear forces, was very slim.

As might be expected, the uncertainty surrounding the future of a joint armed forces had a major impact on the other issues discussed in this study. To begin with, it was clear that whatever remained of the Soviet Army would be much smaller than it was prior to the coup. In October, for example, Shaposhnikov stated that the army would be cut to around three million in coming years, while First Deputy Defense Minister Pavel Grachev claimed that it would be down to around two million by 1994.[22] The problem was, how could one be certain of the final number when it was not clear how many of the fifteen republics would still be part of a joint armed forces?

The situation was similar when it came to the militia question. How could the General Staff intelligently address this issue absent a decision on the relationship between Moscow and the various republics, as well as some certainty over the nature of the national guard formations that were being set up? What kind of weapons would they have? How big would they be? There were some signs of interest in this topic, but they were few in number.[23]

Of all the issues facing the High Command, military doctrine was the most undefined, confused problem it was forced to deal with during the CIS interregnum. Without a clearly defined doctrine, Soviet military specialists felt naked. How could they design a force structure, battle plans, or even a personnel system if they did not have a doctrine to rely on? In fact, in the aftermath of the coup there was no clear understanding of what "defensive" doctrine meant, nor was there any sign that the issue would be resolved in the near future. The only thing that was clear was that major changes were in order. Shaposhnikov, for example, stated that "our doctrine currently does not fully accord with the new political realities." To develop a doctrine, Shaposhnikov noted, "we need to involve the republic defense committees."[24] The difficulty, however, was that the nature of the relationship between the republics and the center had still not been worked out. Lobov put the issue in focus in an interview in September when he stated that "as for the new Soviet military doctrine, it seems to me that discussion on this is something for the future."[25]

The future was not long in coming. Two types of articles began appearing. First, there were those published in the mass media. They stressed the need for a coherent military doctrine to guide military planning. For example, toward the end of December, Colonel Klimenko noted that the General Staff was aware of the problem and was busy developing a doctrine for the CIS states.[26] Suggestions that the General Staff was working on a new military doctrine, however, did not satisfy a number of senior military officers. Toward the end of January, three military theoreticians published another article in *Red Star* in which they argued that reform of the armed forces could not proceed until a doctrine was developed. As they put it, "a reform of the army is only possible on the basis of an officially accepted doctrine." To be meaningful, they maintained, such a doctrine must cover four points. First, who will do the defending? Second, who is our enemy? Third, with what will we defend ourselves? Fourth, how will we go about defending ourselves?[27] General Gareyev, one of the former Soviet Union's most renowned theorists, entered the fray in February. Writing in *Red Star*, he argued in favor of a unified doctrine that would help defend all of the states of the CIS. "Only after having exhausted all possibilities for establishing a defensive alliance at the CIS level," could the Russian Federation "undertake to establish its own Armed Forces."[28] Despite the efforts—and some might say wishful thinking—on the part of these former Soviet officers to create or force the creation of a military doctrine, the preconditions for such a situation were not present. General Skvortsov hit the nail on the head when he observed,

> There is no basic disagreement . . . that military doctrine should provide clear and precise answers. However, in my opinion, up to now the mechanism itself which is needed for its working out, its elaboration and confirmation, has not been clearly established, and this has had a negative effect on deciding many military-political problems in recent years.[29]

The fact was that as long as the CIS existed and could not agree on the missions or structure of an armed forces, there was little chance that a military doctrine could be constructed.

The military academic press contained a second approach to the issue. These articles could be separated into two categories. On the one hand, there were articles devoted to specifically operational issues.[30] In addition, there were the academically oriented articles that, even in the absence of agreement on the missions or structure of the armed forces, began to call for the use of history as a model in formulating doctrine.

In December General I. Vorobyev, a well-known military theorist, drew parallels in a *Red Star* article between the present situation and the military reforms of the nineteenth century and the 1920s. According to Vorobyev, the whole exercise in military reform would be a waste of time if the country did not first come up with a historically based military doctrine. "Contrary to historical experience, the present military reform, it seems to me, from the very beginning began to be conducted 'not from the right end'; that it is being carried out prior to the development of fundamental doctrinal positions on questions of defense structuring."[31] Three other theorists published articles in the January issue of *Voennaya mysl'* adopting the same line; to be effective and relevant, the new doctrine had to be understood in light of Russian and Soviet military history.[32] This was followed the next month by an article in the *Military Historical Journal* which argued that in instituting a reform, the country's leaders should look to the experience of the 1860s and 1870s.[33] A similar approach was adopted in March by an author who, in his attempt to determine the meaning and significance of nonoffensive defense, noted that such questions had already been discussed in the 1920s. To summarize, Russian writers felt that the key to the future of a Russian force structure was a historically based military doctrine, and were concerned that so little progress had been seen to this point in developing such a doctrine.[34]

Unlike the confusion that surrounded doctrine at this time, the leadership was making considerable progress on professionalizing the armed forces. Compulsory military service was reduced to 18 months, and it became clear that even the generals now supported a gradual transition to a professional military. As Shaposhnikov himself stated in an interview shortly after the aborted coup,

> I think that, at the present time, we have reached a state in which our army must be professional. That is a very serious process, very lengthy, very responsible. One cannot simply say it will be professional from tomorrow onward. No. There will be some transitional period, in which I think there will exist both a compulsory service . . . and elements of a professional service.[35]

In effect, what Shaposhnikov was talking about was the implementation of the contract system that had been discussed prior to the coup. The difference was that, unlike Yazov, Shaposhnikov was committed to the eventual elimination of conscription.[36] The important aspect of this decision, insofar as civil-military relations were concerned, was that it was being left up to the generals to implement the program.

In addition to the dismissal of officers who had supported the coup as part of the force reduction, large numbers of senior officers were forcibly retired to make way for younger ones. As Shaposhnikov put it, "the retirement of a large number of over-age officers will make it possible for us to appoint an even greater number of young officers and generals to their posts, ones who are capable of tackling the tasks *in today's conditions.*"[37]

Of even greater importance than the retirement of the old guard was the further depoliticization and departization of the armed forces. As mentioned earlier, soon after the coup was put down two decrees were issued: one banning activity by any political party in the military, and the other abolishing all military-political organs in the armed forces. Unlike during the Gorbachev period, the military leadership was solidly behind these steps. Shaposhnikov stated that "there should be no parties in the military," and

Grachev argued that "under a multiparty system, the army should do its main constitutional duty—defend the motherland."[38]

General Volkogonov, the former political officer who had been fired from his post as director of the Institute of Military History because of his "liberal" views, was appointed to head a commission to reorganize the former political departments in the military. The commission decided to make lower-level political officers assistants for educational and personnel work, to close large numbers of political officer schools, to restructure the Political-Military Academy (now called the Humanitarian Academy of the Armed Forces), and to forcibly retire large numbers of senior officers. According to Volkogonov, "320 of the 345 generals formerly serving in the MPD (Main Political Directorate) will be discharged, while the corps of political officers as a whole will be cut by 40-45 percent. The number of military-political academies is also slated to be cut drastically."[39]

Despite the progress made in creating a professional military and depoliticizing the armed forces, centripetal forces continued to grow. In January 1992 a dispute over ownership of the Black Sea Fleet began to exacerbate Russian-Ukrainian relations.[40] Kiev ordered the fleet and all ground forces stationed in the republic to swear an oath of loyalty to Ukraine. Some Russians agreed to take the oath, while others, led by Admiral Kasatonov, commander of the Black Sea Fleet, flatly refused. Then a dispute erupted over what was strategic and what was not—with the Russians attempting to make almost everything strategic, including in one case construction units, while the Ukrainians tried to minimize the list of such weapons and troops. The result was a further heightening of tensions, leading to a refusal by Kasatonov to meet with Ukrainian officials and Kiev's refusal to deliver supplies to the fleet. Numerous discussions were held between the two sides, but without success.

In February the eleven heads of state held another summit in Minsk at which they were once again unable to resolve the basic military issues. The CIS leaders could not agree on such issues as how to define the powers of CIS bodies in defense matters, the nature of the High Command of the armed forces, and the principles for manning the armed forces. They also found it impossible to agree on how to divide up weapons systems.[41] As a consequence, Shaposhnikov reportedly stated, "I think in the end our army will split into national armies."[42]

Another summit was held in Kiev in March. If anything, the Kiev summit deepened differences between the Russians and the Ukrainians. Kravchuk publicly attacked Russia for failing to solve any military or political problems. In addition he observed that "the Commonwealth is doomed. . . . The situation among Commonwealth countries has been considerably aggravated since the first meeting in Minsk."[43] As a consequence, it should come as no surprise that the eleven leaders failed to come to grips with the most pressing and serious military issues. The agreement was limited to providing for the material and technical support of the military, and the appointment of a number of senior generals to positions of authority within the CIS.

With the writing on the wall, Yeltsin took a step both he and the generals had tried to avoid; on March 16 he ordered the creation of a Russian Defense Ministry. While technically subordinate to the CIS High Command, the establishment of this ministry marked the effective end of the CIS. It would remain in existence until all of the nuclear weapons had been destroyed or removed to Russian soil, and there would be efforts to get it involved in peacekeeping operations, but its limited effectiveness as a military institution was at an end. As one press report noted, "Many observers here and abroad now describe the CIS as little more than a divorce court, a forum to ease the breakup of the Soviet and Russian empires."[44] In any case, the existence of the Ministry of Defense meant that the Russians now could get about the business of constructing an army of their own.[45]

## Conclusion

The unsuccessful effort to create effective CIS forces meant that little of a concrete nature was done to come up with a meaningful military doctrine. Lacking that, and a predictable military budget, there was not much the Kremlin's senior generals and admirals could do when it came to constructing a realistic force structure. They not only lacked any idea of how large a military force they would have at their disposal—and the degree of authority they would exercise over these forces—but there was a serious question of to whom they were subordinated.

In the beginning, for example, Marshal Shaposhnikov was named defense minister—a position that was primarily symbolic in nature, and one that had as its primary function trying to find a way to salvage as much as possible from the former Soviet Army by convincing the other republics to cooperate with the Kremlin in the military area. Meanwhile, General Lobov as chief of the General Staff focused on more technical matters—i.e., how to design a force structure that would be militarily effective. The two eventually clashed and Lobov was removed.

To make matters worse, Shaposhnikov was appointed commander of the CIS forces in December 1991. Russia lacked a defense minister, although for practical purposes Grachev was fulfilling that role. Nevertheless, there was considerable confusion within military ranks over who was in charge. In time, it became obvious that Grachev was *primus inter pares*. But the main point was that it was almost impossible to develop a stable form of civil-military relations at a time of such flux and change. If anything counted, it was personal relationships between the senior military officers and the political leadership.

From the standpoint of the models utilized in this book, it is important to emphasize that they were constructed to deal with the Soviet period. Hence, expecting them to fit with the post-Communist era would be asking too much. Nevertheless, there are some aspects of them which demonstrate just how difficult it is to apply any model to a period of rapid change such as the collapse of the USSR. For example, was the military a unitary actor? In this case it clearly was not. Consequently, any model similar to that proposed by Kolkowicz, which presupposed that the armed forces were a cohesive, integrated political actor would have little relevance for our understanding of the events of the CIS period. In this sense, it would also be hard to apply a model similar to that suggested by Colton to this period. How does one go about charting increases or decreases in military participation at a time when it is difficult to determine what is military and what is not? At that point in time, I doubt that the generals themselves knew what their core interests were. Their world was changing so fast that what seemed like a core interest yesterday was quickly overtaken by events.

The same is true of a model like that proposed by Odom. His assumption that the political and military leadership had a unitary relationship obviously had no relevance here—the party ideology that he considered so important no longer played a key role. The point is that while the undifferentiated nature of the lines separating the civilian from the military worlds was so marked that it was difficult to draw lines between the civilian and military worlds, there were clearly military officers who viewed themselves first and foremost as professionals—not as merely executants for the political leadership.

Indeed, this period was one of reaction on the part of both civilian and military leaders. Insofar as the relationship between civilian and military officials was concerned, it was as confused as the rest of Russian society.

# X

## THE RUSSIAN ARMY FACES AN UNCERTAIN FUTURE

> The plans that we had . . . for reforming the
> army need to be rethought because of the
> financing which has been cut to below the
> limit at which we can exist, because of the
> shortage of personnel and because of the
> changes in the domestic political and foreign
> situation and other changes.
>
> Defense Minister Pavel Grachev

Since its creation in 1992, the Russian military has faced three major problems, all of which have major implications for the evolution of civil-military relations. First, the armed forces are operating within a political system in which there is no basic agreement on the nature of the policy process. During the Soviet period, the generals knew who was in charge. They may not always have liked the decisions that Gorbachev made, and they did not always support his policies. But there was one central point in the political system to which they could turn for support. Now, however, there is no clear center and the political situation borders on chaotic. In fact, the efforts of Russian military officers often appear aimed primarily at creating a stable political environment in which the armed forces can function.

Second, the military is no longer the apolitical institution that it was during the Soviet regime. In the past, the generals saw themselves as public servants, and while they would fight as hard as any other military for resources, the overwhelming majority were not active participants in the political process. Indeed, one of the strongest impressions one had in talking with numerous Soviet officers was how clearly they drew a line between military issues (which they were often prepared to discuss) and political questions (to which they almost always replied, "I don't know, that is a political question").[1] The situation has changed. A large number of Russian military officers are now very political—they comment openly on political matters and are more than prepared to disagree publicly with their military superiors, as well as with politicians—including the president himself. In a nutshell, the military has become politicized as it never was in the past.[2]

A third major factor with an impact on civil-military relations has been the increasing disintegration of the armed forces as an institution. From almost any perspective, the armed forces are no longer a viable military organization. The army's ability to carry out military operations, as demonstrated in Chechnya, is suspect—not only because of a lack of funds, which has led to all kinds of problems, but also because of the deep splits that have developed within the armed forces. Different parts of the military are constantly being drawn into the political process—on different sides of an issue. In short, there are serious questions about the military's reliability in a crisis situation. It has lost most of the institutional coherence and stability it had in the early 1990s.

While the three problems noted above have important implications for the future of civil-military relations in Russia, the last two are most important from the standpoint of the armed forces. There is little the military can do about the country's political decision-making process. On the other hand, the armed forces must resolve the questions of politicization and institutional coherence if the army is to become a viable, effective institution.

## The Russian Army Is Established

On April 4, 1992, Yeltsin signed an instruction creating a state commission, headed by General Dmitri Volkogonov, which was charged with defining the status and creating the basis on which the new Russian Army would be established.[3] The commission recommended that the new Defense Ministry be based on the existing General Staff and Defense Ministry and that a treaty on collective security be concluded with the other countries of the CIS. Such an agreement was signed on May 15.[4]

From a conceptual standpoint, the Russian military was at ground zero. It had been on the verge of collapse. The armed forces still had vast supplies of armaments and fairly modern weapons, not to mention a competent officer corps. Nevertheless, a major reorganization was necessary if the army was not to disintegrate.[5] The general's task was to begin rebuilding what many considered one of the most influential and cohesive institutions in the USSR. Until the military began to reemerge as a viable institution with clearly defined lines of authority, civil-military relations would not be a major concern for the simple reason that Moscow's political authorities were dealing with individual generals—not the armed forces as an influential interest group.

On May 7, Yeltsin signed a decree formally establishing the Russian

Army. General Pavel Grachev was appointed defense minister. He subsequently announced that a draft of the country's new military doctrine would be submitted to Yeltsin by July 1, 1992, and a concept for the Russian Army by September 1. He further stated that the reform process in the Russian Army would go through three stages; the first foresaw the creation of the Russian Defense Ministry. The second, which would take two to three years, involved the removal of all Russian troops from former socialist countries. The third envisaged the withdrawal of all Russian troops from former Soviet republics and the reduction of the armed forces to 1.5 million troops.[6] Despite some civilian involvement on the periphery, the generals were in charge of drawing up the new doctrine.

The draft doctrine published in May 1992 contained a number of new twists. First, it noted that because modern war was so destructive it would have catastrophic consequences. Second, it omitted any reference to the class struggle. Finally, the Russians used the concept of national security, which in essence meant that military doctrine was a part of national security.

Compared with the draft military doctrine of December 1990, it was obvious that the new document contained many assumptions from the old period—not surprising considering the fact that many of the men who drew up the new document came from the "old school," educated in the spirit of the Cold War. For example, the document viewed the world through the eyes of ideological hostility, although this was implicit rather than explicit. It also persisted in arguing a worst-case analysis. In addition, when it came to details its vagueness meant that the military would have to spend considerable time on working out specifics.[7]

A second document on military doctrine was issued in November 1993.[8] In comparison with the 1992 draft document, this one was equally ambiguous but less ideological. The document made it clear that Russia's military doctrine was primarily defensive; unlike the 1992 document it argued that the most important threats to Russia's security were local conflicts and the spread of nuclear and other weapons of mass destruction. It emphasized that military means would always take a back seat to political and diplomatic efforts in the resolution of conflicts. Nuclear forces were viewed primarily as a deterrent and special mention was made of the importance of participation in peacekeeping operations.[9]

Insofar as the implications of this doctrine for force structure were concerned, Yeltsin probably said it best when he observed that the main components of the new doctrine were: flexible organization; compactness; mobility; highly technical weaponry; and highly professional personnel.[10] However, there were two problems with this doctrine insofar as the generals were concerned. To begin with, it did little more than provide a broad guideline on how to proceed with force planning. What, for example, was meant by flexibility? Or compactness? Or even mobility? To be sure, one could assume that the new Russian Army would be smaller, less rigid in structure, and more mobile—but what would that mean in practice? Much would depend on the military's ability to convince an increasingly skeptical political leadership of the need to allocate scarce resources to maintaining the country's armed forces, as well as on Grachev's success in rebuilding a sense of institutional coherence within the military as a whole.

### Politicizing the Military

When Grachev took over as defense minister, the level of politicization within the military was already alarmingly high. This was a consequence of developments during the Gorbachev period, when reform-minded military officers had broken ranks with the generals and led the fight for change under the old regime. The problem was that many of them resisted reintegration into the military bureaucracy after the USSR collapsed. They had tasted power and enjoyed it. They wanted to continue to play a political role in spite of the fact that they wore uniforms.

Grachev's response was to force these politicized officers to choose between a military and a political career. If they selected the former, they would have to conform to military discipline. A case in point was Vladimir Lopatin, a major assigned to the Naval Air Forces who served as a deputy in the Supreme Soviet. During the Gorbachev era, he played a key role in undermining the authority of the country's senior officers. From Grachev's standpoint, Lopatin may have been useful previously, but as long as he was in a position to openly advocate policies that differed from those of the High Command, he threatened to violate military discipline. As a consequence, Grachev forced him to make a choice between careers:

> No one drove Lopatin out of the army. After his deputy's powers came to an end he, like many other army representatives in the USSR Supreme Soviet, was offered several posts to choose from in accordance with his education and experience of service. I remind you that the major was a political worker and chief of a university of Marxism-Leninism.
>
> Many officers who are deputies continued their service but he refused. He wanted to stay in Moscow, as close as possible to the White House and the government, in the apartment allocated to him for the duration, and to travel abroad on official trips. . . . Well, a free man gets what he wants. That is his choice. What has the army to do with it?[11]

For his part, Yeltsin made no effort to protect officers like Lopatin from military discipline. As far as he was concerned, this was a military problem—how could the military function effectively if every officer was free to advocate his own defense policy? By mid-1993 the "military reformers" had disappeared as a political force.[12]

For a while, it appeared that Grachev would be successful in keeping the military out of politics. Despite the battle raging between the president and the Duma over their relative powers, Grachev worked hard to keep the military from becoming involved in the political struggle. He pushed the de-partization of the army and stated on more than one occasion that "I will not permit the incidents that occurred previously and were permitted. . . . I am talking about drawing the armed forces into a battle against their own people."[13] Or as he put it on another occasion, "Any attempts to appeal to the Armed Forces in the political struggle are criminal and are fraught with the most serious consequences."[14]

Despite Grachev's efforts, the military became directly involved in the political struggle in October 1993. At that time, a coup was launched against the Yeltsin government by members of the Russian Parliament, led by Ruslan Khasbulatov and Vice President Aleksandr Rutskoi. The key question during this incident, marked by conflict on the streets of Moscow between pro- and anti-Yeltsin forces, was what would the Russian Army do? In 1991 it had remained neutral, with the result that the coup aimed at Gorbachev failed. Now, however, a number of observers believed that if the army remained on the sidelines, the Yeltsin government would fall.

Yeltsin ordered the army to attack the coup plotters, who were assembled in the White House, the building from which he had led resistance against the coup in 1991. Grachev believed that the military had no choice but to storm the White House. If they had not, the ultra-conservatives would have taken over the country.[15] Thus, in the end, Yeltsin's order was obeyed, the army opened fire on the rebels, and the coup collapsed.

This use of military force for internal political purposes signaled a major break with the past. During the Soviet period, the military had carefully avoided crossing the line between political advocacy and direct involvement in the political struggle. Even in the case of Marshal Zhukov during the mid-1950s the military as an institution was not a factor. Rather, the affair played out primarily a personality clash between Khrushchev and Zhukov.[16]

With the storming of the White House, however, the civil-military equation changed. The army became a direct participant in the political process. Indeed, the new military doctrine adopted in November 1993 made provision for the army to become involved in internal politics "to remove the effects of internal social, ecological, and other upheavals," and also to provide support to border and Internal Security Ministry troops.[17]

A clear sign of how politicized the military became in the aftermath of the storming of the White House was the increasingly outspoken attitude adopted by a number of senior officers. General Aleksandr Lebed, for example, openly criticized Grachev. Toward the end of 1994, he observed that "Grachev must go, if only to safeguard the honor of the Army and its morale."[18]

When the Kremlin ordered Russian troops to invade the break-away province of Chechnya in late 1994, the splits in the military became even more evident. General Eduard Vorobyev refused to lead his troops into battle because he believed his soldiers were inadequately trained. General Ivan Babichev, who was in command of three divisions, stopped his unit's advance on Grozny because he did not believe it was appropriate "to use tanks against the people."[19]

To make matters worse, senior Russian military officers repeatedly criticized Yeltsin and Grachev for their decision to send troops into Chechnya. Lebed, for example, claimed not only that the Chechnya operation was a model of incompetency, but also maintained that it resolved nothing. In fact, Lebed went beyond the Chechnya campaign and argued that what happened in 1991 with the collapse of communism "was no new Russian Revolution. The regime, which was rotten through and through, simply collapsed like an old wooden hut. However, nothing changed."[20] Two other senior military officers, Generals Boris Gromov and Georgiy Kondratyev, also openly criticized the use of Russian troops in Chechnya.[21]

In fact, splits in the Russian military were not limited to a few well-known generals. A survey of Russian officers conducted in late 1994 showed that "less than one in five of mid-level and senior officers expressed trust in Defense Minister Grachev; over half express mistrust." Both Lebed and Gromov were rated much higher.[22] A survey conducted in late 1995 indicated continued dissatisfaction in the ranks of the military. According to this poll of servicemen in the Leningrad Military District, the most popular military leaders included both Lebed and Gromov, among others. Almost 90 percent of the respondents expressed dissatisfaction with their material support. "And behind this entire 'screw-up,' as one polled officer put it, they see the figures of Yeltsin, Chernomyrdin and Grachev."[23]

This sense of dissatisfaction and confusion over the nature of the policy-making process was one of the primary factors behind the strong military support given to the extreme nationalist Vladimir Zhirinovskiy in the 1993 elections. Many military men were simply tired of being misused by politicians and were sympathetic to his simple-minded answers to complex questions. Frustration with the policy process was also one of the reasons for the military's decision to run a slate of military candidates in the 1995 Duma election campaign.[24] Grachev's idea that those military candidates who were elected would represent military interests and thereby create a more stable and predictable as well as friendly environment seemed far-fetched. Not only was there the example of rebels like Lopatin and his colleagues during the Soviet period, the military was even more politicized and split internally at this point than it had been at that time. Those elected might decide to go their own way when it came to advocating various policies—thereby further fractionalizing and politicizing the military.

The bottom line as the military moved into the latter part of the 1990s was that it was not only politicized, but that there were serious questions about its loyalty to the political system itself. This was evident from a 1995 survey of some 600 field-grade Russian officers. This survey showed that questions concerning the army's reliability were pervasive throughout the officer corps.[25] According to this survey, "officers were particularly adamant in their opposition to using the military to quell a separatist rebellion in one of the regions of the Russian Federation." Only 7 percent supported such an action. In addition, when asked if they would follow Moscow's orders if one of the republics declared independence, 39 percent "admitted that they probably or definitely would *not* follow orders."[26]

While it is impossible to foretell the future, from the perspective of the mid-1990s, it is clear that Grachev's successor has his work cut out. Rebuilding military cohesion will be a long-term undertaking.

## A Disintegrating Military?

If the splits within the military and questions about its reliability were not serious enough, by the end of 1995 the material and organizational situation within the armed forces was also critical. In fact, the miserable showing by the Russian Army in Chechnya was indicative of just how far the level of combat readiness within the armed forces had fallen.

In addition to the effects of increasing politicization, the main reason for the decline of the Russian Army over the 1992-1996 period was budgetary. Without money it was impossible to field a modern combat-ready military. Indeed, it was difficult for Western observers to understand just how bad the financial situation was in the Russian military. It led to what could aptly be called a fiscal disaster. As Grachev noted in 1994:

> Our budget for 1994 was corrected in an attempt to tackle, first, the social problems of 120,000 homeless officers, thousands of people without jobs. This will consume 56 percent of our resources. At the same time, we cannot reduce beyond a certain point cash expenditures on technical and military modernization. But unless the Finance Ministry yields, we will be able to purchase only 25 percent of the weapons planned, which means the collapse of the military industries, and an army of unemployed men.[27]

In one sense, the situation has worsened. The portion of the military budget allocated to social programs increased to 60 percent by 1995, thus leaving even less money available for such items as operations and maintenance and the purchase of new weapons.[28]

In spite of all the efforts to improve social services within the military, the problems continued to grow. For example, because of the withdrawal of hundreds of thousands of troops from Eastern Europe and parts of the former Soviet Union (now outside of Russia), housing continued to be a major problem. To cite Grachev:

> The entire budget allocated for us for social needs for 1992 was all spent on the construction of housing for servicemen. We have now given up the construction and upgrading of various facilities like testing grounds, tank training areas, and training grounds, into which, incidently, the main amounts in the budget once went. We have put all this into construction.[29]

During 1993 about 30 billion rubles were earmarked for salaries and benefits to servicemen and civilian employees. This meant, Grachev noted, that there were "no funds for combat and operational training of troops, upkeep of equipment, command posts, air bases, etc." In fact, as a result of the fiscal problems encountered from 1993 to 1995, the military continued to fall far short of its housing construction plan. According to the 1993-1995 plan, the military was to build 220,000 apartments. However, the necessary funds were not provided. Noted Grachev, "In 1993 it was 83 percent financed, last year 46 percent and in the first six months of this year we received from the Finance Ministry only 26 percent of the funds allocated for this year." The result: less than half of the promised 220,000 apartments were built by the end of 1995.

The financial situation within the armed forces was so bad by the middle of 1995 that the Defense Ministry owed "more than 9 billion rubles" to its creditors.[30] A Defense Ministry spokesman claimed in August that the MOD's debt for food was 715 billion rubles. In fact, to that point, the military had been utilizing its emergency reserve to feed its troops. But by August that was gone. The military was in a position where it could not even feed its troops.[31] A senior officer warned that if additional funds were not forthcoming, it would become necessary to evacuate personnel from remote, but key posts in the Far East.[32] The war in Chechnya further worsened the military's financial situation. According to a senior officer, this conflict had cost the military 1.9 trillion rubles by August 1995, more than its entire budget for that fiscal year.[33]

The precarious financial situation also had a major impact on the weapons acquisition process. In fact, Russian arms procurement fell by more than 80 percent between 1991 and 1994.[34] The impact of this cutback was nothing short of disastrous when it came to maintaining a modern military. For example, in 1991 the military ordered and received 585 combat aircraft. In 1995, by contrast, the MOD ordered only *two* combat aircraft—and this for a country that only a few years earlier was considered a superpower.[35] The same was true with regard to the other services.

The situation was particularly bleak in the Navy. As one senior naval officer put it,

> In the past two years no new construction work has been completed apart
> from a single submarine. Everything that we accepted in 1993-1994 was
> laid down previously. Last year we received 10 out of 26 ships, and 16
> have been carried over to this year. By all accounts, they will be partially
> carried over to 1995 owing to lack of funding.[36]

The situation continued to worsen. Of the five destroyers under construction in Baltiysk in 1995, Russian officers expected only two would be completed. The remainder would be cut up for scrap.[37]

This down-turn in acquisitions meant that the country's arsenal would deteriorate to the point where almost all of the weapons systems would soon be obsolete. For example, Russian sources claimed that in most of the developed countries, between 60 and 80 percent of all weapons were new; in Russia the figure was 30 percent. The same source claimed that if this situation remained unchanged, by the year 2005 the military would have only 5-7 percent new weapons. "Gradually we will slide toward the category of armies of third-world countries."[38] The lack of funds for new weapons also undermined Russia's ability to earn hard cash through weapons sales abroad. Who would purchase weapons that were 10-15 years old?[39]

The maintenance of existing weapons systems also posed serious problems. One of Yeltsin's aides complained in September 1995 that only 20 percent of the country's tanks were functioning and added that the supply of combat aircraft had fallen twenty times.[40] Another source claimed in December that only 50 percent of the Russian Air Force's aircraft were serviceable because of a lack of money to pay for repairs and spare parts.[41]

During its first four years, the Russian military relied on reserves to compensate for the cutback in weapons acquisitions. By the beginning of 1996 the situation had deteriorated to the point that senior officers complained that there were almost no reserves. The problem was especially acute in the areas of air defense and aviation.[42]

What forces the generals had at their disposal were stretched thin by the need to participate in peacekeeping operations, both abroad (in the former Yugoslavia) and in what the Russians call the "Near Abroad" (areas formally part of the USSR which have a significant Russian population). In addition to the crisis in Chechnya, there were other flash points. In the early 1990s Grachev was locked in a bitter struggle with General Lebed over the status of the 14th Army. The ostensible purpose of this division, located on the eastern bank of Dniester River in what is now Moldova, was to maintain peace between ethnic Russians and Moldovans in the region. Apart from the personal battle between Lebed and Grachev, this situation highlighted the difficulty of maintaining peace and stability in former parts of the Soviet Union with significant Russians populations. Given the persistence of tensions such as those in Moldova, as well as repeated outbreaks of violence in the Transcaucasus and Central Asia—not to mention the dispatch of Russian troops to the former Yugoslavia—there is no doubt that that provision of peacekeeping forces will remain a major preoccupation of the military leadership for some time to come. Indeed, in light of the increased need for peacekeeping forces around the world, as well as the inclination to deploy them in the "Near Abroad," the struggle to accomplish these tasks under an austerity budget could become the Russian Army's primary focus for the next several years.

Further adding to the military's woes have been personnel problems, aggravated by the lack of funds. To begin with, draft dodging has been a major headache. In 1992, for example, only 7 percent of those called to the colors reported for induction.[43] Only every tenth or eleventh young man entered military service. In practical terms this meant that by June 1992 most military units were only 60 percent manned. By September it was claimed that the level was down to 50 percent and in October former vice-president Rutskoi stated that some units had only 8-10 percent of the personnel they needed.[44] In fact, the situation was so bad in the Moscow Military District that "officers and warrant officers are forced to pull guard duty on military installations in order to relieve the extreme loads on extended service personnel."[45]

By the end of 1995 the personnel situation had improved somewhat—the ground forces were manned at between 65 to 68 percent, while the other services were at levels varying from 70 to 75 percent.[46] Draft dodging, however, remained a problem—during 1994 800 young men were prosecuted for refusing military service, while 23,000 conscripts failed to show up for induction.[47]

Part of the reason for the army's improved ability to fill its ranks was the High Command's decision to place greater reliance on volunteers, who agreed to serve for extended periods in exchange for special training and pay. This process began on December 1, 1992, and was directed at soldiers with certain specialties, who were offered two- and three-year contracts. By the beginning of April 1993, the number of contract soldiers stood at 45,000.[48] By the first part of June the number was up to 110,000 and in January 1994 Yeltsin signed a decree authorizing the recruitment of an additional 150,000 contract service personnel.[49] This meant that by 1995 up to 30 percent of the army's non-officer component were serving under contract. However, between 1993 and the end of 1995 about 50,000 contract servicemen resigned.[50]

The reason for these resignations was not hard to understand. The average monthly wage in Russia in September 1995 was 550,000 rubles, whereas a contract serviceman earned 278,000 rubles (including supplements). The subsistence minimum per person in Russia was 300,000 rubles—and in some regions two or three times that.[51] Not surprisingly, large numbers of contract personnel left the military. The personnel problems confronting Moscow's military decision makers involved officers as well as enlisted personnel. Not only were officers resigning their commissions at an alarming rate, competition among applicants for officers' schools had declined from 1.9 applicants per space in 1989 to 1.35 in 1993.[52] In spite of some improvements in the manning system, significant shortages remained in the first part of 1996. In late 1995, for example, one source reported that there were only 60 contract servicemen, 116 women, and 12 conscripts in a regiment located on the remote peninsula of Kamchatka.[53]

The army's personnel problems involved more than recruiting enough bodies to fill its ranks. Indeed, there were problems in almost every area, especially training. Take, for example, a pilot's flying time. In May 1993 Grachev observed that "whereas in 1991 pilots were getting in only 20-25 hours flying time, and some only 12, the average is already 30-35 hours—practically 50 percent of the norm."[54] Vorobyev, on the other hand, noted at the end of 1995 that

> Pilots are now doing only one-tenth of the statutory flying hours. You do not have the full complement of air defense fighters on alert duty. Aviation school students cannot go into the forces, because they cannot fly. Some 80 per cent of airfields lack fuel stocks for current needs. The Army is doing practically no combat training and exercises are performed entirely on maps.[55]

In practice, this meant that pilots were still flying only 30-35 hours a year instead of the 100-120 necessary for them to retain proficiency. Shortages were endemic throughout the Russian armed forces. For example, during 1994 70 percent of all military exercises and maneuvers had to be scrapped because of a lack of fuel.[56]

The budgetary situation was so bad that on several occasions civilian companies (e.g., power stations) cut off electricity to military installations—at one time threatening the country's primary means of deterrence—the Strategic Rocket Forces. In another case the commander of the Northern Fleet sent in armed sailors to force the engineer on duty at the Kola power plant to restore power to a submarine base, thereby averting a potential nuclear disaster. Incidents of this type led Prime Minister Viktor Chernomyrdin to sign a resolution on September 23, 1995, banning civilian plants from turning off power to military facilities—regardless of how much money the latter owed.[57] To make matters worse, younger officers were resigning at a rapid rate, to the point where "more than 28 percent . . . have served in their positions for less than a year."[58] As long as this high rate of turnover among officers continued, it would be impossible to improve the combat-readiness of the army.

Corruption, crime, and discipline were also major headaches for the generals. By the end of 1992, for example, it was obvious that a number of Russian officers were engaged in the illegal sale of Russian military assets. This forced Grachev to clamp down. As he put it,

> I do not deny the fact that there are abuses in the army. . . . Some 459 men have been dismissed from the army for abuses in the sphere of commerce banned by my edict and in trade. Some 3,711 have been disciplined while criminal charges have been brought against 31 men, especially major leaders, including in the Western Group of Forces.
>
> Here we have dismissed 106 men for various transgressions while 559 have been disciplined and criminal charges have been brought against 10.[59]

The situation with regard to discipline among the troops was no better. One source reported that during the first eight months of 1992 there were 854 crimes (versus 498 in the previous year) recorded in military units in the Moscow area alone.

> The number of premeditated homicides increased (by 71.4 percent; 26 servicemen have already died), as well as rapes (up by 60 percent), thefts of state property (by 125 percent) and personal property (by 300 percent), and crimes associated with the acquisition, possession, and sale of narcotic substances (by 80 percent).[60]

As Yeltsin himself put it, "The embezzlement of weapons and military hardware with a view to their resale has acquired menacing proportions."[61]

By the end of 1995 the situation with regard to discipline appeared to be improving somewhat. In discussing the state of discipline in the Russian Army Grachev noted proudly:

> According to data from the first ten months of this year, there were no incidents of crime in 40 percent of regiments, in 36 percent of ships of first class, in 51 percent of ships of second class, or in 30 percent of educational institutions.[62]

It is important to emphasize that Grachev was speaking of crimes and not merely disciplinary violations. Nevertheless, this marked an improvement over the situation that existed a few years earlier.

One of the worst aspects of the discipline problem was the incidence of suicide. According to Grachev, "suicides make up six to eight percent of the overall number of deaths."[63] By 1993 "practically every fourth death in the armed forces is the result of suicide," and it was reported in July that 140 servicemen committed suicide in the first six months of 1994.[64] Another source reported that almost 3,000 servicemen had died as a result of "criminal incidents" during 1994.[65]

Problems with training and discipline led to a number of serious accidents during the Russian Army's first four years. In early 1993, for example, several Russian sailors starved to death on a remote island base in the Far East. Grachev reacted by firing the commander of the Pacific Fleet. In early 1994 two Russian nuclear submarines from the Northern Fleet collided. Soon afterward civilian authorities in the Far East charged that the navy was not complying with safety standards for storing nuclear waste—resulting in a rise in radiation levels in the region. Two months later the Russian media reported that a private on guard at a strategic missile site had gone berserk and killed two fellow servicemen and wounded two others.[66]

These incidents were a harbinger of a worse disaster. On May 14, 1993, an ammunition depot in the Far East blew up. According to Russian authorities, the blast had the explosive power of a nuclear bomb. The area where it occurred was described as looking "like a war zone." An investigation showed that it was the result of "negligence and lax discipline on the part of the guards."[67] As a result, the new Pacific Fleet commander, Admiral Georgiy Gurinov, was relieved of his command.

The situation remained very serious at the beginning of 1996. Russian sources reported that soon hundreds of Russian submarines would be tied up at various inlets along the Kola coast waiting for the navy's shipyards to remove their nuclear cores. By the year 2000 approximately 100 nuclear submarines would have to be decommissioned and have their cores removed. Slowly rusting, each of these submarines was a potential Chernobyl. The reason: insufficient funds to dismantle them safely.[68]

Given all of these problems, it was not surprising that morale in the armed forces dropped significantly. According to one source "more than 95,000 [young officers] left the armed forces in 1990-1993 because of the disorder and loss of prestige in the military."[69] Indeed, how could morale be expected to be anything but low? Officers were openly attacked by civilians, almost no one wanted to attend an officers' school, and many in the country seized on the problems in the military to argue that it should be severely cut.

All indications are that the situation with regard to junior officers is not improving. Speaking at the end of 1995, Grachev noted that, as a result of a shortage of funds, "It was forecast that we might lose 2,500 officers this year in the rank of lieutenant to captain, but as many as 11,000 have already gone."[70] As any general knows, without good junior officers the military will not only be starved of its future leaders, it will lose those who are closest to the troops and provide their main day-to-day guidance.

Meanwhile, Russian forces were being down-sized throughout this period—although at a much slower rate than the resignations of junior officers would suggest. For example, on May 1, 1992, just prior to the creation of the Russian military, the armed forces were allocated 2.6 million slots. By June 1994 General Kolesnikov, the chief of the General Staff, reported that the number of slots had been decreased to 2.2 million. By mid-1994, some estimates placed the overall number of troops as low as 1.5 million.[71] Meanwhile, the size of the Russian military apears to have stabilized. As Grachev put it, "we have reduced the Army by 1,220,000 men over three years. This is nearly one-half of its entire strength. As of 1 January 1996 we will have 1,700,000 men in the Army."

### Optimism for the Future?

While it would be premature to suggest that the military's situation will improve in the future, there are some signs that when it comes to the budget the worst may be over. To begin with, General Vasily Vorobyev was dismissed from his post as head of the Defense Ministry's Main Department for Military Budget and Finance in late 1995. The reason: "crude financial violations and the unsatisfactory implementation of a decision of the Russian Federation Government." The message to those dealing with financial matters within the armed forces was clear—either you make efficient use of the money allocated to the armed forces or you will be looking for a new job.[72]

At the time Vorobyev was fired, the first deputy finance minister declared, first, that the state had been able to finance 95 percent of the military budget for 1995 and second, that by the end of the year the government would pay off all of the debts incurred by the military.[73]

If the government follows through, this latest action would mark an important breakthrough for the financing of the Russian Army. At the same time, comments by Grachev indicated that major differences remained between the Defense and Finance Ministries. Grachev stated in November 1995 that the military estimated that it needed 134 trillion rubles to "finance the minimum expenditures related to the maintenance of the Army's battleworthiness." In fact, he maintained, the Finance Ministry was proposing a budget of only 77.1 trillion rubles.[74] The battle over the budget and all that it signifies for the future of the Russian military will continue. Its resolution will have a major impact on what kind of armed forces Moscow fields in the year 2000.

The important point to keep in mind is that during the Russian armed forces' first four years of existence, everything was in constant flux. For most of this time the generals themselves did not know how much money they would have in their budgets. They also had no way to predict how many troops would be under their command, nor what kind of weapons systems they would have at their disposal. Such a situation made rational planning impossible.

## Conclusion

The Russian Army of the mid 1990s was a far cry from the Soviet Army that preceded it. There was no doubt that Grachev and his colleagues had done their best to try to restore cohesion and institutional identity. In spite of these efforts, however, the Russian armed forces remained beset by numerous problems. Budgetary allocations were insufficient, discipline was poor, training was far below Soviet—not to mention Western—standards, the army's equipment and weapons systems were aging, little effort was being made to keep up with modern technological developments, and the military's resources were being stretched beyond the breaking point to fulfill its peacekeeping missions. In short, the new Russian Army bore little resemblance to its predecessor—an army that struck fear in the hearts of most of the rest of the world.

From the standpoint of civil-military relations, however, this was an important period of change. When Grachev became defense minister, civil-military relations were primarily a reflection of his personal relationship with Yeltsin. Grachev's primary task was to stem the tide of institutional disintegration while he—and the political leadership—worked to bring about a smooth transition to a more democratic form of civil-military relations. Despite the best efforts of all concerned, the attempt failed. Disagreement about the national security decision-making process, the politicization of the military, and the loss of institutional cohesion meant that by the end of 1995 Grachev was presiding over an organization that was in worse shape than the one he inherited in 1992.

The average Russian soldier was not certain whom to obey in a crisis—the Duma, the president—or perhaps a retired, but highly popular general such as Aleksandr Lebed. Second, Grachev—or his successor—could not be certain that the troops that served under him would obey him in a crisis. The polling data cited above could not help but give him and his colleagues cause for alarm. What if another crisis occurred in the near future and he again ordered his troops into action? What would they do? No one could be certain.

The Russian military has continued to deteriorate in the post-Soviet period. In 1992 the military had vast reserves and a cadre of well-trained apolitical professionals. By 1996 so many officers and servicemen had left the military that questions were inevitably raised about the qualifications of those who staffed its ranks. Similarly, the equipment was in such bad shape that the Russian Army had to cannibalize units elsewhere in the country in order to mount a campaign against rebels in Chechnya. Even if the country's president could count on the military in a crisis, serious questions remained about the army's ability to carry out the tasks assigned to it.

In the context of the post-Soviet period, all three of the models utilized in this book came up short. Odom's paradigm assumed a unity of values on the part of both civilian and military leaders. With the politicization of the military, any semblance of a unified set of values was gone. Furthermore, there existed no party ideology to help unify them.

Kolkowicz's model also was inapplicable because the military was anything but a unified, cohesive institution. Any idea that all military officers thought alike was destroyed by the very different reactions to the changing situation in Russia on the part of officers such as Grachev, Lebed, and Gromov, to name only a few. If nothing else, their reactions to the events in Chechnya destroyed whatever was left of the myth of a unified military outlook. Grachev certainly saw himself as a military officer and went along with the use of force in Chechnya. But this was a case of a single individual, who surrounded himself with like-minded officers. Others were prepared not only to disagree with their senior officer, but to oppose him openly as well.

Colton's model didn't fit precisely because it assumed a dichotomy between civilians and military officers. How could the military leadership protect what it considered core interests when Grachev and his colleagues were not even sure of what these interests were? Sometimes they seemed to shift daily. Nonetheless, Colton's model retains some utility because of its emphasis on participation. If one were to chart military participation in politics from 1992 to 1996 it would be obvious that officers were trying to gain greater control over a variety of areas. How successful they will be in the long run, however, is anyone's guess.

# CONCLUSION

> If . . . a model departs too far from reality, it
> becomes useless.
>
> Kenneth Waltz

It is now time to return to the question raised at the beginning of this study:
how useful were the three models—of Kolkowicz, Odom, and Colton—in
analyzing civil-military relations in Russia and the former Soviet Union?

## Assumptions

As I see it, the three models rely to varying degrees on five different assumptions to explain why the relationship between the military and civilian worlds is either conflictual or cooperative.

*The Military as Distinct Institution.* The first assumption concerns the
degree to which the military is a cohesive, highly integrated institution. If
the military is a separate, cohesive organization, then there is a much greater
probability that military officers will consider themselves different from
civilians. The line separating the military from the civilian worlds will be
clear. On one side of the line will be the military, while on the other will be
found the outsiders—the civilians.

Assuming the military perceives itself to be a separate caste, isolated
from the rest of the world with a distinctive outlook on issues, then the
chances for a conflictual civil-military relationship increase. To varying
degrees, both the Kolkowicz and Colton models argued that this was the
case. Both saw the military and civilian worlds as distinct. They differed in
that Kolkowicz believed that this situation inevitably led to conflict, while
Colton believed that would be the case only if the military's core values
were threatened. Odom, on the other hand, believed that the idea of distinct civilian worlds was exaggerated. Military officers, he argued, were
becoming more like managers; i.e., the line separating the civilian and military worlds was blurring. As a consequence, he believed the relationship
was more cooperative than conflictual.

This study suggests that there is evidence to support both sides on this issue. Certainly, if one looks at the actions of Yazov and Moiseyev, they believed there was a military approach to national security issues. This is one of the reasons why Yazov—and Grachev after him—was so upset with the "heretical" actions of Lopatin and Lobov. The latter were breaking ranks with the military on issues of key importance to the future of the armed forces. Who did they think they were?

At the same time, it is important to recognize that the existence of military officers like Lopatin and Lobov indicated that the Soviet military was far from a monolithic organization when it came to military questions. Discipline may have been strict in the Soviet military, but it did not prevent officers from holding opinions at variance with those of the army's senior officers. In fact, as the discussion on a professional military showed, even senior officers were prepared to differ with Yazov and Moiseyev on issues of considerable importance.

The situation is not likely to change in the near future. Current indications are that the willingness of officers to express views not shared by the military leadership is even more pronounced than it was in the Soviet Army. This was certainly the case with former General Aleksandr Lebed, who was more than willing to continue to disagree publicly with the views and policies of the country's defense minister right up until his retirement. If there was a "military approach" to Russia's problems and Lebed did not agree with it, he was certainly prepared to speak out.

In this sense Odom was right—there was an overlap between the civilian and military worlds. The situation is not as simplistic as Kolkowicz's model suggested. At the same time, it would be wrong to argue that a "military mind" does not exist. The vast majority of Russian and Soviet military officers tend to be uncomfortable around civilians, and appear to support whatever policy the generals advocate. In addition, the generals have not been bashful about expressing their preference for policies that often differ from those advocated by the civilian leadership. The problem comes in trying to make this characteristic into an analytical concept. As Odom argued, the line between a military and a non-military mind is too blurred for the concept to be of much use.

*Resenting Outside Interference?* A second assumption—especially prominent in the Kolkowicz and Colton models—was the idea that because they identified themselves as a separate group, military officers resented interference by civilians in their internal affairs. If this was the case, then one could expect a conflictual relationship between military and civilian authorities whenever the latter attempted to dictate internal military policy.

The record indicates that there is considerable evidence to support this assumption. It did not matter which of the three periods we analyzed. During the 1920s regular military officers, e.g., Svechin and his colleagues, certainly resented interference by political officials in areas such as military doctrine. The result, as one might expect, was a conflictual relationship. Similarly, during the Gorbachev period, Yazov and Moiseyev were not happy about efforts by civilians to dictate military doctrine, not to mention greater reliance on a militia concept, or the departization of the military. The same was true of the post-Communist era. Grachev clearly opposed the extreme budgetary cutbacks that the military has been saddled with. How could Yeltsin expect him to field a military capable of protecting the country when his budget was being cut drastically?

The problem, however, is to determine which issues will cause the military to be most resistant to outside interference. Colton's answer was that the military would become a problem once "core interests" were threatened. The problem with this approach—aside from his loose definition of "core interests"—is that looking at both the Communist and the post-Communist period, it would be hard to argue that the military's core values have not been trampled on. A lack of housing, no pay, a drop in prestige, unexpected retirements, etc., have devastated morale. Yet the Colton model suggested that the military would have revolted by this point. In fact, they have gone along with civilian authority, in spite of considerable grumbling. Indeed, if it were not for the positions adopted by the armed forces, ultra-conservatives would have triumphed in 1991 and in 1993.

A similar problem arises with Odom's paradigm. His basic assumption was that there would never be a case in which conflict characterized the relationship because of the shared values between the military officers and civilian authorities. The problem was that his model was based on the Stalinist period, and in that context he was correct—the military went along with whatever Stalin wanted.

A look at the three time periods covered by this study suggests that the Stalinist period may have been unique. Soviet military officers were more than ready to stand up to civilians when the occasion required it. Senior military officers consistently argued, fought, and openly disagreed with civilian authorities on a whole variety of issues. Odom's suggestion that military officers viewed themselves as "executants" of policy, and not its framers, is not verified by the facts presented in this study.

*Ideology.* A key assumption underlying Odom's model was that since both civilian and military authorities shared the same ideology (value system) during the Soviet period, civil-military relations were bound to be more cooperative than conflictual. While one could argue that the lack of a value consensus helped explain the conflictual relationship during the early 1920s, it did little to help us understand why the relationship was so conflictual during the Gorbachev era.

By the time Gorbachev came to power, Marxism-Leninism had been the dominant ideology for more than sixty years. The officer corps had long ago accepted Marxism-Leninism—the main reason why political officers lost their primary role as political watchdogs. In addition, the vast majority of military officers were party members.

Party membership, however, was not sufficient to cause military officers to become "executants." The minute Gorbachev and his allies began their attempt to undermine military autonomy in order to change the direction in which the country was heading, the generals started fighting back. In the end, they lost the battle as well as the war. But the important point is that they fought, every step of the way, in an effort to maintain military autonomy regardless of whether it involved doctrine, force structure, or the role played by the party in military affairs. The same is true of post-Communist affairs. The generals continue to resist interference in their internal affairs—even though they claim to be committed to the democratic political system. In short, this study suggests that even when both civilian and military authorities share a set of values, it is no guarantee that the relationship will be harmonious.

*External Control Devices.* If one assumes that the military resents interference in its internal affairs, that it is jealous of its autonomy, and that civilian authorities cannot live with an autonomous military, then it should come as no surprise that civilians came up with control devices aimed at undermining the military's autonomy. For Kolkowicz this was the primary purpose for the political organs.

Looking at the early 1920s, one could make a convincing case that the political structures (e.g., especially the commissar) were primarily intended to be control devices. The Bolsheviks considered regular officers—most of whom had served in the Imperial Army—unreliable. Since the military situation demanded their presence, the Bolsheviks' only alternative was to create supervisory organs. Those who were unreliable were eliminated or at least dismissed from the service.

The problem, however, was that this was only a temporary interlude in the evolution of the Soviet Army. By the end of the 1920s, the situation had changed significantly. Political commissars had become political officers. They worked for regular officers, and while the former could cause problems for the latter, by and large they worked together. In short, Odom and Colton were right: the relationship was far more harmonious during the late 1920s than Kolkowicz's model hypothesized.

By the time of the Gorbachev era, the military leadership had co-opted the political structures in the armed forces. Furthermore, they carried out a critical function: helping maintain unity and morale at a time when ethnic nationalism was on the rise. Indeed, one of the last things one would expect, relying on the Kolkowicz model, is what actually happened—the generals fighting hard to keep the political apparatus. Had these structures been primarily aimed at controlling the actions of regular officers at this time, I doubt that Yazov and Moiseyev would have struggled so hard to keep them. The Gorbachev period was one of conflict between civilian and military authorities over questions concerning doctrine, personnel, and force structure—but not because of the existence of political structures. It is also noteworthy that when Gorbachev sought to undermine the autonomy of the military he did not use the political structures. Rather, he relied on a group of individuals made up of both civilians and officers. He knew only too well who controlled the military's political structures.

*Technical Expertise.* One of the most dubious assumptions underlying the Kolkowicz model was that as technology became more complex, the military would become even more jealous of its bureaucratic prerogative and would fight even harder for its organizational autonomy. After all, since the weapons were so complex, how could civilians hope to understand military affairs? This was a matter best left to experts, and professional military officers were the experts.

In fact, there did not appear to be much of a correlation between advanced technology and conflict between civilians and the military. During the 1920s, for example, conflict was only remotely related to technology. Svechin certainly felt that his knowledge of military affairs set him apart from amateur soldiers such as Voroshilov or Frunze. Nevertheless, this was not the main source of conflict. Instead, it resulted from a lack of value consensus on the part of military and civilian elites. Svechin and others disagreed on some technical questions, but what really upset them was the Bolsheviks' tendency to politicize all aspects of military affairs. This, as Svechin correctly foresaw, led to distortions in everything from doctrine to force structure.

The situation was similar under Gorbachev. The military objected to his interference in key areas not because military systems were becoming more complex, although concerns over technology certain influenced the attitude of the military leadership toward national armies and a militia. The main problem was that by trying to make doctrine more benign, less threatening, the generals believed that Gorbachev was upsetting a whole carefully thought-out, well-constructed, military structure. This included not only force structure, but operational plans and training procedures as well. True, Yazov and Moiseyev complained about amateurs interfering in areas they did not understand, but the same complaints could be found in the 1920s—a period when technology was far less sophisticated. Indeed, if technology was a major concern one would have expected the generals to lobby for a professional military—after all, professional soldiers can be better trained to handle complex technology than is the case with conscripts.

The situation has been the same in the post-Communist era. The generals object to much of what civilians have to say. But those objections stem not so much from a concern for modern technology—in many respects the Russian Army is less technological now than its predecessor was—but because they are faced with an impossible situation, and they fear that meddling by civilians will only make a bad situation worse.

Looking back at these assumptions, it is clear that none of them hold up in all instances when compared with the three time periods analyzed in this study. In some instances the military showed an amazingly high degree of cohesion and corporateness—for example, during the early stages of the battle with Gorbachev over doctrine or the discussions concerning territorial/national forces. In other cases, however, the opposite was the case. The generals were all over the map when it came to a professional military, and a few military officers led the charge against the High Command for a militia.

The same is true for opposition to outside interference in military affairs. It was moderately strong during the 1920s and especially strong during the Gorbachev period—at least on the part of Yazov and Moiseyev. However, it was weaker during the post-Communist era.

The other three assumptions seldom had any explanatory relevance. Ideology was only a factor in the 1920s when there was a difference in values. By the Gorbachev era, values had been so deeply internalized that they played only a minor role. Bureaucratic concerns and personalities were more important. The same is true of external control devices. They were important in the 1920s, but they were soon absorbed into the military structure. Finally, the question of increased technology never played the role in civil-military relations that Kolkowicz assumed it would.

This then leaves open the question, why conflict or cooperation? If one cannot make analytically precise assumptions (e.g., that the former Soviet/ Russian military is a corporate entity with a corporate identity), then what factors give rise to conflict or cooperation between military and civilian authorities?

## Why Conflict/Cooperation?

If one accepts the suggestion that none of the three models discussed above was particularly helpful in understanding the full range of civil-military relations in Russia or the Soviet Union, the question then arises, where do we go from here? To begin with, I believe that this study provides us with a number of insights that could be the starting point for further analyses.

*A Lack of Value Congruence.* While one can question the utility of Odom's suggestion that value congruence in a totalitarian system leads to a cooperative relationship between civilian and military authorities, it is clear that the opposite greatly increases the chances of conflict. For example, in my view the main reason for the conflictual relationship during the 1920s can be traced back to the lack of a value consensus on the part of civilian and military authorities. To be sure, the battle between Trotsky and Stalin played an important role. Nevertheless, the Bolsheviks introduced political commissars to deal with a real and serious problem—how to ensure the loyalty of officers from the old army.

Yeltsin confronted a similar problem. He was part of a new, more democratic polity. Many Russian military officers, who were socialized under the old Communist system, did not share the same "democratic" values as the country's new civilian leaders. Rather than introducing a whole structure to ensure loyalty, Yeltsin and his colleagues decided to keep the bulk of the Russian officer corps in tact. Yeltsin and Grachev forced those who indicated that they were not prepared to live with the new system to retire or resign. The bottom line was that to remain in the military, an officer had to convince his superiors that he was committed to the new polity. The difference with the 1920s in the post-Communist era was that he was assumed to be loyal until his actions proved differently.

*Periods of Change.* The common variable uniting all three periods has been change. The 1920s represented systemic change, while the 1980s were characterized by a more gradualistic modification in the nature of civil-military relations. The post-Gorbachev period is in many ways similar to the 1920s. The major difference, however, is that the new system is built upon the old; in contrast to the 1920s, the leadership did not carry out a full-scale purge of the existing officer corps.

The key point here is that in every instance in which change occurred, conflict in civil-military relations was the result. This is not surprising. The military is as much a part of society as any other group. It will experience—and in many cases resist—change just like other institutions. In the 1920s it was the introduction of a new political system. In the 1980s it involved a new approach to national security affairs. In the 1990s we see the emergence of another new polity. In short, it seems safe to say that based on the Russian and Soviet cases, change produces conflict (of varying degrees) in civil-military relations.

*Issues.* One of the most useful aspects of Colton's paradigm was his focus on issues. There was some of the interest group model in his approach (i.e., conflict results when core interests are involved), but by and large his effort to isolate key issues was helpful. For example, having examined the Soviet and Russian experiences, it is clear that the key question in civil-military relations revolves around military doctrine. The reason is simple: in the Russian system it determines all of the other aspects of military structure and policy—from force structure to personnel. There is no question that other issues, such as the budget, play a key role. This is certainly the most important equation in Russian civil-military relations as this book goes to press. Nevertheless, the budget is important from a military standpoint because it provides the necessary predictability on which to build a military doctrine. If the money is not available, it will be impossible to construct a meaningful doctrine—a problem for any Russian defense minister—or if a doctrine exists, it will not be possible to implement it. Furthermore, given Russian military culture, doctrine is the key factor in training, exercises, and combat.

The point I am making is that if one wants to understand the nature of the civil-military relationship in this polity, the most important issue will be doctrine. Everything else branches out from it. This is not to suggest that other issues are not important—for example, peacekeeping. But even when it comes to peacekeeping, the key question in a Russian military officer's mind is, what is our doctrine? Once he understands it, he can begin to plan for the various contingencies. Without a doctrine, most Russian military officers feel lost.

*Personalities.* While the role of personalities does not play a significant role in any of the three models analyzed in this book, this review suggests that it is much more important than many specialists acknowledge. While the roles played by Stalin and Trotsky were obvious to everyone, Svechin was not as well known. Yet during the 1980s it became obvious that he was one of the major actors—through his books and articles. Similarly, one could argue that individuals like Kokoshin, Larionov, Lobov, Lopatin, Grachev, and Lebed also played key roles. What I am suggesting is that in addition to key issues, in the Russian case the analyst is well advised to ask the age-old question "kto kogo" (who against whom). Institutions play an important role in Russian politics, but my experience suggests that personalities have a major impact on how these institutions act. For example, what if the assertive and efficient Ogarkov had been chief of staff instead of Moiseyev? What if instead of Yazov the Defense Ministry had been led by a strong and competent leader like Grechko?

*So What?* By now it should be obvious to the reader that based on the Russian/Soviet case, I do not believe that any single model will suffice in explaining civil-military relations in that country at this time. There are a number of reasons for this conclusion.

First, there are simply too many variables involved for one paradigm to include them all. We can look at issues or personalities, or the nature of the institutions, and come up with a general impression, but we are not likely to be able to construct a model that will satisfactorily explain this complex reality—a part of it perhaps, but not the overall nature of the relationship.

Second, the problem of constructing a model is made more difficult in a situation characterized by a high rate of change. In the 1920s, the Soviets themselves did not know where they were going. They were making decisions on the spur of the moment. Lacking any kind of rationality in the system—other than an effort to enforce a value congruence on the officer corps—it would have been hard for anyone to come up with a generalizable proposition. During the Gorbachev period, when change was slower, more gradual, one might have expected one of the models discussed in this study to be useful. All were to some degree, but none would have explained the situation under Gorbachev—both the high degree of military autonomy and the combative way in which the military responded.

Third, one of the reasons two of these models found it so difficult to deal with change (Colton's paradigm is an exception) was that they took a given point in time and universalized it. Odom took the totalitarian model—which was an ideal type of the Stalinist period—and then assumed it was indicative of the entire Soviet period. One has the impression that Kolkowicz did much the same. Civil-military relations during the 1920s were based on conflict, so that must be the case during all periods. In this sense, Colton's model is superior to the others because by focusing on participation by the military in a variety of areas it was sensitive to change.

Fourth, one of the problems for all Western analysts is the tendency to take models based on the Western experience and then to superimpose them on other polities and cultures. This is what Kolkowicz did in part. Drawing on a study of the American military he assumed that increased technology would lead to greater demands for institutional autonomy. Not surprisingly, that was exactly what he found. Such a practice reminds one of what Marxists have done for years. If reality did not suit them, they would come up with a paradigm that would change reality by selectively collecting data to prove their basic hypothesis.

### Modeling the Post-Soviet Experience

What then do we do when it comes to the post-Soviet era? Is there a model currently available to help explain the evolving nature of civil-military relations? In this writer's opinion, the answer is no, for two reasons.

The first problem with modeling civil-military relations in Russia at present is that the military is not a cohesive institution. Russia is suffering from a lack of "institutionalization," to use Huntington's phrase.[1] Few of Russia's institutions have the stability, and especially the coherence, that Huntington noted was a prerequisite for institutionalization. This is certainly true of the military, as this study has shown. In fact, seen from the perspective of early 1996, the level of institutionalization within the military is lower than it was in 1992. This may change in four or five years, but for the present the generals have a long way to go in their effort to rebuild the Russian military. The low state of discipline, the lack of a meaningful training program, the obsolescence of most of its equipment, the absence of a minimally adequate budget—even questions about the willingness of the armed forces as a whole to obey orders given by Grachev's successors—raise serious questions about both the military and political effectiveness of this institution.

Until the military begins to reflect more closely the level of institutionalization present in the Soviet armed forces of a decade ago, civil-military relations will remain in flux. At this point, the political leadership is less concerned about the military as an institution than it is with the ability of Grachev's successors to maintain control of the armed forces—or a significant segment of it—during a crisis situation. Assuming the political leadership is able to co-opt the country's senior military officers, will the average soldier or sailor follow their orders in the event of societal chaos? Twenty years ago this would not have been a major concern. By the end of the Gorbachev period, the military as an institution had deteriorated to the point where the loyalty and cohesion of the armed forces were open to question. In the post-Soviet period, problems with political reliability worsened significantly.

A second problem facing anyone trying to model the current situation in Russia is the lack of societal agreement on the country's political-military decision-making process. If one thing is clear it is that there is little or no agreement among Russian voters on what kind of "democratic" political system they should have. What if the Communists take over? Russia's Communists are not the Social Democrats that the East European Communists have become. What if a nationalist group comes to power? The main point is that the process of national security decision-making in Russia is far from determined. Until it is, it will be difficult to construct any kind of conceptual framework.

Once the political process has stabilized and the level of institutionalization has increased (by which for the military I mean that it begins to take on more of the characteristics of corporateness and cohesion of the old Soviet military), it will be possible to again ask the old question: Should the military be looked upon as a tightly structured institution along the lines of Kolkowicz's model or should it be seen as one characterized by greater permeability? Any model that is constructed to deal with post-Soviet civil-military relations will have to take into consideration the fact that the military sometimes fits both patterns.

## Model Building in General

The foregoing discussion raises a key question—what is the value of models? To begin with, I would suggest that this study shows that they have limited utility during periods of change. The greater the change, the less useful they are. If those involved in the process see no logical relationship between what they are doing and their end goals, it seems highly presumptive to me for an outsider—even a political scientist—to believe that the "power" of one's paradigm will be sufficient to explain change.

Second, although it has been stated many times, all of the models used to date to analyze Soviet and Russian reality have tended to oversimplify reality. It seems to me questionable to assume that institutions necessarily played the key role in the USSR. On some occasions they did; in other instances, however, they did not. Perhaps it is the issue itself, external factors such as another country's action, or even personalities that are the variables most heavily impacting on the decision-making process. It will vary according to each individual case.

Third, this study raises the question of the cultural sensitivity of many of our models. Kolkowicz attempted to apply a model developed in the U.S. to the USSR, while Odom's paradigm was intended to explain Soviet civil-military relations on the basis of totalitarian theory. Because issues are so important in Russian and Soviet politics, Colton's model was the most culturally relevant. It avoided any prejudicial assumptions about the nature of the system.

### Forget Models?

Despite my criticisms of models, I still believe they are useful. We are constantly faced with the need to conceptualize complex reality—and in the process to simplify it. The problem is that some analysts tend to exaggerate the relevance of their findings. For example, let us assume a model suggests that there is a relationship between doctrine, force structure, budget, and personnel; i.e., the more clearly stated the doctrine, the greater the chance one will be able to predict the other three. Even if this finding holds true for Russia or the former Soviet Union, it does not follow that it will hold true in another polity. Similarly, just because one concludes that history plays an important role in the decision-making process in Russia, it does not follow that this will be the case with other polities. Based on my experience, neither doctrine (as defined in a Russian context) nor history (as the Russians understand it) play a significant role in the American national security decision-making process. In essence, what I am arguing is that the analyst must avoid becoming too closely tied to any paradigm. Similarly, he or she should keep in mind that any set of findings is tentative at best. It may hold for today but could be only tangentially relevant tomorrow.

Another value of models is that they serve as heuristic devices for conceptualizing problems. For example, although I have criticized all three of the models discussed in this book, I acknowledge that political scientists are in debt to Kolkowicz, Odom, and Colton. Without Kolkowicz, political scientists might not be as sensitive to the importance of institutional identity in an organization such as the military. Similarly, Odom reminds us that the military is not as homogeneous as some specialists believe. They may say the same thing in public—although that is clearly not the case at present in Russia—but if given the opportunity, their different views become readily apparent. Finally, scholars are in Colton's debt because of his emphasis on the importance of issues and participation in the political process. His was the only model that dealt with change with any degree of success.

So where do political scientists go from here? In my opinion, the situation in Russia is too fluid at present to come up with meaningful models. Whatever variable one selects today could well be irrelevant tomorrow. Does that mean that scholars will stop trying to apply models to better understand civil-military relations? Hardly. Like my colleagues I will continue to try to find a way to conceptualize this relationship. This book suggests, however, that as soon as a model is devised, reality will have changed sufficiently to raise questions about its utility. Nonetheless, models do organize knowledge about how the process works. This will help us to begin to make some generalizations—even if tentative and partial—about civil-military relations in post-Communist Russia.

# NOTES

## Introduction

1. While the three models discussed below were the most influential and most clearly articulated approaches to civil-military relations in the former USSR, there were a number of other studies that dealt with Soviet civil-military relations as well. For a discussion of some of the earlier approaches, see David E. Albright, "A Comparative Conceptualization of Civil-Military Relations," *World Politics* 32, no. 4 (July 1980): 553-76. Recent book-length studies include Timothy J. Colton and Thane Gustafson, eds., *Soldiers and the State* (Princeton: Princeton University Press, 1990); Bruce Parrott, *The Dynamics of Soviet Defense Policy* (Washington, D.C.: Woodrow Wilson Center Press, 1990); Kenneth M. Currie, *Soviet Military Politics* (New York: Paragon, 1991); William C. Green and Theodore Karasik, *Gorbachev and His Generals* (Boulder: Westview, 1990); Roy Allison, *Radical Reform in Soviet Defence Policy* (London: Macmillan, 1992); and Thomas M. Nichols *The Sacred Cause; Civil-Military Conflict over Soviet National Security, 1917-1992* (Ithaca: Cornell, 1993).

2. Roman Kolkowicz, *The Soviet Military and the Communist Party* (Princeton: Princeton University Press, 1967). For further articulation of his views on this topic, see "Military Intervention in the Soviet Union: Scenarios for Post-Hegemonical Synthesis," in Roman Kolkowicz and Andrzej Korbonski, eds., *Soldiers, Peasants, and Bureaucrats* (London: Allen and Unwin, 1982); "The Military," in H. Gordon Skilling and Franklyn Griffiths, eds., *Interest Groups in Soviet Politics* (Princeton: Princeton University Press, 1971); "The Impact of Modern Technology on the Soviet Officer Corps," *Orbis* 11, no. 2 (Summer 1977); and "Interest Groups in Soviet Politics: The Case of the Military," in Dale R. Herspring and Ivan Volgyes, eds., *Civil-Military Relations in Communist Systems* (Boulder: Westview, 1978).

3. Samuel P. Huntington, *The Soldier and the State* (New York: Vintage, 1964), pp. 12, 15, 16.

4. Kolkowicz, *The Soviet Military and the Communist Party*, p. 21.

5. Ibid., p. 10.

6. William E. Odom, "The Party-Military Connection, a Critique," in Herspring and Volgyes, *Civil-Military Relations in Communist Systems*, p. 28. See also his "A Dissenting View on the Group Approach to Soviet Politics, *World Politics*, 27, no. 4 (July 1976): 542-67.

7. See Morris Janowitz, *The Professional Soldier* (New York: Free Press, 1960), p. 6.

8. Odom, "The Party-Military Connection," pp. 37, 44.

9. Timothy J. Colton, *Commissars, Commanders and Civilian Authority: The Structure of Soviet Military Politics* (Cambridge: Harvard University Press, 1979), and "The Party-Military Connection: A Participatory Model," in Herspring and Volgyes, *Civil-Military Relations in Communist Systems*, pp. 53-75, 62.

10. See Jack Snyder, *The Ideology of the Offensive* (Ithaca: Cornell University Press, 1984).

11. The Stalinist period is not included because it was a period in which the Soviet armed forces were decimated as an organizational entity.

12. (Princeton: Princeton University Press, 1944). Pioneering works by these three authors include Raymond Garthoff, *Soviet Strategy in the Nuclear Age* (New York: Praeger, 1958); Garthoff, *Soviet Military Policy* (New York: Praeger, 1961); Thomas Wolfe, *Soviet Strategy at the Crossroads* (Boston: Harvard University Press, 1964); and Herbert Dinnerstein, *War and the Soviet Union* (New York: Praeger, 1959).

13. (London: Macmillan, 1962); (Ithaca: Cornell, 1990).

14. I. B. Berkhin, *Voennaya reforma v SSSR, 1924-1925.*

(Moscow: Voennoe Izdatel'stvo, 1958); A. G. Kavtaradze, *Voennye spetsialisty na sluzhbe Respubliki Sovetov, 1917-1920 gg.* (Moscow: Nauka, 1988); V. N. Konyukhovskiy, *Territorial'naya sistema voennogo stroytel'stva* (Moscow: Voennoe Izdatel'stvo Ministerstva Oborony Soyuza SSR, 1961). Among the more important book-length biographies of the key personalities from the 1920s and their ideas in the military sphere available in English are the following: Thomas G. Butson, *The Tsar's Lieutenant* (New York: Praeger, 1984) (on Tukhachevsky); Walter Darnell Jacobs, *Frunze: The Soviet Clausewitz, 1885-1925* (The Hague: Martinus Nijhoff, 1969); George Breitman, ed., *Leon Trotsky, Military Writings* (New York: Merit, 1969); and Kent D. Lee, ed., *Aleksandr A. Svechin, Strategy* (Minneapolis: East View, 1992).

15. This is only a partial list. For additional works on the contemporary period, see note 2 above.

## 1. Devising a New Military Doctrine

1. D. Fedotoff-White, *The Growth of the Red Army* (Princeton: Princeton University Press, 1944), p. 158.

2. M. N. Tukhachevsky, "Strategiya natsional'naya i klassovaya," in M. N. Tukhachevsky, *Izbrannye proizvedeniya,* vol. 1 (Moscow: Voennoe Izdatel'stvo Ministerstva Oborony SSSR, 1964), p. 31.

3. The theses cited here are found in S. I. Gusev, "Reorganizatsiya raboche-krest'yanskoy Krasnoy Armiy," in *Grazhdanskaya voyna i Krasnaya Armiya* (Moscow: Voennoe Izdatel'stvo, 1958), pp. 120, 127. Lest the reader get the impression that the question of military doctrine first arose in 1920, it is important to note that it had been discussed widely in military journals. For example, this writer counted 16 articles published in *Voennoe delo* on the topic between July 1918 and September 1919.

4. Gusev, *Grazhdanskaya voyna i Krasnaya Armiya,* pp. 123-24, 127.

5. M. V. Frunze, "Edinnaya voennaya doktrina i Krasnaya Armiya," in M. V. Frunze, *Sobranie sochinenii,* vol. 1 (Moscow: Gosudarstvennoe Izdatel'stvo, 1929), p. 210.

6. Frunze, "Edinaya voennaya doktrina i Krasnaya Armiya," in M. V. Frunze, *Izbrannye proizvedeniya* (Moscow: Voennoe Izdatel'stvo, 1984), pp. 34-35.

7. Ibid., pp. 45-46.

8. Ibid., pp. 47-48. Throughout his writings, Frunze uses the terms "offense" and "maneuver" interchangeably.

9. Svechin understood military history and its impact on areas such as doctrine and strategy better than any other military writer at this time. He served in the Russo-Japanese War, and as a member of the General Staff joined the Bolsheviks and spent most of the 1920s as a professor at the General Staff Academy. His biggest fame, however, came from the many articles and books he wrote on military issues—especially the interrelationship between history and military theory. For example, his three-volume *History of Military Art,* published in 1922-1923, discussed in considerable detail the evolution of military thought and the importance of the past for the present. See *Istoriya voennogo iskusstva,* Ch. 1, Klassicheskiy mir i srednie veka (Moscow: Vysshiy Voennyy Redaktsionnyy Sovet, 1922); *Istoriya voennogo*

*iskusstva*, Ch. 2, Novye veka (Moscow: Vysshiy Voennyy Redaktsionnyy Sovet, 1922); and *Istoriya voennogo iskusstva, Ch. 3, Noveyshee vremya* (Moscow: Vysshiy Voennyy Redaktsionnyy Sovet, 1923).

10. Kent D. Lee, ed., *Aleksandr A. Svechin, Strategy* (Minneapolis, 1992), p. 145. This is a translation of the 2nd edition of Svechin's *Strategiya*, originally published in 1927. Svechin reiterated this point later in the book, "An army cannot help but be a reflection of the class factions existing in a country, and elementary logic demands that the ruling class guide the thinking of an army in accordance with the requirements of its policies" (p. 175).

11. A. Svechin, "Chto takoe voennaya doktrina?" *VD*, 1920, no. 2, p. 39. See also Redaktsiya, "Osnovy voennoy doktriny," ibid., pp. 38-39.

12. *The Growth of the Red Army*, pp. 160-61.

13. *Strategy*, p. 62.

14. L. Trotsky, "Voennaya doktrina ili mnimo-voennoe doktrinerstvo," in L. Trotsky, *Kak vooruzhalas' revolyutsiya* (Moscow: Vysshiy Voennyy Redaktsionnyy Sovet, 1925), vol. 3, book 2, p. 212; L. Trotsky, "Vstupitel'noe i zaklyuchitel'noe slovo na diskussii o voennoy doktrine," in ibid., pp. 201-208.

15. L. Trotsky, "Voennaya doktrina ili mnimo-voennoe doktrinerstvo," pp. 214-15; L. Trotsky, "Sovremennoe polozhenie i zadachi voennogo stroytel'stva," in Trotsky, *Kak vooruzhalas' revolyutsiya*, vol. 3, book 2, p. 168. Emphasis in the original.

16. Trotsky, "Vstupitel'noe i zaklyuchitel'noe slovo na diskussii o voennoy doktrine," pp. 201-209. This and a number of other speeches by Trotsky are available in English in Leon Trotsky, *Military Writings* (New York: Merit, 1969). Emphasis in the original.

17. Trotsky, "Vystupitel'noe i zaklyuchitel'noe slovo na diskussii o voennoy doktrine," p. 205; Trotsky, "Voennaya doktrina ili mnimo-voennoe doktrinerstvo," p. 228.

18. As will be discussed in chapter 4, military specialists refer to former officers from the Imperial Army, such as Tukhachevsky, who voluntarily joined the Red Army, in many cases openly embracing the new regime and its ideology. Such officers contrasted with those who joined the Red Army primarily because of their belief in and commitment to the new ideology, but had only a rudimentary knowledge of military technical things.

19. Fedotoff-White, *The Growth of the Red Army*, pp. 167-68, 179.

20. M. V. Frunze, "Voenno-politicheskoe vospitanie Krasnoy Armii," in M. V. Frunze, *Izbrannye proizvedeniya* (Moscow: Voennoe Izdatel'stvo, 1984), pp. 51-83.

21. Frunze, "Voenno-politicheskoe vospitanie Krasnoy Armii," pp. 51-83; "Osnovye voennye zadachy momenta," in ibid., pp. 88-89, 90, 89, 92, 98.

22. Frunze, "Voennoe-politicheskoe vospitanie Krasnoy Armii; Frunze, "Osnovye voennye zadachi momenta." For a discussion of Frunze's attitude toward offensive strategy, see A. Golubev, "Obrashchena li byla v proshloe nasha voennaya teoriya v 20-e gody?" *VIZ*, no. 10 (1964): 40-42.

23. Frunze, "Voenno-politicheskoe vospitanie Krasnoy Armii," p. 63; Frunze, "Osnovnye voennye zadachi momenta," pp. 92-93.

24. See M. N. Tukhachevsky, "Voyna kak problema vooruzhennoy bor'by," in M. N. Tukhachevsky, *Izbrannye proizvedeniya*, vol. II (Moscow: Voennoe Izdatel'stvo Ministerstva Oborony SSSR, 1964), pp. 3-23.

25. Born in 1881, Voroshilov participated in the Civil War in command of the 5th and 10th armies and at this time was commander of the North Caucasus Military District. Having developed close ties with Stalin during the Civil War, he was destined to become one of the latter's closest colleagues during the 1930s and 1940s.

26. "Doklad na XI S"ezde P. K. P. (bol'shevikov)," in L. Trotsky, *Kak vooruzhalas' revolyutsiya* (Moscow: Vysshiy Voennyy Redaktsionnyy Sovet, 1924), vol. III, book

2, pp. 248, 258-60. See also Sally W. Stoecker, "The Historical Roots of the Current Debates on Soviet Military Doctrine and Defense," *JSMS* 3, no. 3 (September 1990): 366-67.

27. Trotsky, "Doklad i zaklyuchitel'noe slovo na soveshchanii voennykh delegatov XI s"ezda P. K. P. 1-go aprelya 1922 g.," vol. III, book 2, pp. 247, 256, 264-65, 267.

28. Svechin, *Strategy*, p. 241.

29. Svechin had held that the defense would play an important role in any future conflict for some time. In 1913 he argued that a future conflict would probably be protracted, a view that World War I served only to confirm. See A. A. Svechin, "Bolshaya voennaya programma," *Russkaya mysl'*, book VIII (August 1913), pp. 19-29, as cited in Menning, *Bayonets before Bullets* (Bloomington: Indiana University Press, 1992), p. 216.

30. The militia-regular army controversy is the topic of the next chapter. In essence, it asks the question to what degree should the Red Army rely on a large standing army rather than a militia system, according to which individuals are called up for training for short periods of time and activated in the event of a war?

31. Svechin, *Strategy*, pp. 247, 248, 251.

32. For Svechin, positive goals were associated with offensive actions, negative with defensive. "The advancement of a series of positive goals characterizes a strategic offensive, while a series of negative goals characterizes a strategic defense," *Strategy*, p. 250. The quote in the text is from ibid., p. 252.

33. *Strategy*, p. 98.

34. Stoecker, "The Historical Roots of the Current Debates on Soviet Military Doctrine and Defense," pp. 369-70.

35. Fedotoff-White, *The Growth of the Red Army*, p. 181.

36. Frunze died in October 1925 under suspicious conditions. Despite differences between Voroshilov and Tukhachevsky, the latter remained chief of staff of the Red Army until 1928. Throughout the remainder of the 1920s, he continued to supply most of the intellectual brain power for those, including Voroshilov, who supported the call for a proletarian offensive military doctrine.

37. The best discussion of these changes on Soviet force structure is contained in Stoecker, "The Historical Roots of the Current Debates on Soviet Military Doctrine and Defense," pp. 374-79. See also Erickson, *The Soviet High Command*, pp. 182-83.

38. This discussion of the 1925 *Provisional Field Regulations* is based on Erickson, *The Soviet High Command*, p. 207; Thomas G. Butson, *The Tsar's Lieutenant; The Soviet Marshal* (New York: Praeger, 1984), p. 169; and Erich Wollenberg, *The Red Army* (London: Secker and Warburg, 1940), p. 191. In June 1925 the word "provisional" was dropped from the regulations as they were affirmed by Frunze. They remained operative until 1929 when they were superseded by the *Field Service Regulations* of that year.

39. Erich Wollenberg, *The Red Army*, p. 191; Erickson, *The Soviet High Command*, p. 207.

40. This analysis is based, in part, on Jacob Kipp, "General-Major A. A. Svechin and Modern Warfare: Military History and Military Theory," in *Aleksandr A. Svechin, Strategy*, pp. 23-56.

41. Ibid., p. 45. The suggestion that a defensive strategy is a recipe for the defeat of the USSR at the hands of imperialism is contained in R. A. Estreykher-Egorov, "M. V. Frunze i uchenie o revolyutsionnoy klassovoy voyne," *Voyna i Revolyutsiya*, nos. 10-11 (1927): 221-24.

42. G. Isserson, "Zapiski sovremennika o M. N. Tukhachevskom," *VIZ*, no. 4 (1964): 65-67. See also R. A. Savushkin, "Zarozhdenie i razvitie sovetskoy voennoy doktriny," *VIZ*, no. 1 (January 1988): 25.

43. Butson, *The Tsar's Lieutenant*, p. 171. This is the best biography on Tukhachevsky available in English.

44. Erickson, *The Soviet High Command*, p. 288, 289. Erickson does not provide the source for the Voroshilov statement.

45. This reference is taken from Linda Lord, *Marshal Tukhachevskii* (Paris: Lev, 1978), p. 64.

46. B. M. Shaposhnikov, *Mozg Armii*, 3 vols. (Moscow, 1927-1929).

47. M. N. Tukhachevsky, "Voyna kak problema vooruzhennoy bor'by," in M. N. Tukhachevsky, *Izbrannye proizvedeniya* (Moscow: Voennoe Izdatel'stvo Ministerstva Oborony SSSR, 1964), vol. 2, p. 4.

48. Tukhachevsky, "Voyna kak problema vooruzhennoy bor'by," pp. 15, 17. ; D. Fedotoff-White, "Soviet Philosophy of War," *Political Science Quarterly*, vol. 51, no. 3 (September 1936): 344, 345.

49. *From the First Five Year Plan. A Symposium* (Moscow-Leningrad, 1933), p. 351, as cited in Erickson, *The Soviet High Command*, p. 303. The latter quote is from E. Yu. Lokshin, *Ocherk istorii promyshlennosti SSSR* (Moscow, 1956), p. 276, as cited in Erickson, *The Soviet High Command*, pp. 304, 47 ff. Emphasis in the original.

50. *Polevoy Ustav RKKA 1929* (Moscow-Leningrad, 1929), vol. 1, pp. 17, 60. This document is available in English, *Field Regulations of the Red Army, 1929*, USSR Report, *JPRS*, March 13, 1985.

51. See *Protiv reaktsionnykh teoriy na voennonauchnom fronte* (Moscow: Gosudarstvennoe Voennoe Izdatel'stvo, 1931). The information on Svechin's arrest and execution is taken from A. A. Kokoshin and V. V. Larionov, "Origins of the Intellectual Rehabilitation of A. A. Svechin," in *Aleksandr A. Svechin, Strategy*, pp. 1-13, and Aleksey Khorev, "Vozvrashchenie Svechina," *KZ*, December 5, 1992.

## 2. Deciding on a Force Structure

1. See, for example, Carl Bleibtreu, "Die zunkunftige Uberlegenheit des Milizsystems," *Sozialistische Monatshefte*, no. 10 (1899): 510-18.

2. The importance of morale in combat was not a new idea. The great Russian theorist Mikhail Dragomirov—who was not a socialist by any stretch of the imagination—also stressed the importance of morale. As Fuller put it, "At the Nicholas Academy of the General Staff, which he headed from 1878 to 1889, and thereafter in countless articles and pamphlets, Dragomirov tirelessly argued that the decisive factor in warfare was morale, not technology." William C. Fuller, Jr., *Civil-Military Conflict in Imperial Russia, 1881-1914* (Princeton: Princeton University Press, 1985), p. 6.

3. A. Shifres, "Frants Mering i militsionnaya sistema," *Voennaya mysl' i revolyutsiya*, no. 6 (1923): 117. After presenting arguments advanced by Mehring and others, Shifres proceeds to argue that a militia system is possible. Just as Communists and the party organization played a decisive role in the Reds' victory in the Civil War, they would also play the key role in ensuring that the militia units were militarily competent. Ibid., pp. 123-25.

4. Ibid.

5. S. M. Klyatskin, *Na zashchite oktyabrya, 1917-1920* (Moscow: Nauka 1965), p. 56. The idea of universal military service was not unique to the Bolsheviks. In fact, it was a key aspect of the reforms advocated by General Dmitri Miliutin, and became official policy in the conscription law of January 1, 1874. In essence, the real debate was not over whether or not universal service should be adopted (although some Bolsheviks opposed it), but over the existence of a large professional officer and noncommissioned officer corps, which would super-

vise the conscripts. For a discussion of the Miliutin reforms, see Bruce W. Menning *Bayonets before Bullets* (Bloomington: Indiana University Press, 1992), pp. 6-38.

6. For an English translation of Lenin's speech, in which he also defends the recently concluded treaty, see *V. I. Lenin, Speeches at Party Congresses* (1918-1922) (Moscow: Progress Publishers, 1971), pp. 7-31. The Russian version is contained in Institut Marksa-Engel'sa-Lenina-Stalina, *Kommunisticheskaya Partiya Sovetskogo Soyuza v rezolyutsiyakh i resheniyakh s"ezdov, konferentsiy i plenumov TsK*, Part II (Moscow: Gosudarstvennoe Izdatel'stvo Politicheskoy Literatury, 1954), pp. 332-53. The October quote from Lenin is contained in Lenin, *Collected Works* (in Russian), vol. 26, p. 238 as cited in Klyatskin, *Na zashchite oktyabrya*, p. 57.

7. For a discussion of the General Staff's role in developing a militia strategy at this time, see John Erickson, *The Soviet High Command, a Military-Political History* (London: Macmillan, 1960), p. 28.

8. For a discussion of the role played by the Red Guards during the October Revolution, see Rex A. Wade, *Red Guards and Workers' Militias in the Russian Revolution* (Stanford: Stanford University Press, 1984).

9. General Yuri Danilov, "The Red Army," *Foreign Affairs* 7, no. 1 (October 1928): 102.

10. Lenin, *Collected Works*, vol. 30, p. 126 as cited in Klyatskin, *Na zashchite oktyabrya*, p. 153, 32 ff. The role played by the military specialists, or *voenspets*, is discussed in greater detail in chapter 4.

11. Erickson, "Some Military and Political Aspects of the 'Militia Army' Controversy, 1919-1920," p. 206.

12. Erickson, *The Soviet High Command*, p. 40.

13. The 1918 report is taken from the Central State Archives of the Red Army, archive 4, folder 1, document 7, p. 40 as cited in Klyatskin, *Na zashchite oktyabrya*, p. 202; reference to the Fifth All-Russian Congress resolution is from ibid., p. 204.

14. In utilizing the term "militia," it is important to note that Soviet writers often make no distinction between militia units and territorial units. Militia units as used in this book refer to non-regular military units that were set up in the 1920s, primarily in the RSFSR or around major cities. Territorial or national units, on the other hand, refer to militia-type units that were set up in non-Russian regions.

15. See Klyatskin, *Na zashchite oktyabrya*, pp. 251-52.

16. S. Gusev, "Kak stroit' sovetskuyu armiyu," in S. I. Gusev, *Grazhdanskaya voyna i Krasnaya Armiya* (Moscow: Voennoe Izdatel'stvo Ministerstva Oborony Soyuza SSSR, 1958), pp. 31, 32.

17. V. Sorin and A. Kamenskiy, "Komandiry i komissary v deystvuyushchey armii," *Pravda*, November 29, 1918; A. Kamenskiy, "Davno pora," *Pravda*, December 25, 1918.

18. *Protokol s"ezdov i konferentsiy vsesoyusnoy kommunisticheskoy partii(b), Vos'moy s"ezd RKP(b)* (Moscow: Partiynoe Izdatel'stvo, 1933), pp. 146-48.

19. Ibid., pp. 402-403.

20. Ibid., p. 405.

21. Erickson, "Some Military and Political Aspects of the 'Militia Army Controversy,' " p. 208.

22. L. Trotsky, "Programmy militsii i ee akademicheskiy kritik," in L. Trotsky, *Kak voourzhalas' revolyutsiya*, vol. 2, book 1 (Moscow: Vysshiy Voennyy Redaktsionnyy Sovet, 1924), pp. 117, 120.

23. Klyatskin, *Na zashchite oktyabrya*, pp. 439-40.

24. Ibid., pp. 430-31.

25. A. Svechin, "Militsiya kak ideal: Kritika tezisov L. Trotskogo," *VD*, nos. 11-12 (40-41) (1919): 436-38.

26. The military's position was evident in articles published in the pages of *Voennoe delo*. As one writer put it, "The only means for avoiding that threat [i.e., the external threat facing the country] is to support a standing army and to utilize it to destroy those houses of cards [*kartochnie gosudarstva*] while their reinforced Entente has not yet become a fortress." Or as he put it later in the article, "It is clear that as long as we have a state, it is necessary to have a standing army, that has been built to the disadvantage of a militia." N. Valentinkov, "Militsiya ili postoyannaya armiya," *VD* 2, nos. 34-35 (63-64) (1919): 1042, 1043.

27. See "Devyatyy s"ezd RKP(b)," in *KPSS v rezolyutsiyakh i resheniyakh*, vol. 1, pp. 501-502. Based on a report of his speech to the congress, Trotsky accepted this compromise arrangement, but argued that the country was in "a transition period." In the end, the country would move toward a militia system. See "Doklad L. Trotskogo o perekhode k militsionnoy sisteme na 9 s"ezde RKP," *VD* 3, no. 11 (75) (1920): 347-50.

28. Klyatskin, *Na zashchite oktyabrya*, 451-54.

29. Ibid., pp. 456-59.

30. Erickson, "Some Military and Political Aspects of the 'Militia Army' Controversy, 1919-1920," pp. 221-22.

31. L. Trotsky, "Stroytel'stvo krasnoy vooruzhennoy sily," in Trotsky, *Kak vooruzhalas' revolyutsiya*, vol. 2, book 1, pp. 123, 127.

32. K. Marx in F. Engel's, *Sochineniya*, vol. III, p. 277, as cited in Berkhin, *Voennaya reforma v SSSR*, p. 29.

33. Ibid., pp. 30-31.

34. S. Gusev, "Uroki grazhdanskoy voyny," in S. I. Gusev, *Grazhdanskaya voyna i Krasnaya Armiya* (Moscow: Voennoe Izsdatel'stvo Ministerstva Oborony SSSR, 1958), p. 103.

35. The resolution of the Second All-Russian Meeting of Political Workers of the Red Army and Fleet, is contained in T. F. Karyaev, et. al., *Vsearmeyskie soveshchaniya politrabotnikov. 1918-1940* (Moscow: Izdatel'stvo Nauka, 1984), p. 32.

36. Tukhachevsky's discussion of this issue is contained in M. Tukhatschewsky, *Die Rote Armee und die Miliz* (Leipzig: Kleine Bibliothek der Russischen Korrespondenz, 1921), esp. pp. 20-24. For his part, Trotsky continued to oppose the idea of a regular army, arguing later in 1921 that Tukhachevsky's opposition to a militia "is incorrect." By improving the economic conditions in the countryside, Trotsky argued, the preconditions for the creation of a militia were being successfully created. See L. Trotsky, "Vstupitel'noe i zaklyuchitel'noe slovo na diskussii o voennoy doktrine," in Trotsky, *Kak vooruzhalas' revolutsiya*, vol. 3, book 2, p. 205.

37. S. I. Gusev, "Reorganizatsiya raboche-krest'yanskoy krasnoy armii," in *Grazhdanskaya voyna i Krasnaya Armiya*, p. 126.

38. *Uroki grazhdanskoy voyny*, pp. 105-106.

39. The Smilga quote is from A. S. Bubnov, *Grazhdanskaya Voyna, 1918-1921* (Moscow: Voennyy vestnik, 1928), vol. 2, pp. 97-98.

40. "Desyatyy s"ezd RKP(b)," in *KPSS v rezolyutsiyakh i Resheniyakh*, p. 570. See also Z. Grebel'skiy, "X s"ezd partii o dal'neyshem stroytel'stve Krasnoy Armii," *VIZ*, no. 3 (1971): 7.

41. M. V. Frunze, "Edinaya voennaya doktrina i Krasnaya Armiya," in M. V. Frunze, *Sobranie sochineniy*, vol. 1 (Moscow: Gosudarstvennoe Izdatel'stvo, 1929), p. 225.

42. Ibid.

43. I. B. Berkhin, *Voennaya reforma v SSSR*, pp. 39-40.

44. Frunze, *Sobranie sochineniy*, vol. III, p. 289, as quoted in Berkhin, *Voennaya reforma v SSSR*, p. 79.

45. Frunze, *Sobranie sochineniy,* vol. III, pp. 220-21, as cited in Berkhin, *Voennaya reforma v SSSR,* p. 79.
46. Ibid.
47. Berkhin, *Voennaya reforma v SSSR,* p. 79.
48. Ibid., pp. 84-90. Frunze made a similar evaluation, "Krasnaya armiya i oborona Sovetskogo Soyuza," in Frunze, *Izbrannye proizvedeniya,* p. 413.
49. Berkhin, *Voennaya reforma v SSSR,* pp. 57-58.
50. Ibid., pp. 60-67.
51. Ibid., pp. 71-73.
52. Berkhin, *Voennaya reforma v SSSR,* pp. 90-91.
53. Berkhin, *Voennaya reforma v SSSR,* p. 96.
54. Ibid., pp. 98-99.
55. Erickson, *The Soviet High Command,* p. 180.
56. Berkhin, *Voennaya reforma v SSSR,* p. 102.
57. K. E. Voroshilov, *Oborona SSSR* (Moscow: Voennyy Vestnik, 1927), pp. 96-97.

## 3. How to Deal with Non-Russians

1. Bruce W. Menning, *Bayonets before Bullets* (Bloomington: Indiana University Press, 1992), p. 222.
2. V. I. Varennikov, "Iz istorii sozdaniya i podgotovki natsional'nykh voynskikh formirovaniy," *Voennaya mysl',* no. 2, 1990, p. 5.
3. See, for example, Scott R. McMichael, "National Formations of the Red Army, 1918-38," *JSMS* 3, no. 4 (December 1990): 614.
4. The best source for this period is A. V. Krushel'nitskii and M. A. Molodtsigan, "Stanovlenie RKKA kak Armii Druzhby i Bratstva Narodov" in I. I. Mints, ed., *Boevoye Sodruzhestvo Sovetskikh Respublik, 1919-1922* (Moscow: Nauka, 1982). Most of the following comments on the role played by national units during the Civil War were taken from the articles in this book or from I. B. Berkhin, *Voennaya reforma v SSSR* (Moscow: Voennoe Izdatel'stvo, 1958), pp. 116-45.
5. For a discussion of the formation of these units see V. Shorin, "Bor'ba za Ural," in A. S. Bubnov, S. S. Kamenev, and R. P. Eydeman, *Grazhdanskaya voyna v SSSR,* vol. 1 (Moscow: Voenizdat, 1980), pp. 143-44.
6. "National'nye voennye formirovaniya: vchera . . . segodnya? zavtra?," *VIZ,* no. 5 (1990): 48.
7. As one Soviet source put it, "In the Tsarist Army Uzbeks, Tadzhiks, Turkmens, Kirgiz, Karakalpaks, Kazakhs, Azerbaijanis, Kalmyks, Chechens, Ingushs, Jews, Finns, Permyaks, Mariytsy, Chuvashi, Votyaki, Buryat-Mongols, Oyrots and also Yakuts and other Peoples of Northern Russia either did not serve or had serious restrictions." N. Makarov, "Stroytel'stvo mnogonatsional'nykh Vooruzhennykh Sil SSSR v 1920-1939 gg.," *VIZ,* no. 10 (1982): 39.
8. The figures for Muslims fighting for the Reds are taken from P. Shuktomov, "National'nie formirovanie Krasnoy Armii v gody inostrannoi interventsii i grazhdanskoi voiny" *VIZ,* no. 4 (1962): 115. For a discussion of the Soviet experience with Turkestan, see D. Zuev, "Istochniki komplektovaniya Krasnoy Armii v Turkestane," *Voennaya mysl' i revolyutsiya,* no. 4 (1923): 153-70.
9. As cited in S. Lipitskiy, "Voennaya reforma 1924-1925 godov," *Kommunist,* no. 4 (March 1990): 108.
10. Ibid.
11. *Partiya i Armiya* (Moscow: Politizdat, 1980), p. 76. Some Soviet writers continued to argue, however, that these forces did play an important role. It is difficult to know whether such statements were based on a careful analysis of the facts or

were intended for domestic consumption. See, for example, Varennikov, "Iz istorii sozdaniya i podgotovki natsional'nykh voinskikh formirovaniy," p. 6. The latter quote is from Berkhin, *Voennaya reforma v SSSR*, p. 34.

12. "Dvenadtsatyy s"ezd RKP(b)," in *KPSS v Rezolyutsiyakh i resheniyakh*, Part I (Moscow: Gosudarstvennoe Izdatel'stvo Politicheskoy Literatury, 1954), p. 717.

13. Lipitskiy, "Voennaya reforma 1924-1925 godov," p. 107.

14. A. S. Bubnov, *1924 god v voennom stroytel'stve* (Moscow: Gosvoenizdat, 1925), p. 199. According to Berkhin, the idea of creating national formations was mentioned as early as December 22, 1922, in the theses presented by Voroshilov to a meeting of military and political officers. These theses called for providing military education to civilians "according to the territorial principle." *Voennaya reforma v SSSR*, p. 47.

15. V. N. Konyukhovskiy, *Territorial'naya sistema voennogo stroytel'stva* (Moscow: Voennoe Izdatel'stvo Ministerstva Oborony Soyuza SSR), p. 36.

16. L. Trotsky, "Perspektivy i zadachi voennogo stroytel'stva," *Voennaya mysl' i revolyutsiya*, no. 2 (1923): 13-14.

17. M. V. Frunze, "Itogi i perspektivy voennogo stroitel'stva v svyazi s reorganizatsiey tekushchego goda," *Izbrannye proizvedeniya* (Moscow: Voennoe Izdatel'stvo, 1984), p. 219.

18. These figures are from Red Army Archives, archive 9, folder 1, document 431, p. 10, as cited in Berkhin, *Voennaya reforma v SSSR*, pp. 119-20.

19. "Chetvertoe Soveshchanie TsK RKP(b) s otvetstvennymi rabotnikami natsional'nykh respublik i oblasty," in *KPSS v rezolyutsiyakh i resheniyakh*, p. 765.

20. This circular and its significance for mobilizing local parties in support of the creation of territorial units is discussed in Konyukhovskiy, *Teritorial'naya sistema voennogo stroytel'stva*, pp. 37-39. The August 8, 1923, directive is discussed in ibid., pp. 40-42.

21. As quoted in "M. V. Frunze o reorganizatsii Krasnoy Armii v 1924 gody," *VIZ*, no. 6 (1966): 73.

22. Bubnov, *1924 god v voennom stroytel'stve*, p. 231.

23. The plan outlined above is from the Central Archives of the Red Army, archive 9, folder 1, document 54/c, p. 29, as cited in Berkhin, *Voennaya reforma v SSSR*, p. 124.

24. "Plenum TsK RKP(b)," in *KPSS v resolyutsiyakh i resheniyakh*, Part I, p. 813. *Trinadtsatyy s"ezd RKP(b). Stenograficheskiy otchet* (Moscow, 1963), p. 642.

25. *KPSS v resolyutsiyakh i resheniyakh*, Part II, 1924-1930 (Moscow: Gosudarstvennoe Izdatel'stvo Politicheskoy Literatury, 1954), p. 52.

26. M. A. Gareyev, *M. V. Frunze—Voennyy teoretik* (Moscow: Voennoe Izdatel'stvo, 1985), pp. 263-64.

27. Berkhin, *Voennaya reforma v SSSR*, p. 126.

28. In terms of specific units, the plan adopted by the December 1924 plenum foresaw the creation of the following:

From Central Asia:
        Uzbekistan—one rifle and one cavalry division,
        Turkmenistan—one cavalry division,
        Tadjikistan—one cavalry division,
        Kirgizia—one cavalry regiment,
        Kazakh Autonomous Oblast—one cavalry division.
The Transcaucasus:
        Georgia—one cadre division, one national division,
        Armenia—one cadre division,
        Azerbaijan—one national division.

The RSFSR:

Buryat-Mongolian ASSR—one cavalry regiment,
Yakut SSR—one national rifle unit,
Northern Caucasus Military District—one national cavalry division,
Karelia—one jaeger battalion,
Tartar ASSR—one national rifle division and a cavalry regiment,
Bashkir ASSR—one national rifle division with a cavalry regiment.

A copy of the resolution is contained in "Novye dokumenty o reorganizatsii Krasnoy Armii v 1924 gody," *VIZ*, no. 12 (1974): 55-58. The list is taken from Central Archives of the Red Army, archive 7, folder 1, document 46/c, p. 10, as cited in Berkhin, *Voennoe reforma v SSSR*, pp. 129-30. The reason for going into detail concerning the number and type of units assigned to each ethnic group is that it illustrates the seriousness with which the Soviet government took their creation. Careful and detailed plans were a part of the process.

29. M. V. Frunze, "Itogi plenuma Revvoensoveta SSSR," in M. V. Frunze, *Izbrannye proizvedeniya* (Moscow: Voennoe Izdatel'stvo, 1984), p. 275.

30. Frunze, "Itogi plenuma Revvoensoveta SSSR," p. 266.

31. "Novye dokymenty o reorganizatsii Krasnoy Armii v 1924 godu," p. 56.

32. Central State Archives of the Red Army, archive 9, folder 1, document 581, p. 251, as cited in I. M. Ovcharenko et al., *M. V. Frunze: Voennaya i politicheskaya deyatel'nost'* (Moscow: Voenizdat, 1984), p. 200. Another source goes even further arguing that by October 1924 there were a total of 43 territorial divisions and one cavalry brigade. Together these units made up 44 percent of the divisions and brigades in the Red Army. Konyukhovskiy, *Territorial'naya sistema voennogo stroytel'stva*, p. 61, citing unspecified Red Army archival documents.

33. By the end of 1924 the following new schools were in operation:

The Cavalry Command School of the Northern Caucasus Mountain Peoples,
The Sixth All-Arms Tatar-Bashkir School,
The Tatar Military-Political School,
The Eighth All-Arms Kirgiz/Kazakh School,
The Third All-Arms School of Red Communes (for Poles),
The Third All-Arms International School,
The Georgian All-Arms School,
The Armenian All-Arms School,
The Azerbaijani All-Arms School,
The Georgian Military-Political School,
The Armenian Military-Political School,
The Azerbaijani Military-Political School,
The Transcaucasus Military-Political School,
The Fifth All-Service School of Red Senior Noncommissioned Officers,
The Fifth Cavalry School,
The Military-Preparatory School (in Ukraine),
The Seventh All-Arms Byelorussian School, and
The Central Asian School for Command Personnel.

See Central State Archives of the Red Army, archive 7, folder 1, document 42/c, p. 34, as cited in Berkhin, *Voennay reforma v SSSR*, pp. 132-33.

34. Berkhin, *Voennaya reforma v SSSR*, pp. 133-36.

35. M. V. Frunze, "Ocherednye voprosy voennogo dela," in Frunze, *Izbrannye proizvedeniya*, p. 385.

36. M. V. Frunze, "Krasnaya Armiya i oborona Sovetskogo Soyuza," in ibid., pp. 412-13, 441-42.

37. M. V. Frunze, "Ocherednye zadachi politrabotnikov," *Voyna i revolyutsiya*, no. 5 (August-September, 1925): 4.

38. Berkhin, *Voennaya reforma v SSSR*, p. 134.

39. P. F. Vashchenko and V. A. Runov, "Voennaya reforma v SSSR," *VIZ*, no. 12 (1989): 38.

40. "Iz istorii territorial'no-militsionnogo stroytel'stva v Krasnoy Armii," *VIZ*, no. 11 (1960): 93.

41. Frunze emphasized the importance of action in this area in his report to the Third Meeting of the Council of the USSR. M. V. Frunze, "Krasnaya Armiya i oborona Sovetskogo Soyuza," in M. V. Frunze, *Izbrannye proizvedeniya*, p. 441.

42. K. E. Voroshilov, *Oborona SSSR* (Moscow: Voennyy Vestnik, 1927), pp. 104-105.

43. E. Lepin, "Stroytel'stvo natsional'nykh chastey v Uzbekistane," *Voyna i revolyutsiya*, no. 8 (1927): 87. According to Lepin, "part of the regimental commanders are also from the indigenous populace." He admitted, however, that at more senior levels, "Europeans, who have some knowledge of Uzbek or Tadzhik," are being utilized. Ibid. According to Konyukhovskiy, one of the problems that was singled out for special attention at this time was pre-military training. "Local organizations were not giving sufficient attention to political work with future recruits and the liquidation of illiteracy among them was going too slowly." *Territorial'naya sistema voennogo stroytel'stva*, p. 69.

44. Voroshilov, *Oborona SSSR*, p. 100. Berkhin, *Voennaya reforma v SSSR*, p. 140. Lepin places the percentage of illiterates in the Uzbek populace at 90 percent. Lepin, "Stroytel'stvo natsional'nykh chastey v Uzbekistane," p. 92.

45. Voroshilov, *Oborona SSSR*, p. 101.

46. Lepin, "Stroytel'stvo natsional'nykh chastey v Uzbekistane," p. 88.

47. K. E. Voroshilov, "Natsional'noe stroytel'stvo v Krasnoy Armii," in K. E. Voroshilov, *Stat'i i rechi* (Moscow: Partizdat CC VKP(b), 1936), pp. 338-40.

48. See N. Makarov, "Stroytel'stvo monogonatsional'nykh vooruzhennykh sil SSSR v 1920-1939 gg.," *VIZ*, no. 10 (1982): 42-43.

49. Konyukhovskiy, *Territorial'naya sistema voennogo stroytel'stva*, p. 71. Konyukhovskiy states that this directive was issued in 1932. A second source claims it was issued in 1931. The latter source, which contains a copy of the directive, is contained in "Iz istorii territorial'no-militsionnogo stroitel'stva v Krasnoy Armii," pp. 96-97.

50. Fedotoff-White, *The Growth of the Red Army* (Princeton: Princeton University Press, 1944), p. 359.

51. Varennikov, "Iz istorii sozdaniya i podgotovki natsional'nykh voynskikh formirovaniy," p. 8.

52. Konyukhovskiy, *Territorial'naya sistema voennogo stroytel'stva*, pp. 71-72.

53. Ibid., p. 83.

54. The document is contained in "O natsional'nykh chastyakh i formirovaniyakh RKKA," in *KPSS o vooruzhennykh silakh Sovetskogo Soyuza. Dokumenty 1917-1981* (Moscow: Voenizdat, 1981), pp. 286-87.

55. K. E. Voroshilov, *Rech' na XVIII S"ezde VKP(b)*, March 13, 1939, Moscow, 1939, p. 11, as cited in Fedotoff-White, *The Growth of the Red Army*, p. 361.

56. The key source on the role played by these units is N. A. Kirsanov, *Po zovy Rodiny; Dobrovol'cheskie formirovaniya Krasnoy Armii v period velikoy otechestvennoy voyny* (Moscow: Mysl', 1974). See especially pp. 96-112.

57. See *Kommunist*, no. 13 (1977): 77, as cited in Varennikov, "Iz istorii sozdaniya natsional'nykh voynskikh formirovaniy," p. 11.

58. *Po zovy Rodiny*, p. 113.

59. Varennikov, "Iz istorii sozdaniya natsional'nykh voynskikh formirovaniy," pp. 10-12.

60. Frunze, "Itogi plenuma revvoensoveta SSSR," p. 273.

61. M. V. Zakharov, *Natsional'noe stroytel'stvo v Krasnoy Armii* (Moscow, 1927), as cited in Varennikov, "Iz istorii sozdaniya i podgotovki natsional'nykh voynskikh formirovaniy," p. 9.

62. Gareyev, *M. V. Frunze*, p. 266.

63. Leon Trotsky, *The Revolution Betrayed* (Garden City: Doubleday, Doran, 1937), p. 218.

64. M. V. Frunze, "Itogi plenuma Revvoensoveta SSSR," p. 273.

65. F. Engels, *Izbrannye voennye proizvedeniya* (Moscow: Voenizdat, 1956), p. 11.

66. K. E. Voroshilov, *Oborona SSSR*, p. 98.

67. Konyukhovskiy, *Territorial'naya sistema voennogo stroytel'stva*, p. 82.

68. The quote concerning the importance of the national units as a vehicle of political socialization is from Zakharov, "Natsional'noe stroytel'stvo v Krasnoy Armii," pp. 81-82, as cited in Varennikov, "Iz istorii sozdaniya natsional'nykh voynskikh formirovaniy," p. 9. See also Berkhin, *Voennaya reforma v SSSR*, pp. 142-43; D. Fedotoff-White, *The Growth of the Red Army*, p. 273, and Lipitskiy, "Voennaya reforma 1924-1925 godov," p. 107.

69. Varennikov, "Iz istorii sozdaniya natsional'nykh voynskikh formirovaniy," p. 9.

## 4. Red or Expert

1. This discussion is based on John Erickson, *The Soviet High Command* (London: Macmillan, 1962), pp. 16-22.

2. S. I. Gusev, *Grazhdanskaya voyna i Krasnaya Armiya* (Moscow: Voennoe Izdatel'stvo Ministerstva Oborony Soyuza SSR, 1958), p. 28. See also "Pyat' let Krasnoy Armii," *Voennaya mysl' i revolyutsiya*, no. 1 (1923), where the creation of *voenspets* is discussed, pp. 8-9. According to Mark von Hagen, the choice of the term "military specialist" (*Voenspets*) was not accidental. "The officers who volunteered were called 'military specialists,' both to avoid the opprobrium attached to the word 'officer' among the revolutionary soldiers and to distinguish those officers loyal to the Soviet state from the opposite numbers who were joining the White cause." Mark von Hagen, *Soldiers in the Proletarian Dictatorship* (Ithaca: Cornell University Press, 1990), p. 24.

3. A. G. Kavtaradze, *Voennye spetsialisty na sluzhbe Respubliki Sovetov, 1917-1920 gg.* (Moscow: Nauka, 1988), p. 74.

4. N. I. Shatagin, *Organizatsiya i stroytel'stvo Sovetskoy Armii v period inostrannoy voennoy interventsii i grazhdanskoy voyny (1918-1920)* (Moscow: Voennoe Izdatel'stvo, 1954), p. 52. The figure 13, which differs from that reported by other observers, is taken from Kavtaradze, *Voennye spetsialisty na sluzhbe Respubliki Sovetov*, p. 63. According to one Soviet author, Lenin himself called for the use of military specialists as instructors and especially for staff work. See Yu. Korablev, *V. I. Lenin i zashchita zavoevaniy velikogo oktyabrya* (Moscow: Voenizdat, 1979), p. 132.

5. N. A. Kozlov, *Akademiya general'nogo shtaba* (Moscow: Voennoe Izdatel'stvo, 1987), pp. 11-12.

6. Heavy reliance was placed on military specialists at educational institutions not only because of the need for such special expertise, but also because "during the October Revolution the staff of the Military Academy remained neutral and did not participate in counterrevolutionary activities and for that reason Soviet power did not take repressive actions against the teaching staff and students." Kavtaradze,

*Voennye spetsialisty na sluzhbe Respubliki Sovetov,* p. 70. The 90 percent figure is taken from ibid., p. 198.

7. L. Trotsky, "Nam nuzhna armiya," in L. Trotsky, *Kak vooruzhalas' revolyutsiya* (Moscow: Vysshiy Voennyy Redaktsionnyy Sovet, 1923), vol. 1, pp. 27-28.

8. The quote from Krylenko and Podvoyskiy is taken from Kavtaradze, *Voennye spetsialisty na sluzhbe Respubliki Sovetov,* p. 77, who cites Red Army archival sources. Podvoyskiy is the same person, noted in chapter 2, who fought hard against the creation of a regular army.

9. A. F. Danilevskiy, *V. I. Lenin i voprosy voennogo stroytel'stva na VIII S"ezde RKP(b)* (Moscow: Voennoe Izdatel'stvo, 1964), p. 30.

10. The resolution is cited in Kavtaradze, *Voennye spetsialisty na sluzhbe Respubliki Sovetov,* pp. 95, 96, 97. The resolution also contained a warning to former officers that if they used their positions in support of "counterrevolution" or to support "imperialism" they would be subject to the death penalty.

11. Shatagin, *Organizatsiya i stroytel'stvo sovetskoy armii,* p. 52.

12. See also Kavtaradze, *Voennye spetsialisty na sluzhbe Respubliki Sovetov,* p. 166, who cites a number of Soviet sources to back up the 8,000 figure. The 75,000 figure, which differs from the commonly cited one of 48,409, is from Kavtaradze, p. 198. Kavtaradze notes also that of the 75,000 military specialists some 12,000 had previously served the Whites, but had either been taken prisoner or gone over to the Soviets, p. 222. The 130,000 figure is from Shatagin, *Organizatsiya i stroytel'stvo sovetskoy armii,* p. 225.

13. The figures for command positions occupied by military specialists are from Kavtaradze, *Voennye spetsialisty na sluzhbe Respubliki Sovetov,* pp. 207-209. Kavtaradze provides additional figures showing that the vast majority of officers in middle command positions were military specialists.

14. For a discussion of this process and the steps a former member of the Imperial Army who wished to join the Red Army was required to take, see "K.," "Ukomplektovanie armii komandnym sostavom'," *VD* 1, no. 10 (1918): 6-7.

15. Berkhin, *Voennaya reforma v SSSR* (Moscow: Voennoe Izdatel'stvo, 1958), pp. 289, 291.

16. The idea of a military commissar was not a Soviet invention. Such individuals existed in a number of armies, most commonly where the values of the new political leadership were at variance with large segments of the military and the political system as a whole. See, for example, John Ellis, *Armies in Revolution* (London: Croom Helm, 1973). The best Soviet work on the evolution of the Political Organs and the Political Commissar remains Yu. P. Petrov, *Stroytel'stvo politorganov, partiynykh i komsomol'skikh organizatsiy armii i flota* (Moscow: Voennoe Izdatel'stvo Ministerstva Oborony SSSR, 1968). A number of editions of this work have been published.

17. Fedotoff-White, *The Growth of the Red Army* (Princeton: Princeton University Press, 1944), p. 84. See also von Hagen's discussion of the relationship between these two officers at this time, *Soldiers in the Proletarian Dictatorship,* pp. 32-34.

18. Ibid., p. 211.

19. As cited in Kavtaradze, *Voennye spetsialisty na sluzhbe Respubliki Sovetov,* p. 121.

20. L. Trotsky, "Voennye spetsialisty i Krasnaya Armiya," *VD* 2, no. 2 (1919): 71. Or as another writer put it at the same time, "Already the history of our revolutionary war has written the names of Hero-Specialists on its tablets." Malygiev, "O Spetsialistakh," *VD* 2, no. 3 (1919): 151.

21. The speeches are contained in *Vos'moy s"ezd RKP(b)* (Moscow: Partiynoe Izdatel'stvo, 1933). This quote is from pp. 148-49.

22. Ibid., pp. 155-60. Smirnov's biography and the notation that he was the leader

of the military opposition is found on p. 543. Danilevskiy also sees Smirnov as the leader of the military opposition, *V. I. Lenin i voprosy voennogo stroytel'stva na VIII S"ezde RKP(b)*, p. 68.

23. Yu. Korablev, "V. I. Lenin i voprosy stroytel'stva regulyarnoy armii na VIII s"ezde partii," *VIZ*, no. 2 (February, 1969): 4.

24. The quote from Lenin is from *Vos'moy s"ezd RKP(b)*, p. 539. According to Petrov, this was the first time that the idea of introducing the unity of command question was raised formally at a major party meeting. Petrov, *Stroytel'stvo politorganov partiynikh i komsomol'skikh organizatsiy armii i flota*, p. 155, n. 1.

25. The resolution is contained in *KPSS v rezolyutsiyakh i resheniyakh*, Part I (Moscow: Gosudarstvennoe Izdatel'stvo Politicheskoy Literatury, 1954), pp. 430-39.

26. Danilevskiy, *V. I. Lenin i voprosy voennogo stroytel'stva na VIII S"ezde RKP(b)*, p. 76.

27. Smilga, *VD*, no. 2 (1919), as cited in Trotsky, vol. 2, book 1, pp. 76, 453. Smilga was probably making this suggestion with Trotsky's full knowledge, since he mentions Smilga's article in his December speech. This writer has been unable to locate a copy of this article in *Voennoe delo*, as cited by Trotsky. It is cited here because it reflects Trotsky's views.

28. L. Trotsky, "Nashi ocherednye voprosy," in L. Trotsky, *Kak vooruzhalas' revolyutsiya*, vol. 2, book. 1 (Moscow: Vysshiy Voennyy Redaktsionnyy Sovet, 1924), p. 77.

29. D. Fedotoff-White, *The Growth of the Red Army*, pp. 85, 89-90.

30. "I. V.," "Nam nuzhen komandnyy sostav," *VD* 2, no. 3 (1919): 157.

31. Shatagin, *Organizatsiya i stroytel'stvo sovetskoy armii*, p. 225.

32. K. E. Voroshilov, "Desyatiletie Krasnoy Armii," in K. E. Voroshilov, *Stat'i i rechi* (Moscow: Partizdat TsK VKP(b), 1936), p. 228.

33. Berkhin, *Voennaya reforma v SSSR*, p. 38.

34. Ibid., p. 38.

35. The 10. 5 percent figure is from Petrov, *Stroytel'stvo politorganov, partiynikh i komsomol'skikh organizatsiy armii i flota*, p. 156. The important role played by Kraskoms in the Red Army—in spite of their educational deficiencies—is discussed in D. Petrovskiy, "K voprosu o edinonachalii," *Voennaya mysl' i revolyutsiya*, no. 4 (1922): 3-9.

36. "Desyatyy s"ezd RKP(b)in KPSS v rezolyutsiyakh i resheniyakh s'ezdov . . . ," vol. 1, pp. 568-71.

37. For the latter statement, see "O komplektovanii voenno-uchebnykh zavedeniy," in *KPSS o vooruzhennykh silakh Sovetskogo Soyuza* (Moscow: Voennoe Izdatel'stvo Ministerstva Oborony SSSR, 1969), pp. 166-67.

38. A. Yovlev, "Sovershenstvovanie voenno-uchebnykh zavedeniy v 1921-1928 gg.," *VIZ*, no. 2 (1979): 95.

39. Central Archives of the Red Army, archive 32,562, document 218, p. 32, as cited in Berkhin, *Voennaya reforma v SSSR*, pp. 57-58.

40. The source is the Central Party Archives of the Institute of Marxism-Leninism attached to the Central Committee of the Communist party, archive 17, folder 2, document 113, p. 7, as cited in Berkhin, *Voennaya reforma v SSSR*, pp. 61-62.

41. Berkhin, *Voennaya reforma v SSSR*, p. 68.

42. As cited in Fedotoff-White, *The Growth of the Red Army*, p. 199. Fedotoff-White does not list the source of this quote.

43. For details on this directive, see Berkhin, *Voennaya reforma v SSSR*, pp. 239-43.

44. Additional details on the 1924 directive are contained in Berkhin, *Voennaya reforma v SSSR*, pp. 246-48.

45. Ibid., p. 259.

46. Figures are from the Central State Archives of the Red Army, archive 9, folder 1, documents 63/c, p. 73 and 11/c, p. 2, as cited in ibid., p. 155.

47. Petrov, *Stroytel'stvo politoroganov, partiynikh i komsomol'skikh organizatsiy armii i flota*, p. 156.

48. The 562,000 figure is from Berkhin, who states that the number for the armed forces "was fixed at 562,000, including for the army itself 529,865." Berkhin *Voennaya reforma v SSSR*, p. 77.

49. Yovlev, "Sovershenstvovanie voenno-uchebnykh zavedeniy," p. 95. "Otchet Narkomvoenmora na 1923/24," p. 73, 66, and "Otchet Narkomvoenmora na 1924/1925," pp. 116, 127, 316, as cited in Berkhin, *Voennaya reforma v SSSR*, p. 261. For additional educational figures, see ibid., p. 264.

50. "Otchet Narkomvoenmora za 1923/24," pp. 88-89.

51. Berkhin, *Voennaya reforma v SSSR*, pp. 262, 273. Berkhin's figures accord with those supplied by Voroshilov: working-class background, 1921—12 percent; 1927—22 percent; Communist party members, 1921—20 percent; 1927—48.1 percent. Voroshilov, "Stat'i i rechi," p. 230; but differ from those cited by Yovlev: working-class background, 1924—31.5 percent; 1927—39.0 percent, "Sovershenstvovanie voenno-uchebnikh zavedeniy v 1921-1928 gg.," p. 96.

52. Berkhin, *Voennaya reforma v SSSR*, pp. 260, 262, 263.

53. This issue is discussed in von Hagen, *Soldiers in the Proletarian Dictatorship*, pp. 163-64.

54. A. Bubnov, *1924 god v voennom stroytel'stve* (Moscow: Voenizdat, 1925), p. 87. See also "Novye dokumenty o reorganizatsii Krasnoi Armii v 1924 gody", *VIZ*, no. 12 (1974): 54-58. The Bubnov quote was made at the plenum of the Revvoensovet held from November 24–December 1, 1924.

55. M. V. Frunze, "Itogi plenuma Revvoensoveta SSSR," in Frunze, *Izbrannye proizvedeniya*, pp. 265-66.

56. M. V. Frunze, "Ochernye zadachi politrabotnikov," *Voyna i revolyutsiya*, no. 5 (August-September 1925), p. 5. See also Berkhin, *Voennaya reforma v SSSR*, pp. 292-93.

57. Central Archives of the Red Army, archive 9, folder 1, document 110/c, p. 130, as cited in ibid., p. 294.

58. For the Central Committee Statement, see "Ob edinonachalii v Krasnoy Armii," in *KPSS o voouzhennyh silakh Sovetskogo Soyuza*, pp. 228-29.

59. Central Archives of Red Army, archive 9, folder 1, document 110/c, pp. 79, 82, as cited in Berkhin, *Voennaya reforma v SSSR*, pp. 306, 395.

60. Berkhin, *Voennaya reforma v SSSR*, pp. 396-97.

61. Frunze, "Ochernye zadachi politrabotnikov," p. 6.

62. Von Hagen, *Soldiers in the Proletarian Dictatorship*, p. 218.

63. Figures are from Voroshilov, *Oborona SSSR*, p. 152. See also Yu. Petrov, "Deyatel'nost Kommunisticheskoy partii po predvediyu edinonachaliya v Vooruzhennykh Silakh," *VIZ*, no. 5 (1963): 19. Petrov provides figures for September, 1925: Corps commanders, 73. 3 percent; division commanders, 44. 5 percent; commanders of military-educational institutions, 54 percent; and regimental commanders, 33. 4 percent.

64. This directive is discussed in Voroshilov, *Oborona SSSR*, pp. 77-78, and in Petrov, *Stroytel'stvo politorganov, partiynikh i komsomol'skikh organizatsiy armii i flota*, pp. 163-64. The education level of Soviet officers had also risen dramatically. Yovlev reports, for example, that while only 56. 6 percent of commanders had military education in 1921, by 1928 the figure had risen to 90 percent. Likewise, he notes that at the level of military district, corps and division commanders all had a military edu-

cation, while 99. 6 percent and 99. 4 percent of regimental and battalion command-ers had such an education. "Sovershenstvovanie voenno-uchebnikh zavedeniy v 1921-1928 gg," p. 98.

65. Fedotoff-White, *The Growth of the Red Army*, p. 240. Erickson, *The Soviet High Command*, p. 198.

66. Von Hagen, *Soldiers in the Proletarian Dictatorship*, p. 328.

67. For work supporting the latter view, see Timothy J. Colton, *Commissars, Commanders and Civilian Authority; The Structure of Soviet Military Politics* (Cambridge: Harvard University Press, 1979), p. 57.

68. Petrov, "Deyatelnost' Kommunisticheskoy partii po provedeniyu edinonachaliya v Vooruzhennykh Silakh," p. 21. Petrov states that by the middle of 1931 about 70 percent of naval officers enjoyed this status (p. 22).

69. Concerning the reintroduction of the dual command principle, see Erickson, *The Soviet High Command*, p. 460. The unity of command principle was reintroduced throughout the military on August 12, 1940, but lasted less than a year. On July 16, 1941, when large numbers of reservists were called to the colors, the dual com-mand structure reappeared only to be withdrawn in favor of the unity of command principle in 1942.

## 5. Getting Control of Military Doctrine

1. Richard Sakwa, *Gorbachev and His Reforms, 1985-1990* (New York: Prentice-Hall, 1990), p. 315.

2. "Politicheskiy doklad Tsentral'nogo Komiteta KPSS XXVII S"ezdu Kommunisticheskoy Partii Sovetskogo Soyuza," in *Materialy XXVII S"ezda Kommunisticheskoy Partii Sovetskogo Soyuza* (Moscow: Politizdat, 1986), pp. 64, 67.

3. For a discussion of Ogarkov's views on nuclear war, see Dale R. Herspring, *The Soviet High Command, 1967-1989; Personalities and Politics* (Princeton: Princeton University Press, 1990), pp. 169-76. For a discussion of the April Central Commit-tee and Minsk meetings, see Raymond Garthoff, "Continuity and Change in Soviet Military Doctrine," in Bruce Parrott, ed., *The Dynamics of Soviet Defense Policy* (Wash-ington: Wilson Center Press, 1990), p. 170.

4. S. F. Akhromeyev, "Uroki istorii," *Izvestiya*, May 9, 1986.

5. "Rech deputata S. F. Akhromeyeva," *Izvestiya*, November 28, 1985.

6. This journal was classified until 1991. "Konkretnaya programma obespecheniya mira i bezopastnosti," *VM*, no. 6 (June, 1986): 3-4. Akhromeyev used the term "reasonable sufficiency" in June 1986—the only senior military officer to do so—but in spite of his close relations with Gorbachev, even he "failed to endorse the broader concept until after Gorbachev's February 1987 speech." See Malvin Helgesen "Civil-Military Relations Under Gorbachev," in Parrott, ed., *The Dynam-ics of Soviet Defense Policy*, p. 66.

7. "Za bez'yardernyy mir, za gumanizm mezhdunarodnykh otnosheniy," in M. S. Gorbachev, *Izbrannye rechi i staty*, vol. 4 (Moscow: Izdatel'stvo Politicheskoy Literatury, 1987), pp. 376-92.

8. "Perestroyka—krovnoe delo naroda," in ibid., pp. 424-43.

9. S. F. Akhromeyev, "Velikaya pobeda," *KZ*, May 9, 1987 (emphasis in the origi-nal).

10. "O boevoy doktrine gosudarstv-uchasnikov Varshavskogo Dogovora," *Pravda*, May 30, 1987.

11. Raymond Garthoff, "New Thinking in Soviet Military Doctrine," *Washington Quarterly*, vol. 11, no. 3 (Summer 1988): 134.

12. D. T. Yazov, "Voennaya doktrina Varshavskogo Dogovora—doktrina

zashchity mira i sotsializma," *KZ*, July 28, 1987. The document's endorsement of the primacy of the defense over offense marked a major change in Soviet military doctrine. Up to that time Soviet doctrine had seen offense as the main and decisive form of military operations. See Garthoff, "Continuity and Change in Soviet Military Doctrine," p. 175.

13. The key individuals who wrote about the relevance of the past for present understanding of military doctrine were Andrei Kokoshin, Valentin Larionov, and Valentin Lobov. Kokoshin was a long-time analyst of American affairs at the Institute for the Study of the U.S. and Canada, while Larionov, a retired military officer who was a contributor to Marshal Vasily Sokolovskiy's classic *Military Strategy*, was a specialist on military affairs at the same institute. Lobov, meanwhile, was a serving military officer who held the post of chief of the General Staff in the immediate aftermath of the coup. He was subsequently dismissed from this post because of policy differences with Defense Minister Shaposhnikov. Kokoshin was appointed deputy defense minister in the New Russian Defense Ministry on April 3, 1992. These were not the only writers to mention the relevance of the 1920s for the present. They were, however, the most visible and influential non-General Staff writers on the question of military doctrine during this period.

14. A. Kokoshin and V. Larionov, "Kurskaya bitva v svete sovremennoy oboronitel'noy doktriny," *Mirovaya ekonomika i mezhdunarodovye otnosheniya*, no. 8 (1987): 32-40. Larionov made the same points in an article aimed directly at a military audience in his piece entitled "Triumf prednamerennoy oborony," *VM*, no. 7 (1988): 12-21.

15. M. S. Gorbachev, "Real'nost' i garantii bezopasnogo mira," *Izbrannye rechi i staty* (Moscow: Izdatel'stvo Politicheskoy Literatury, 1988), p. 289.

16. Ye Velikov, "Prizyv k peremenam," *Kommunist*, no. 1 (1988): 53.

17. D. T. Yazov, *Na strazhe sotsializma i mira* (Moscow: Voenizdat, 1987), pp. 32-34.

18. M. A. Gareyev, "Sovetskaya voennaya nauka," *Znanie*, no. 11 (1987): 5-6. Even Akhromeyev refused to budge on this issue. "Defense sufficiency means our Army and Navy must possess a military potential sufficient to deter imperialism from unleashing aggression, ensure that they cannot be caught unaware, and in the event of aggression, to reliably rebuff it." S. Akhromeyev, "Watching over Peace and Security," *Trud*, February 21, 1988 in *FBIS SU*, February 22, 1988, p. 87.

19. A. Kokoshin and V. Larionov, "Protivostoyanie sil obshchego naznacheniya v kontekste obespecheniya strategicheskoy stabil'nosti," in *Mirovaya ekonomika i mezhdunarodnye otnosheniya*, no. 6 (1988): 23-31.

20. A. Kokoshin, "A. A. Svechin. O voyne i politike," in *Mezhdunarodnaya zhizn'*, vol. 10 (1988): 133-42.

21. Ibid., p. 140.

22. Ibid., p. 141.

23. Ibid.

24. While he was not cited publicly by military officers prior to the Gorbachev period, Svechin was well known in the armed forces. Articles were published on him and his work in military journals, as well as in encyclopedias. See "Svechin, Aleksandr Andreevich," *Bol'shaya sovetskaya entsiklopediya*, vol. 23 (Moscow: Izdatel'stvo Sovetskaya Entsiklopediya, 1976), p. 75. "Svechin, Aleksandr Andreevich," *VIZ*, no. 9 (1966): 117-18; A. Ageev, "Voennyy teoretik i voennyy istorik," *VIZ*, no. 8 (1978): 126-28.

25. D. T. Yazov, "70 let na strazhe sotsializma i mira", *KZ*, February 23, 1988.

26. "Vooruzhennye sily," *Novoe Vremya*, no. 8 (February 1988): 12-13.

27. V. Lobov, "K voprosu vnezapnosti i neozhidannosti," *VM*, no. 3 (1988): 3-8.

28. V. N. Lobov, "Strategiya Pobedy," *VIZ*, no. 5 (1988): 6.

29. "Studio 9," Moscow Television Service, October 15, 1988, in *JPRS SU*, October 21, 1988, p. 10.

30. See, for example, Yazov's statement of the continued importance of parity in D. T. Yazov, "Kachestvennye parametry oboronnogo stroytel'stva," *VM*, no. 9 (September 1988): 3-10.

31. A. Kokoshin, "Tri 'kita' stabil'nosti," *KZ*, September 16, 1988 (emphasis in the original).

32. M. Moiseyev, "Na strazhe mira i sotsializma," *KZ*, February 23, 1989. For Gorbachev's UN speech, see "Vystuplenie M. S. Gorbacheva v Organizatsii Ob"edinennykh Natsiy," *Izvestiya*, December 8, 1988.

33. D. T. Yazov, "V interesakh obshchey bezopasnosti i mira," *Izvestiya*, February 27, 1989.

34. V. N. Lobov, "Aktual'nye voprosy razvitiya teorii sovetskoy voennoy strategii 20-kh—serediny 30-kh godov," *VIZ*, no. 2 (1989): 41-50.

35. D. T. Yazov, "Na osnove novogo myshleniya," *KZ*, April 13, 1989.

36. For a typical statement of concern by Yazov over the "NATO threat" and the need for the West to take reciprocal steps, see "Neobkhodim politicheskiy dialog," *Izvestiya*, April 22, 1989.

37. "Putting Soviet Troops on the Defensive," *Morning Star*, April 10, 1989 in *FBIS SU*, April 17, 1989, p. 3.

38. "Akhromeyev Explains 'Defensive Military Doctrine,'" *Le Figaro*, June 13, 1989, in *FBIS SU*, June 15, 1989, p. 70.

39. A review of articles published in *Voennaya mysl'* from 1987 to 1989 suggests that Soviet theoreticians were devoting increasing attention to the issue of how to interrelate offensive and defensive actions under battlefield conditions as a result of "the transference of priorities in Soviet miliary doctrine to the sphere of defense." In 1987 there were five such articles, in 1988 eleven, and in 1989 twenty-five. From the purely military standpoint, there was a serious problem, since all of the writers involved in the discussion stressed the fact that "defeating an aggressor is impossible without launching a decisive offensive operation." R. M. Portugalskiy, "K voprosu o perekhode ot oborony k nastupleniyu," *VM*, no. 6 (1990): 15. As one senior Soviet military officer put it to this writer during this period, "How are we expected to repel an enemy if we cannot go over to the offensive? Even Kursk showed that the offense is critical to success. Furthermore, who is to say how far we should go and where we should stop? Many state borders make no sense from a military point of view. Stopping at the border could leave my forces in a very exposed position."

40. A. A. Kokoshin, and V. N. Lobov, "Predvidenie—General Svechin ob evolyutsii voennogo iskusstva," *Znamya*, no. 2 (1990): 170-82.

41. Andrey Kokoshin and Valentin Larionov, "Voennaya doktrina na sluzhbe mira," *Kommunist*, no. 15 (October 1990): 100-10. An article Lobov wrote in a book published in the U.S. in 1992 suggests that while he believed deeply in the ideas of Svechin, he was not prepared to go as far as Kokoshin and Larionov in pushing for a nonoffensive defense, i.e., one without any counteroffensive capability. In discussing Svechin's emphasis on defense, Lobov remarked that "Svechin's statements to the effect that the defense is the strongest form of combat actions are relevant as well, in light of the concept of reasonable (defensive) sufficiency for the USSR." At the same time he made it clear that he, like Svechin, believed that a counteroffensive capability remained critical: "He saw strategic defense as, above all, the totality of operations, including counterstrikes and counterattacks on various lines which had been prepared beforehand." See V. N. Lobov, "The Significance of Svechin's Military-Theoretical Legacy Today," in *Aleksandr Svechin, Strategy*, Kent Lee, ed. (Minneapolis: East View Publications, 1992), pp. 1-14.

42. Vladimir Lobov, "Voennaya reforma: tseli, printsipy, soderzhanie,"

*Kommunist,* no. 13 (September 1990): 14, 17. This criticism was made even sharper by the fact that the article was published in the leading civilian party journal, where Lobov was identified as an army general. Lobov had clearly broken ranks with his fellow officers on this issue.

43. This was not the first time senior military officers, including Yazov and Moiseyev, had accepted the idea of quality as an important measure of military power. See, for example, V. Strebkov, "Kriterii voenno-strategischeskogo pariteta," *Kommunist vooruzhennykh sil,* no. 4 (February 1989): 18-24, and Strebkov, "Voennyy paritet vchera i sevodnya," *KZ,* January 3, 1989. The Draft Military Doctrine document is contained in "O voennoy doktrine SSSR (Proekt)," *VM,* 1990 special issue. This document was sent to press on November 28, 1990.

44. Ibid., p. 27.

45. For an example of the High Command's focus on structural changes as the substance of defensive doctrine, see the interview with Moiseyev, "Voennaya reforma: deystvitel'nost' i perspektivy," *KZ,* November 18, 1990.

46. V. N. Lobov, "Puti realizatsii kontseptsii dostatochnosti dlya oborony," *VM,* no. 2 (1991): 18. On April 7, 1991, Lobov was relieved of his command as Warsaw Pact Chief of Staff and not reassigned until July, as chief of the Frunze Military Academy.

## 6. Restructuring the Armed Forces

1. For a discussion of Khrushchev's militia proposals, see Walter D. Jacobs, "Die kunftige Sowjetarmee: Elite oder Militz?" *Wehrkunde* 10, no. 3 (1960): 126-29; Walter C. Clemens, Jr., "Soviet Disarmament Proposals and the Cadre-Territorial Army," *Orbis* 7, no. 4 (Winter 1964): 778-99; Clemens, "The Soviet Militia in the Missile Age," *Orbis* 8, no. 1 (1965): 84-105.

2. Dale R. Herspring, *The Soviet High Command, 1967-1989* (Princeton: Princeton University Press, 1990), p. 37.

3. "Beseda N. S. Khrushcheva s redaktorom inostrannoyu otdela angliyskoy gazety 'Tayms,'" *Pravda,* February 16, 1958.

4. "Priem v Kremle Tsentral'nym Komitetom KPSS i Sovetom Ministrov SSSR," *Pravda,* March 21, 1958.

5. N. S. Khrushchev, "Razoruzhenie—put' k uprocheniyo mira i obespecheniyu druzhby mezhdu narodami," *Pravda,* January 15, 1960.

6. See P. S. Smirnov, "O nekorotikh politiki partii v voennom stroytel'stve," *Voprosy istorii KPSS,* no. 2 (1964): 42-53.

7. "Armiya i obshchestvo," *Vek XX i Mir,* no. 9 (1988): 22-25.

8. Aleksandr Savinkin, "Kakaya armiya nam nuzhna," *Moskovskie novosti,* November 6, 1988.

9. "Nuzhna li reforma armii," *Moskovskie novosti,* no. 4, January 22, 1989.

10. "Poka sushchestuet opasnost' agressii," *Kommunist vooruzhennykh sil,* no. 2 (January 1989): 19-20. Tabunov is playing with facts here. Frunze clearly preferred a professional military, but given the economic problems facing the state, he felt Moscow had no alternative but to make use of a mixed system. See chapter 2.

11. M. A. Moiseyev, "S pozitsiy oboronitel'noy doktriny," *KZ,* February 10, 1989.

12. V. Serebryannikov, "Armiya. Kakoy ey byt'?" *KZ,* February 12, 1989.

13. "Byt' na ostrie perestroyki. Vsearmeyskoe soveshchanie rukovoditeley organov voennoy pechati," *KZ,* March 7, 1989.

14. D. T. Yazov, "Na osnove novogo myshleniya," *KZ,* April 13, 1989.

15. V. Larionov and A. Kokoshin, "Soviet Military Doctrines," *Soviet Union* (March 1989): 12-13.

16. V. N. Lobov, "Aktual'nye voprosy razvitiya teorii sovetskoy voennoy strategii 20-x—serediny 30-x godov," *VIZ*, no. 2 (February 1989): 43.

17. V. Kuznetsov, "Desantniki: ili stroybat v golubykh beretakh," *Ogonek*, no. 8 (1989): 8.

18. For academic analyses published at the end of 1989 mentioning the role of militias, see N. A. Mal'tsev, "Kadrovaya ili militsionnaya?" *VIZ*, no. 11 (1989): 30-40, and P. F. Vashchenko and V. A. Runov, "Voennaya reforma v SSSR," *VIZ*, no. 12 (1989): 33-40.

19. "Soldiers Take off Their Overcoats," *Pravitel'stvennyy vestnik*, no. 9 (May 1989): 5, in *JPRS SU*, July 20, 1989, pp. 37-38.

20. A. Rogachev, "Kakaya armiya nam nuzhna?" and A. Men'shakov, "Samaya sil'naya logika—logika zhizn," *Morskoy sbornik*, no. 10 (1989): 46-50.

21. V. Makarevskiy, "Professiya—Soldat? Kakoy byt' armii v usloviyakh oboronitel'noy dostatochnosti," *Novoe vremya*, no. 46 (November 10, 1989): 23-24.

22. "Realities of Our Time," *Sovetskiy patriot*, no. 1 (1990): 7, in *FBIS SU*, January 31, 1990, pp. 112-13.

23. "Dialogue. Ask Questions! The 17 Servicemen's Draft," in *Komsomolskaya pravda*, February 11, 1990, in *FBIS SU*, February 18, 1990, pp. 118-19. According to several Soviet sources, including Lopatin, the Ministry of Defense chose to sit on the proposal, thereby forcing Lopatin to go public. See Stephen Foye, "Radical Military Reform and 'The Young Turks.'" *Report on the USSR*, April 13, 1990, p. 9.

24. N. Nikitin, "Polozhenie obyazyvaet," *KZ*, April 13, 1990.

25. "Vasha pozitsiya tovarishchi deputaty?" *Kommunist vooruzhennykh sil*, no. 2 (1990): 61, and "Kakaya armiya nam nuzhna?" *Ogonek*, no. 9 (1990): 29.

26. Lopatin's comments are in "Vtory s"ezd narodnikh deputatov SSSR," *Izvestiya*, December 13, 1989. Additional press commentary noting the harassment that these officers were experiencing at the hands of the Ministry of Defense is found in "Your Move, Minister," *Komsomolskaya pravda*, April 8, 1990, in *FBIS SU*, April 12, 1990, pp. 66-67. To understand the ire felt by senior officers toward individuals like Lopatin, it is important to remember that he went out of his way to attack the military leadership, suggesting repeatedly that they were incompetent and not seriously interested in military reform. He went so far as to suggest to a foreign audience that both Yazov and Moiseyev continued to oppose many of Gorbachev's economic and military reforms. According to a press report, Lopatin told the National Press Club that "success will occur only if Yazov and other military leaders are forced to relinquish their control." See "Soviet Defense Officials Stonewall Efforts to Reform Military Complex," *Inside the Pentagon*, October 18, 1990, p. 7. Given such statements, it is not surprising that the High Command went on a campaign to get him.

27. "One of the Leaders in the Soviet Parliament," *El Pais*, May 17, 1990, in *FBIS SU*, May 24, 1990, p. 6.

28. V. Lopatin, "Payasnitel'naya zapiska k proektu kontseptsii voennoy reformy," *Mirovaya ekonomika i mezhdunarodnye otnosheniya*, no. 9 (1990): 122-24.

29. "On Guard of the Motherland," *Selskaya zhizn*, February 23, 1990, in *FBIS SU*, March 6, 1990, p. 86.

30. V. Yermakov, "Tri voprosa komanduyushchemy," *KZ*, July 14, 1990.

31. "On the Eve of Military Reform," *Trud*, February 23, 1990, in *FBIS SU*, March 7, 1990, p. 92.

32. "Za konstruktivnye peremeny," *KZ*, February 22, 1990.

33. "Kakoy byt' armii 90-x?" *Argumenty i fakty*, February 24–March 2, 1990, p. 8.

34. A. Shevchenko, "Moe mnenie: nuzhna reforma," *Morskoy sbornik*, no. 3 (1990): 16-17.

35. "Kakaya armiya nam nuzhna?" *Kommunist vooruzhennykh sil*, no. 6 (March, 1990): 18.

36. "Armiya i voennaya reforma," *KZ*, June 27, 1990.

37. "Armiya budet s narodom!" *KZ*, July 14, 1990.

38. "Oboronnaya moshch'—kakoi ei byt?" *Mirovaya ekonomika i mezhdunarodnye otnosheniya*, no. 1 (1990): 105-10; "Kakaya armiya nam nuzhna?" *Kommunist vooruzhennykh sil*, no. 9 (1990): 34, 36.

39. "Ob usnovnykh napravlenniyakh voennoy politiki partii na sovremennom etape," *Pravda*, July 11, 1990. The hardline position taken by Yazov and Moiseyev on this and similar positions did not come without a cost. At the Twenty-Eighth Party Congress, for example, both were criticized for being more concerned with protecting their privileges than with the welfare of the armed forces. See "Yazov, Moiseyev Criticized," *RFE/RL Daily Report*, July 13, 1990.

40. "Kontseptsia voennoy reformy," *VM*, special issue, 1990, pp. 3-23.

41. "Voennaya reforma," *KZ*, June 3, 1990.

42. "Voennaya reforma: deystvitel'nost' i perspektivy," *KZ*, November 18, 1990.

43. "Military Reform: Generals and Radicals", *Komsomolskaya pravda*, November 13, 1990, in *FBIS SU*, November 16, 1990, p. 53.

44. Gelyy Batenin, "Kak preodelet' sindrom 41-go,", *Novoe vremya*, February 26–March 4, 1991: 12-14.

45. "Starovoitova Calls for Professional Army," *RFE/RL Daily Report*, March 5, 1991; Sergei Rogov, "Kakoy budet voennaya reforma?" *Kommunist*, no. 8 (April 1991): 88-89; L. G. Ivashov and A. S. Emelin, "Opyt voennoy reformy 1924-1925 godov," *VM*, no. 4 (1991): 17.

46. Vladislav Yanelis, "What Kind of Army Don't We Need?" *Literaturnaya gazeta*, no. 2 (January 1991), in *JPRS SU*, April 3, 1991, pp. 40-41.

47. "Who's Who Program with Dmitry Yazov, USSR Defense Minister and Marshal of the Soviet Union," Moscow Central Television Program Network, March 30, 1991 in *FBIS SU*, April 1, 1990, pp. 26-41.

48. M. Moiseyev, "Voennaya reforma: real'nosti i perspektivy," *KZ*, June 12, 1991.

49. V. Chirvin, "Zdravyy smysl ili diletantstvo?" *Kommunist vooruzhennykh sil*, no. 2 (1991): 15. The key exception was Akhromeyev, who perhaps because he was now retired and therefore could be said to be speaking for himself, reiterated the standard line; i.e., the Lopatin plan was too expensive and would not produce the necessary reserves. See S. F. Akhromeyev, "There is a Struggle Underway for Power," *Rabochaya gazeta* (Kiev), January 31, 1991 in *JPRS SU*, June 5, 1991, p. 1.

50. V. Achalov, "A Professional's View on the Prospects and Problems of Military Reforms in the USSR," *IAN Military Bulletin*, nos. 4-5 (February–March 1991): 1-5, in *FBIS SU*, May 23, 1991, pp. 9-11.

51. Interview with A. M. Makharov, "A zavtra byla voyna," *Kommunist vooruzhennykh sil*, no. 6 (1991): 93.

## 7. The Revival of National Military Forces

1. Territorial armies refer to ethnically based militaries subordinate to Moscow's central control, while national armies relate to independent ethnically based armed forces.

2. "But Problems Remain. On 'Regional Cliques,' and the Russian Language in the Army," *Argumenty i Fakty*, 27, August–September 1988, in *JPRS SU*, September 15, 1988, p. 1.

3. "Voynskiy mnogonatsional'nyy kollektiv," *KZ*, March 12, 1987.

4. Ibid.

5. "Sovetskiy Voin Discussion Club," *Sovetskiy voin*, no. 4 (1989), in *JPRS SU*, May 26, 1989, p. 4.

6. Ibid.

7. "Ikh zhdut voennye vuzy," *Zarya Vostoka* (Tbilisi), August 1, 1986.

8. "Sovetskiy Voin Discussion Club," p. 5.

9. "Pochemu eta izbiratel'nost'?" *KZ*, May 18, 1989.

10. See "Voynskiy mnogonatsional'nyy," *KZ*, March 12, 1987.

11. "Internatsional'nomy vospitaniyu—bol'she partiynogo vnimaniya", *Kommunist vooruzhennykh sil*, no. 5 (1989): 7.

12. Ibid., pp. 8-9.

13. See "The Sons Were Indignant in Response to a 'Letter on Behalf of Their Mothers' to the Minister of Defense," *KZ*, April 6, 1990 in *JPRS SU*, May 22, 1989, p. 1.

14. "Perestroyka trebuet dela," *KZ*, December 25, 1988.

15. A. Lizichev, "V tsentre perestroyka—chelovek," *KZ*, February 3, 1989.

16. "So What Happened with Our Army?," *Komsomol'skaya pravda*, January 18, 1989, *JPRS SU*, p. 36.

17. "Internatsional'nomy vospitaniyu—bol'she partiynogo vnimaniya," p. 8.

18. "Rezolyutsii XIX Vsesoyuznoy Konferentsii KPSS," *Pravda*, July 5, 1988.

19. Aleksandr Savinkin, "Kakaya armiya nam nuzhna," *MN*, November 6, 1988.

20. "Byt li natsional'nym armeiskim formirovaniiam?" *Sovetskaya Litva*, January 13, 1989.

21. "Gde sluzhit' parniu iz Litvy?" *Sovetskaya Litva*, December 23, 1988; "Voennye voprosy v programme kandidata," *KZ*, February 26, 1989.

22. Captain Sergey Khrapko, "Soldat—eto professiya," *MN*, January 8, 1989.

23. "Nakaz generalu," *Pravda*, February 12, 1989; V Serebryannikov, "Armiya. Kakoy ey byt'" *KZ*, February 12, 1989.

24. "V chest' godovshchiny," *KZ*, February 24, 1989.

25. "Kommunisty—avangard perestroyki," *KZ*, March 12, 1989.

26. "Poka sushchestvuet opasnost' agressii," *Kommunist vooruzhennykh sil*, no. 2 (1989): 18-25.

27. "Internatsional'nomy vospitaniyy—bol'she partiynogo vnimaniya," p. 8.

28. V. Kulpinskas, "A Defense Shield or 'Poteshniy Troop'"? *Sovetskaya Latviya*, April 20, 1989 in *JPRS SU*, July 20, 1989, p. 2.

29. "Open Letter to the Population of the LaSSR," *Sovetskaya Latviya*, July 9, 1989 in *JPRS SU*, September 6, 1989, pp. 8-9.

30. "Ostankino Radio Studio on the Line" Moscow Domestic Service, May 7, 1989, in *FBIS SU*, May 8, 1990, p. 81.

31. V. Varennikov, "U nashey armii—odna pochetnaya funktsiya," *KZ*, June 15, 1989.

32. "Yazov Notes Ethnic Tensions in Military," *Sankei Shimbun*, October 15, 1989, in *FBIS SU*, November 20, 1989, pp. 4-5.

33. D. T. Yazov, "Zashchita otechestva ne terpit mestnichestva, egoizma, svoekorystiya," *Pravda*, November 13, 1989.

34. M. A. Moiseyev, "Nasha armiya—armiya vsego naroda," *KZ*, December 17, 1989.

35. "Lithuania and the Army—In Search of Points of Contact," *Tiesa*, December 15, 1989, in *FBIS SU*, January 10, 1990, pp. 61-65.

36. "Proekt voennoy reformy", *Izvestiya*, April 11, 1990.

37. "Kakaya armiya nam nuzhna," *Ogonek*, no. 9 (1990): 30.

38. "Perestroyka v strane—perestroyke v armii," *Pravitel'stvennyy vestnik*, no. 6 (1990).

39. "Zadachi u nas odin," *KZ*, February 11, 1990.

40. V. I. Varennikov, "Iz istorii sozdaniya i podgotovka natsional'nykh voynskikh formirovaniy," *VM*, no. 2 (1990): 3-13.

41. "On Guard of the Motherland," *Sel'skaya zhizn*, February 23, 1990, in *FBIS*

*SU,* March 6, 1990, p. 86. It is noteworthy that Yefimov openly disagreed with Yazov on the question of professionalization in the same article.

42. "Interview with Dmitri Semenovich Sukhorukov, USSR Deputy Defense Minister," Moscow Television Service, February 23, 1990, in *FBIS SU,* February 25, 1990, p. 82.

43. "Military Chief Discusses Armed Forces Manning," *TASS International Service,* March 15, 1990, in *FBIS SU,* March 16, 1990, p. 94.

44. "Kakoy byt' armii 90-x?" *Argumenty i fakty,* February 24–March 2, 1990, p. 2.

45. V. Ermolin, "Zatyanuvshiysya monolog," *KZ,* March 4, 1990.

46. D. Yazov, "Vesenniy prizyv," *Izvestiya,* March 12, 1990.

47. S. Lipitskiy, "Voennaya reforma, 1924-1925 godov," *Kommunist,* no. 4 (1990): 109.

48. "Natsional'nye voennye formirovaniya: vchera . . . segodniya? zavtra?," *VIZ,* no. 5 (1990): 47-51.

49. Stephen Kux, *Soviet Federalism: A Comparative Perspective* (New York: Institute for East-West Studies, 1990), p. 13.

50. Rasma Karklins, "Nationalities and Ethnic Issues," in Anthony Jones and David E. Powell, eds., *Soviet Update, 1989-1990* (Boulder: Westview Press, 1991), p. 86.

51. D. T. Yazov, "Klyuchevaya zadacha voennoy reformy," *KZ,* September 2, 1990.

52. M. A. Moiseyev, "Voennaya reforma: Deystvitel'nost' i perspektivy," *KZ,* November 20, 1990.

53. For a copy of the draft Union Treaty, see "Proekt soyuznyy dogovor," *Pravda,* November 24, 1990, and for a discussion of the plan to combine all-Union strategic forces and republic forces, see V. Ochirov, "Soyuznyy dogovor. Chto zhdet armiy?", *KZ,* October 31, 1990.

54. "Soviets Moved Warheads, Top General Confirms," *Washington Post,* September 28, 1990.

55. "Gorbachev Acts to Retain Control of Nuclear Arms," *Washington Post,* November 28, 1990.

56. "Armiya i politika: press-konferentsiya Marshala Sovetskogo Soyuza D. T. Yazova," *KZ,* December 21, 1990.

57. "Nelizia peredelat' armiyu na skoruyu ruku," *Izvestiya,* December 23, 1990.

58. Yazov in *Komsomolskaya pravda,* as cited in *RL/RFE Daily Report,* December 3, 1990.

59. D. Volkogonov, "Man, Society, and State: The Army in the Political System," *Narodnyy deputat,* no. 1 (January 1991) in *JPRS SU,* August 22, 1991, p. 2.

60. Karklins, "Nationalities and Ethnic Issues," p. 88. Yazov disclaimed any responsibility by blaming the local commander, who was reportedly reprimanded. See "Defense Minister Interviewed," *RFE/RL Daily Report,* March 5, 1991.

61. "My Opinion: We Have the Strength to Keep an Army," *Edebiyat gezeti,* February 22, 1991, in *JPRS SU,* July 25, 1991, pp. 12-13.

62. "Cossack Units in the Soviet Army," *RFE/RL Daily Report,* May 13, 1991.

63. Sergei Rogov, "Kakoy budet voennaya reforma?" *Kommunist* (April 1991): 98-99.

64. "Voennaya reforma: priobreteniya i poteri," *VV,* no. 7 (1991): 6.

## 8. Cadre and Party

1. N. V. Ogarkov, "Teoreticheskiy arsenal voennogo rukovoditelya," *KZ,* September 10, 1971.

2. S. Akhromeyev, "Prevoskhodstvo sovetskoy voennoy nauki i sovetskogo voennogo iskusstva—odin iz vazhneyshikh faktorov pobedy v velikoy

otechestvennoy voyne," *Kommunist*, no. 3 (1985): 50, 62. Some of the material used in this section is covered from a different perspective in this author's *The Soviet High Command, 1967-1989; Personalities and Politics* (Princeton: Princeton University Press, 1990), pp. 236-44.

3. "O sozyve ocherednogo XXVII S"ezda KPSS i zadachakh, svyazannykh s evo podgotovkoy i provedeniem," in M. S. Gorbachev, *Izbrannye rechi i staty*, vol. 2 (Moscow: Izdatel'stvo Politicheskoy Literatury, 1987), pp. 155, 164-65.

4. "Navstrechu XXVII S"ezdu KPSS," *KZ*, April 25, 1985.

5. "Partiynaya trebovatel'nost'," *KZ*, June 6, 1985.

6. "Lichnaya otvetstvennost'," *KZ*, June 11, 1985.

7. A. Sorokin, "XXVII S"ezdu KPSS—dostoynuyu vstrechu," *KZ*, June 25, 1985.

8. In the Soviet military, and in the Communist party as well, formalism refers to the process whereby an individual carries out the tasks assigned to him in a bureaucratic, formal manner. Sorokin's comments are contained in "Povyshat' deystvennost' politicheskikh zanyatiy," *KZ*, July 2, 1985.

9. "Gorbachev: What Makes Him Run," *Newsweek*, November 18, 1985.

10. M. Gorbachev, "Politicheskiy doklad Tsentral'nogo Komiteta KPSS XXVII S"ezdu Kommunisticheskoy Partii Sovetskogo Soyuza," in *XXVII S"ezd kommunisticheskoy partii Sovetskogo Soyuza: Stenograficheskiy Otchet*, vol. 1 (Moscow: Politizdat, 1986), pp. 24, 98.

11. "Ostree otsenivat' reshitel'no deystvovat'" *KZ*, November 15, 1986.

12. "O perestroyke i kadrovoy politike partii," *KZ*, January 28, 1987.

13. "V Politburo TsK KPSS," *Pravda*, May 31, 1987.

14. D. Yazov, "Voennaya doktrina Varshavskogo Dogovora—doktrina zashchity mira i sotsializma," *Pravda*, July 27, 1987.

15. D. T. Yazov, "Perestroyka v rabote voennykh kadrov," *VIZ*, no. 7 (1987): 3-12.

16. Ibid.

17. The special role played by the party in implementing Gorbachev's policy of perestroyka was followed in the civilian world as well.

18. "O khode realizatsii resheniy XXVII S"ezda KPSS i zadakh po uglubleniyu perestroyki," *Pravda*, July 5, 1988. For Yazov's speech, see "Kachestvennye parametery oboronnogo stroytel'stva," *KZ*, August 9, 1988.

19. "Sluzhim Sovetskomu Soyuzy!" *Pravda*, January 22, 1989.

20. "S positsiy oboronitel'noy doktriny," *KZ*, February 10, 1989; "V tsentre perestroyki—chelovek," *KZ*, February 3, 1989.

21. M. Moiseyev, "Na strazhe mira i sotsializma," *KZ*, February 23, 1989.

22. "O rabote s kadrami," *KZ*, February 12, 1989.

23. "The Army in the Mirror of Restructuring," *Agitator*, no. 2 (January 1989), in *JPRS SU*, March 16, 1989, p. 1.

24. Dale R. Herspring, "The Soviet Military and Change," *Survival* (July/August 1989): 325.

25. "Out of Uniform," *Sovetskaya Rossiya*, March 8, 1989, in *FBIS SU*, March 10, 1989; V. Lobov, "Vysokoe kachestvo—glavnyy kriteriy boevoy podgotovki," *Kommunist vooruzhennykh sil*, no. 1 (1989): 14.

26. See the interview with General Konchits, former commander of the Frunze Military Academy, "Kuznitsa voennykh kadrov," *VV*, no. 12 (1988): 6-12.

27. "Shipy dogmatizma," *Sovetskiy voyn*, no. 1 (1989): 8.

28. For a discussion of the role the High Command expected the officer meetings to fulfill, see A. Mironov, "Ofitserskoe sobranie, Kakim emy byt'?," *KZ*, January 19, 1989.

29. See "Ofitserskoe sobranie. Kakim emy byt'?," *KZ*, May 17, 1989. The latter quote is taken from "Ofitserskoe sobranie: pervye shagi," *KZ*, September 13, 1989.

30. "Supreme Soviet overrules Yazov on students," *Janes Defence Weekly*, May 13, 1989, p. 174.

31. "Vooruzhennym Silam—novoe kachestvo," *Kommunist vooruzhennykh sil*, no. 15 (1989): 3-13.

32. "Vysoko nesti chest' ofitsera, byt' v avantgarde perestroyki," *KZ*, December 8, 1989.

33. "Perestroyka v strane—perestroyka v armii," *Pravitel'stvennyy vestnik*, no. 6 (1960): 1.

34. Ibid. As one Soviet admiral put it to this writer, "Political officers are useless on ships. They don't even stand watch. On the other hand, we have nothing to replace them or the party."

35. "Dialogue, Ask Questions," *Komsomolskaya pravda*, February 11, 1990, in *FBIS SU*, February 21, 1990, p. 118.

36. "Zashchitit' zashchitnika," *Kommunist*, no. 3 (1990): 54-58.

37. "Zadachi u nas odin," *KZ*, February 10, 1990. Moiseyev's decision to publicly challenge Gorbachev on this issue was unusual even for these heady days of glasnost. Soviet generals did not generally criticize the country's president or first secretary, who bore ultimate responsibility for determining the procedures utilized at the plenum.

38. "Kakoy byt' armii 90-kh?" *Argumenty i fakty*, February 24, 1990.

39. "Armiya na poroge reformy," *Literaturnaya gazeta*, March 7, 1990.

40. "The Army and Society: Who Serves Whom?" *Sovetskaya kultura*, March 31, 1990, in *JPRS SU*, May 17, 1990, p. 17.

41. "Aktivnost' mysli i deystviya,", *KZ*, March 13, 1990.

42. "Voennaya reforma: opyt, problemy, perspektivy," *VM*, no. 5 (May 1990): 50.

43. "Skvoz' spektr mneniy," *KZ*, May 27, 1990.

44. V. N. Ponikarovskiy and A. M. Mikhaylovskiy, "Zametki po proekty voennoy reformy v SSSR," *VM*, no. 4 (1991): 22.

45. "To Serve the People and Not Parties," *Nedelya*, May 28, 1990, in *FBIS SU*, June 19, 1990, p. 69. There are two logical explanations for the change in Lopatin's position. First, the move toward a multiparty system throughout Soviet society was accelerating and his proposal simply took note of that phenomena. Second, Lopatin had been attacked by the High Command for his stance on military reform, including his position vis-à-vis the political organs, up to the point where he was temporarily excluded from the party. Thus bitterness may have influenced his position.

46. D. T. Yazov, "Voennaya reforma," *KZ*, June 3, 1990.

47. "Armiya i perestroyka," *Pravda*, June 22, 1990.

48. "Idti dal'she putem perestroyki," *Pravda*, July 3, 1990.

49. "Obosnovykh napravlenyakh voennoy politiki partii na sovremennom etape," *Pravda*, July 11, 1990.

50. For Yazov's statement of opposition to depoliticization at the congress, see "Podlinno narodnaya armiya," *KZ*, July 4, 1990.

51. "Politorgany: vremya radikal'nogo obnovlenia," *KZ*, July 20, 1990.

52. S. F. Akhromeyev, "Ne syp'te sol' na rany . . . ," *Komsomolskaya pravda*, August 4, 1990.

53. D. T. Yazov, "Klyuchevaya zadacha voennoy reformy," *KZ*, September 8, 1990.

54. Valeriy Pogrebenkov, "The USSR President's Decrees and Army Restructuring," *Polska zbrojna*, October 24, 1990, in *FBIS SU*, November 2, 1990, pp. 58-59.

55. V. Lopatin, "Poyasnitel'naya zapiska k proekty kontseptsii voennoy reformy," *Mirovaya ekonomika i mezhdunarodnye otnosheniya*, no. 9 (1990): 124. That Lopatin and his group had support from at least some in the upper ranks of the armed forces is evident from an article by Lobov, who stated that "In our view, there should

be a review of the previous principles concerning the leadership of the CPSU in policies related to the defense and security of the country." See Vladimir Lobov, "Voennaya reforma: tseli, printsipy, soderzhanie," *Kommunist*, no. 13 (1990): 18.

56. "Voenn-politicheskie organy i osnovy strukture i organizatsii raboty i zadachy," *KZ*, January 23, 1991.

57. "Interview with Colonel General Shlyaga," Moscow Central Television First Program, January 12, 1991 in *FBIS SU*, January 14, 1991, p. 38.

58. "Novyy status, novye funktsii," *KZ*, January 16, 1991.

59. "Logika vybora," *KZ*, January 29, 1991.

60. This is based on Stephen Foye, "Committee Suspends CPSU Control over Armed Forces," *RFE/RL Research Paper*, April 10, 1991, pp. 1-3.

61. See, for example, L. Shlyaga, "Ot Politiki partii—k politike gosudarstva," *Kommunist vooruzhennykh sil*, no. 12 (1991): 13-21; "Utverzhdat'sya konkretnym delom," *KZ*, June 8, 1991; "Aftoritet vozvrashchaetsya delom," *KZ*, July 3, 1991.


### 9. The Post-Coup Period and the Commonwealth of Independent States

1. The list of such top-level officers includes General Konstantin Kobets, a former member of the General Staff, Col. Aleksandr Rutskoy, the RSFSR vice president; General Yevgeniy Shaposhnikov, the chief of the Air Force; General Pavel Grachev, the commander of Soviet Airborne Forces; Admiral Vladimir Chernavin, the commander of the Navy; General Viktor Samsonov, Commander of the Leningrad Military District; and even General Boris Gromov, the Hero of Afghanistan, a purported a hard-liner, who at that time was assigned to the Interior Ministry. According to Grachev, the forces which surrounded Yeltsin's headquarters were sent there in response to a request to him from Yeltsin. "He asked me to provide paratroopers for guarding the White House to which I responded positively." "Desantniki protiv naroda ne poschli," *KZ*, August 31, 1991.

2. "Limited Support for the Coup," *RFE/RL Daily Report*, August 22, 1991.

3. "Gorbachev Praises Army's Role in Thwarting Coup," Moscow TASS, August 28, 1991, in *FBIS SU*, August 29, 1991, p. 70.

4. "Shaposhnikov on Army's Involvement," Moscow TASS International Service, February 18, 1992 in *FBIS SU*, February 19, 1992, p. 56. For a list of the top military officers involved, see "Rodionov Explains Military Personnel Dismissals," Moscow *TASS*, September 16, 1991 in *FBIS SU*, September 17, 1991, p. 30.

5. See "Gorbachev Bans Political Activity in Armed Forces," *RFE/RL Daily Report*, August 26, 1991.

6. "Against Force to Maintain Union," Vienna Oesterreich Eins Radio Network, August 26, 1991 in *FBIS SU*, August 27, 1991, p. 58.

7. "Armiya nuzhna korennaya reforma," *Trud*, August 29, 1991. Shaposhnikov adopted a similar line in an interview at that time. "We are doing everything we can in order that the military will be radically reformed, while at the same time retaining a unified Armed Forces." "Sluzhit' narody," *Armiya*, no. 18 (September 1991): 9.

8. See "Marshal Shaposhnikov predlagaet ego kontsepsiyu voennoy reformy," *Izvestiya*, September 11, 1991, and "Ukrainian Defense Minister on Meeting," Radio Kiev, September 10, 1991, in *FBIS SU*, September 13, 1991, p. 56.

9. "Shaposhnikov, Republic Envoys," Moscow Central Television, First Program, October 10, 1991, in *FBIS SU*, October 10, 1991, 26-29.

10. "Minoborony provodit konsul'tatsii. Respubliki prinimayut resheniya," *Izvestiya*, October 10, 1991.

11. "Ukraine Plans to Create Army of 450,000," *RFE/RL Daily Report*, October 8, 1991.

12. "V krugu slozhneyshikh problem," *KZ*, October 9, 1991.

13. "Novyy nachal'nik sovetskogo genshtaba," *Nezavisimaya gazeta*, September 3, 1991.

14. See, for example, "Armiyu delit' ne budem," *Pravda*, September 9, 1991; "Politika, Doktrina, strategia vmenyayushchemsya mire," *KZ*, October 23, 1991; "Lobov Advocates Collective Defense Structure," Moscow Central Television First Program, October 17, 1991 in *FBIS SU*, October 18, 1991, p. 33. "Vooruzhennye sily otechestva segodnya i zavtra," *KZ*, November 29, 1991.

15. See "Lobov Removed over Disagreements on Reform," Moscow, *TASS*, December 9, 1991 in *FBIS SU*, December 10, 1991, p. 35. For a discussion by Lobov of why he was removed from office, see "Kak snimali nachal'nika genshtaba," *Nezavisimaya gazeta*, December 21, 1991.

16. "Text of Accords by Former Soviet Republics Setting Up a Commonwealth," *New York Times*, December 22, 1991.

17. "Russia to Create National Guard," *Washington Post*, December 30, 1991.

18. Shaposhnikov singled out the word "joint" to describe the concept favored by the High Command. See "Defense Ministers Hold Conference 27 December," Moscow Central Television First Program, December 27, 1991 in *FBIS SU*, December 30, 1991, p. 11.

19. "Text of Armed Forces Agreement," Moscow TASS, December 31, 1991 in *FBIS SU*, December 31, 1991, p. 18.

20. "Sud'ba nashey bezopasnosti," *Sovetskaya Rossiya*, January 4, 1992.

21. "Kravchuk Interviewed on Commonwealth, Defense," *Corriere della sera*, December 29, 1992 in *FBIS CE*, January 3, 1992, p. 6.

22. Shaposhnikov's statement is contained in Marshal Shaposhnikov, "Povinuyus' sovesti i zakony . . . ," *Pravda*, September 25, 1991. The Grachev statement is in "Soviet Set Cuts in Size of Army, Missile Readiness," *Washington Post*, September 30, 1991.

23. It is clear from discussion in the media that thought was being given to using national guard formations as militia formations. Shaposhnikov, for example, stated that "in my view, these formations should carry light firearms without any military equipment. In wartime they could provide reserves for the Armed Forces." Shaposhnikov, "Povinuyus' sovesti i zakony . . . ," *Pravda*, September 25, 1991.

24. Ibid.

25. "Armyu delit' ne budem," *Pravda*, September 9, 1991.

26. "SNF: Nuzhna li emu obshchaya voennaya doktrina," *KZ*, December 26, 1991.

27. "Razumnaya voennaya reforma bez voennoy doktriny nevozmozhna," *KZ*, January 29, 1992.

28. "Est' li u Rossii svoy interes," *KZ*, February 29, 1992.

29. A. Skvortsov, "Kto dolzhen utverzhdat' voennuyu doktrinu," *KZ*, March 19, 1992.

30. See, for example, V. A. Sapozhinskiy, "K voprosy ob oboronnoy dostatochnosti," *VM*, no. 10 (1991): 37-40; G. V. Kirilenko and D. V. Trenin, "Razmyshleniya nad proektom voennoy doktriny," *VM*, no. 10 (1991): 11-18; I. V. Erokhin, "O razrabotke kontseptsii voennoy reformy," *VM*, nos. 11-12 (1991): 36-45.

31. I. Vorobyev, "Ternii voennoy reforma," *KZ*, December 27, 1991.

32. V. Ya. Petrenko, "Chto pokazyvaet analiz proekta voennoy doktriny," *VM*, no. 1 (1992): 11-16; V. P. Mironov and Yu. A. Nikolaev, "Kharakter vzaimosvyazi i vzaimozavisimosti i razvitii vooruzheniya i voennogo iskusstva," *VM*, no. 1 (1992): 40-45.

33. M. N. Osipova, "Posle Krymskoy voyny," *VIZ*, no. 2 (1992): 4-13.

34. S. L. Pechorov, "Nenastupatel'naya oborona: Vykhod iz tulpika?" *VM*, no. 3 (1992): 13.

35. "Shaposhnikov Discusses Army's Future Role," Moscow Russian Television Network, August 28, 1991, in *FBIS SU*, August 29, 1991, p. 73.

36. See Shaposhnikov's interview where he discusses the subject in some detail, "Defense Minister Shaposhnikov Gives Interview," Moscow Russian Television Network, September 9, 1991, in *FBIS SU*, September 10, 1991.

37. "Shaposhnikov Comments on Defense Ministry Tasks," Moscow Radio Rossii Network, September 18, 1991, in *FBIS SU*, September 20, 1991, p. 32 (emphasis added).

38. Shaposhnikov, "Povinuyus' sovesti i zakonu," *Pravda*; "Desantniki protiv naroda ne poshli . . . ," *KZ*, August 31, 1991.

39. "Chairman Remarks," Moscow Radio Rossii Network, November 19, 1991, in *FBIS SU*, November 22, 1991, p. 39.

40. One of the best discussions of the origins of the dispute is contained in Douglas L. Clarke, "The Saga of the Black Sea Fleet," *RFE/RL Research Report*, January 24, 1992, pp. 45-49.

41. See "A CIS General Looks at the Minsk Summit," *RFE/RL Daily Report*, February 21, 1992.

42. "Commonwealth Military Chief Predicts Split-up of Ex-Soviet Force," *Washington Post*, February 19, 1992.

43. As cited in "Ex-Soviet Leaders Fail to Settle Disputes," *Washington Post*, March 21, 1992.

44. "Commonwealth: How Much Longer?", *Washington Post*, May 15, 1992.

45. In fact, on June 15 the defense ministers of six post-Soviet republics announced that they were disbanding the Commonwealth Joint Armed Forces and replacing them with a loosely organized "United headquarters for coordinating military cooperation." See "Ex-Soviet States End Joint Forces," *Washington Post*, June 16, 1993.

## 10. The Russian Army Faces an Uncertain Future

1. "Ja nie znayu, eto politicheskiy vopros." This is based on hundreds of discussions the author had with Soviet military officers over the years.

2. Politicization in this context does not refer to the political indoctrination process described in previous parts of this book. Instead, it refers to the active participation in the political process by Russian/Soviet military officers.

3. See "Sopernichestvo Ukrainy i Rossii za armiyu, flot i Krym obostryaetsya," *Nezavisimaya gazeta*, April 9, 1992.

4. See, for example, "Volkogonov Urges Collective Security Accord," Moscow Radio, March 18, 1992, in *FBIS CE*, March 19, 1992, p. 35.

5. As only one sign of how far things had deteriorated in the Russian military, at the time of the creation of the Russian Army the military numbered only 1. 22 million men—down from around four million a few years earlier. "Minister oborony Rossiykoy Federatsii general armii Pavel Grachev: Vooruzhennym Silam ochen' trudno, no s zadachami oni spravlyayutsya," *KZ*, November 17, 1995.

6. See "Military Doctrine Formation Predicted," Moscow, ITAR-TASS, May 30, 1992, in *FBIS CE*, June 2, 1992, p. 15.

7. Two of the best Western analyses of this document are Scott McMichael, "Russia's New Military Doctrine," *RFE/RL Research Report*, October 9, 1992, pp. 45-50, and C. J. Dick, "Initial Thoughts on Russia's Draft Military Doctrine and Russia's

Draft Military Doctrine, 10 Months On," Soviet Studies Research Center, RMA Sandhurst, July 14, 1992.

8. See "Basic Provisions of the Military Doctrine of the Russian Federation," *FBIS CE*, November 19, 1993, pp. 1-11.

9. For a good discussion of the relevance of this document for Russian foreign policy, see Andrey Kozyrev, "Voennaya doktrina strany i mezhdunarodnaya bezopastnost'," *KZ*, January 14, 1994.

10. "Yeltsin Addresses Military Students," ITAR-TASS, February 23, 1994, in *FBIS CE*, February 24, 1994, p. 34.

11. "Pavel Grachev, Armii sgodnya trudno, kak i vsemu narodu."

12. Grachev lashed out not only at reformers such as Lopatin, but at other military critics from both the left and the right who were attacking the way the military was operating.

13. "Grachev Comments on Army Situation," Moscow Russian Television Network, February 28, 1993, in *FBIS CE*, March 1, 1993, p. 33.

14. "Pavel Grachev: Armiya—garant stabil'nosti," *Rossiyskie vesti*, March 6, 1993.

15. For an argument to this effect, see "Armiya byla vynuzhdena deyztvovat' reshitel'no," *KZ*, October 8, 1993.

16. See Timothy J. Colton, *Commissars, Commanders and Civilian Authority: The Structure of Soviet Military Politics* (Cambridge: Harvard University Press, 1979), pp. 175-95.

17. "The Army is Not a Policeman," *Nezavisimaya gazeta*, October 29, 1993, in *FBIS CE*, November 2, 1993, p. 51.

18. "Interview with General Lebed," *Le Figaro*, November 5-6, 1994, as cited in S. G. Simonsen, "Going His Own Way: A Profile of General Aleksandr Lebed," *Journal of Slavic Military Studies*, vol. 8, no. 3 (September 1995), p. 539.

19. As quoted in Deborah Yarsike Ball, "The Unreliability of the Russian Officer Corps: Reluctant Domestic Warriors," in Kathleen Bailey and M. Elaine Price, *Director's Series on Proliferation*, November 17, 1995, UCRL-LR-114070-9, p. 19.

20. "General Lebed: Russia Is an Empire," *Trud*, July 26, 1995, in *FBIS CE*, August 3, 1995, p. 23.

21. See, for example, "Defense Ministry Personnel Changes Still 'Unsettled,'" Moscow, ITAR-TASS, January 23, 1995, in *FBIS CE*, January 24, 1995, pp. 26-27.

22. James H. Brusstar and Ellen Jones, "Attitudes within the Russian Officer Corps," *Strategic Forum*, no. 15, January 1995, p. 3.

23. "For Whom Will the Military Vote?" *Novaya Yezhednevnaya gazeta*, October 18–25, no. 39, p. 2, in *FBIS CE*, November 2, 1995, p. 55.

24. See "Pavel Grachev: 'Emphasis on Force in Chechnya Should Be Retained,'" *Nezavisimoye voyennoye obozreniye*, no. 3, November 1995, in *FBIS CE*, November 23, 1995, p. 32.

25. Data from this survey is taken from Ball, *The Unreliability of the Russian Officer Corps: Reluctant Domestic Warriors*, pp. 19-29.

26. Ibid. Emphasis in the original.

27. "Grachev: 'Russian Army Loyal to Constitution,'" *La Repubblica*, March 18, 1994, in *FBIS CE*, March 18, 1994, pp. 20-21.

28. "Conversation without Middlemen," Moscow Television, September 14, 1995, in *FBIS CE*, September 18, 1995, p. 19.

29. "Radio Rossii Interviews Grachev on Military Issues," Moscow Radio Rossii, February 23, 1993, in *FBIS CE*, February 24, 1993, p. 26.

30. "Conversation without Middlemen," p. 19.

31. "Army Faces Disruption in Food Supply," INTERFAX, August 27, 1995, in *FBIS CE*, August 28, 1995, p. 36.

32. "Conversation without Middlemen," Moscow Television September 14, 1995, in *FBIS CE*, September 18, 1995, p. 19.

33. "Chechen War Bankrupting Armed Forces," *OMRI Daily Digest,* August 25, 1995.

34. "Defense Ministry on Reform Efforts, Budget," *RFE/RL Daily Report,* August 22, 1994.

35. "Conversation without Middlemen," p. 19.

36. "Moryaki derzhatsya na entusiazme," *Pravda,* July 30, 1994.

37. "Conversation without Middlemen," p. 20.

38. Ibid., p. 19.

39. "Yeltsin Aide Favors Cossack Military Service," INTERFAX, *FBIS CE,* September 8, 1995, p. 32.

40. Ibid.

41. "In 1996 the State Will 'Give' the Russian Army New Debts and Promises," *Financovyye izvestiya,* December 28, 1995, in *FBIS CE* January 3, 1996, p. 26.

42. "Conversation without Middlemen," p. 20.

43. Stephen Foye, "Rebuilding the Russian Military: Some Problems and Prospects," *RFE/RL Research Report,* November 6, 1992, p. 53.

44. "Rutskoy: Army has 8-10 percent of Personnel Needed," INTERFAX, October 8, 1992, in *FBIS CE,* October 9, 1992, p. 20.

45. "Lyubit' Rossiyo i v nepogodu," *KZ,* December 10, 1992.

46. "Grachev Addresses Army Recruiting Problems," Moscow Public Television, September 11, 1995, in *FBIS CE,* September 12, 1995, p. 34.

47. "Figures for Evasion of Military Service Reported," Moscow 2X2 Television, August 25, 1995, in *FBIS CE,* August 29, 1995, p. 29.

48. "Armed Forces' Contract Soldiers Number 45,000," Ostakino Television First Channel, April 8, 1993, in *FBIS CE,* April 9, 1993, p. 42.

49. "Grachev: Quota for Contract Personnel Fulfilled," Ostakino Television First Program, June 9, 1993, in *FBIS CE,* June 9, 1993, p. 48.

50. "Conversation without Middlemen," p. 21.

51. "Chinovnich'ya volokita tormozit povyshenie denezhnogo soderzhaniya voennosluzhashchikh," *Krasnaya zvezda,* September 12, 1995.

52. "Officers! Russian Federation of Ministry of Defense Information Publishes Data on Armed Forces' Officer Corps," *Rossiyskaya gazeta,* August 26, 1995, in *FBIS CE,* August 31, 1995, p. 31.

53. Given the negative Russian attitude toward women serving in the military, the message to the average reader was that the situation was even worse than a Western observer reading this material might assume. See "Grachev Cited on Personnel Levels in the Army," Moscow Public Television, September 11, 1995, in *FBIS CE,* September 12, 1995, p. 35.

54. "Reforma v armii: orientiry dla voennoy pressy," *KZ,* May 25, 1993.

55. "Battalions Want Something to Eat. The 'Invincible and Legendary' Is on Starvation Rations." *Trud,* November 4, 1995, in *FBIS CE,* November 7, 1995, p. 26.

56. "The Defense Minister Has It in for Everyone," p. 33.

57. "Government Bans Shut Down of Power to Military," *OMRI Daily Digest,* September 24, 1995.

58. "Armiya budet takoy, kakim budet ee ofitserskiy korpus," *KZ,* May 17, 1994.

59. "Pavel Grachev: Armii segodnya trudno, kak i vsemu narodu," *KZ,* February 23, 1993.

60. "Letter to the Editor," *Argumenty i fakty,* October 1992, p. 8.

61. "Preds"ezdovskie khlopoty vlastey," *Nezavisimaya gazeta,* November 25, 1992.

62. Grachev, "Vooruzhennym Silam ochen' trudno, no s zadachami oni spravlyayutsya," *KZ,* November 17, 1995.

63. "General Grachev ob armii i o soldate," *Argumenty i fakty,* February 1993, pp. 1-2.

64. Trevor Waters, "The New Russian Army One Year On—Hopes and Fears," *Jane's Intelligence Review,* July 1993, p. 305, and "Official Reports 518 Servicemen Killed in 1994," INTERFAX, July 12, 1994, in *FBIS CE,* July 13, 1994, p. 23.

65. "Suicide a Problem in the Military," *OMRI Daily Report,* July 8, 1995.

66. "Posle ubiytstva u raketnogo kompleksa," *Izvestiya,* May 14, 1994.

67. "Explosion 'Equivalent' to Nuclear Bomb," Vladivostok Radio, May 16, 1994, in *FBIS CE,* May 16, 1994, p. 28.

68. "Spisannye atomokhody poka eshche zhut gosprogrammy utilizatsii. No uzhe grozyat katastrofoy," *Krasnaya zvezda,* July 13, 1995.

69. See, for example, V. A. Yakovlev, "Sluzhba, k sozhaleniyu, ne samoe prestizhnoe delo," *KZ,* July 2, 1994.

70. "Pavel Grachev: 'Emphasis on Force in Chechnya Should Be Retained,'" *Nezavisimoye voyennoye obozreniye,* November 3, 1995, in *FBIS-CE,* November 20, 1995, p. 32.

71. "A dukh v kazarmakh vse krepchaet," *Komsomolskaya pravda,* April 19, 1994.

72. See "Yeltsin Fires Military Budget Department Head," ITAR-TASS, November 24, 1995, in *FBIS CE,* November 24, 1995, p. 31.

73. "Dolgi 'silovikami' budut pogasheny do kontsa goda," *KZ,* December 6, 1995.

74. "Pavel Grachev: 'Emphasis on Force in Chechnya Should Be Retained,'" p. 32.

## Conclusion

1. Samuel Huntington, *Political Order in Changing Societies* (New Haven: Yale University Press, 1971), pp. 12-24.

# INDEX

DALE R. HERSPRING is Professor and Head of the Department of Political Science at Kansas State University. A former Foreign Service Officer with the Department of State, he is the author/editor of six books and more than forty articles dealing with civil-military relations in the former Soviet Union and Eastern Europe. He is currently working on a book to be entitled *Requiem for an Army: The Case of the East German Military.*